BOOK FOUR

THE MASTERS OF HORSEMANSHIP
SERIES

Dressage in

Harmony

From Basic to Grand Prix

◆

Foreword by Egon von Neindorff

WALTER ZETTL

The Masters of Horsemanship Series, Book Four

Dressage in Harmony: From Basic to Grand Prix

by Walter Zettl

© 1998 Walter Zettl

Illustrations © 1998 Paul Schopf

Published in the United States of America by
Half Halt Press, Inc.
P.O. Box 67
Boonsboro, MD 21713

Printed in the United States of America

Library of Congress Cataloging-in-Publication Data

Zettl, Walter A.
    Dressage in harmony : from basic to Grand Prix / Walter A. Zettl.
        p. cm. -- (The masters of horsemanship series ; bk. 4)
    ISBN 0-939481-54-5 (hardcover)
    1. Dressage.   I Title.   II. Series.
SF309.5 Z48   1998
    798.2'3--dc21   98-46028
                                                          CIP

Table of Contents

Thanks

This book is dedicated to my wife Heide, for her patience and understanding during the long process of writing. I would like also to thank my friends in Munich, Drs. Hans and Christiane Hebel. Through forty years of friendship, they have always been there for me when I needed advice or a sounding board.

Cindy Sydnor gave me the push to write this book almost 10 years ago. She said I should write about my experiences, and that she would translate, if I would dictate in German. Through her enormous effort and her own experience in dressage, a first draft was produced that made a wistful dream turn into the start of a real book.

Undying thanks go to my long-time students and friends, Professor Paul Schopf and his wife Jane Seigler who own Reddemeade Farm in Maryland. Through their expertise in riding, their deep understanding of my philosophy, and their experience in writing and editing, the seed of the first draft grew and flourished into the present book. Over the past years, we have spent countless hours discussing, musing, and merging into printed text our responses to the questions raised by their experiences in their riding and teaching. The discussions were long and enjoyable as we searched for the proper details to include, and the proper wording to convey my meaning. The longer I worked with them, the more impressed I became. It has been a source of joy to see the principles set forth in this book reflected in their students' riding, and confirms my belief that the classical principles have an unending validity in the modern age. I also thank them for taking time from their busy professional schedules to bring this book to life.

Along the way, many people have helped in many ways: Kay Shaw Whitlock suggested the title; Margo Isbister, JoAnn Young, Diana Creech, Kathleen Terry Mobley, and Marion Adoranti provided many early photographs and drawings. Final hand drawings were prepared by Liz Lockett. Prof. Schopf provided the computer illustrations. His artistic talent and computer skills could have produced sufficient figures, but his understanding of riding and horsemanship brings the most subtle detail to these illustrations.

Special thanks to Elizabeth Carnes at Half Halt Press for her enthusiastic support of the book, and her help along the way. Many thanks also to Riding Master Egon Von Neindorff for his support and forward to this book. He has always provided a model of a life devoted to the service of classical horsemanship. He is one of the very few great masters who is still active and influencing the ideals of the sport.

This book is in a very real sense a monument to the life and horsemanship of my teacher, Col. Herbert W. Aust. A gentleman of the old school, he exemplified and applied in his own conduct the highest standards of character and behavior. He inspired the same in those around him.

I came to him when I was sixteen years old. He not only taught me the classical arts of dressage and jumping, he built my character and ethic. He taught me that it is indeed possible to achieve success through a life that is guided by integrity and dedicated to the preservation of the beauty of the horse. From him I learned that any act of force or violence would violate that principle and that most precious gift, the temporary custodianship of one of nature's most exquisite creatures. I could go to him at anytime for advice, counsel, encouragement and direction. He was always my role model, in both riding and in daily life, and was to me always, until his death, a father figure and a friend. Much of what I have achieved in my life and what I am today, I owe to him. I will never forget him.

A Horse's Prayer

*Give me to eat, give me to drink, and worry about me when
the day's work is done, give me shelter, a clean bed and a
wide box, talk to me, often your voice substitutes for the
reins, be good to me and I will gladly serve you and love
you. Don't jerk the reins, and forego the whip when we go
up a rise. Don't hit or kick me should I not understand you,
give me time to understand. Don't think me disobedient
should I not follow your orders, perhaps the harness and
hooves are not in order. Examine my teeth should I not eat,
perhaps I have a bad tooth. You know how much that can
hurt. Don't tie me too short and don't braid my tail, it is my
only weapon against flies and mosquitos. And at the end,
dear master, when I am no longer useful, don't let me go
hungry and cold and don't sell me. Don't give me to a new
master, one who will torture me to death and let me starve,
but give me a quick and compassionate death, dear master,
and God will reward you, in this life and the next. Let me
ask this of you, not in disrespect, when I request it in the
name of Him who too was born in a stable, your savior
Jesus Christ*

Amen

From an inscription in an old English barn

Foreword

"Dressage in Harmony" ---what does this mean? Dressage training is systematic, structured, and nature-oriented education---both the teaching and the being taught. Dressage does not mean total submission of the horse, nor overtaxing him forcefully, nor getting into useless arguments. Harmony means sensibility, synchronization, consistency and unison. "Dressage in Harmony" means to solve together a task in such a manner that rider and horse are enjoying the work. Then and only then will you feel the wonderful natural ease and subtle relaxation which every rider seeks in his or her daily work.

The modern sportsman knows how much the body and soul are connected with one another. But in riding we ask two totally different personalities to become one in unison--a path which one can only master successfully in small steps with the help of a very experienced teacher and with a lot of patience.

I have known Walter Zettl for over forty years, from his earlier many successes in competitive dressage as well as in jumping, through his extremely fruitful work as a trainer. Teaching has always been one of his strong points. His lessons require close attentiveness and are very interesting at the same time. His immediate corrections are efficient and precise, and his sense for achieving harmony between horse and rider is impeccable.

Although he uses modern teaching methods such as head phones, he has never left the path of true classical riding. It gives me great pleasure and satisfaction that Walter Zettl will pass on to the dressage riders of North America the experience and knowledge of our great riding masters, as years ago my honored teacher Richard Waetjen did.

If you are not fortunate enough to be taught by Walter Zettl personally, he gives you in this book a very valuable guide to the art of classical riding. In clearly worked out and easy to understand chapters, he takes you through each step of the training stages, discusses problems that occur, and assists with competent, sensible corrections, from Beginner to becoming a Master. With Walter Zettl's guidance, it is made possible.

I pleaded with Walter Zettl to publish this book in Germany as well. It is a wonderful aid from starting with the basics to reaching the pinnacle of the art of classical riding. It will show you how to ride your horse at all training stages in balance and rhythm.

I wish Walter Zettl lots of success with this wonderful book and I am sure his book will answer many questions and clear any misunderstandings, helping you to achieve personally "Dressage in Harmony."

E.v. Neindorff

List of Figures

Chapter 1

Introduction

For those who love horses, the sight of horse and rider in perfect harmony is a thing of beauty: moving in perfect balance and grace, an effortless performance, yet energetic and fluid. Through imperceptible aids, the rider guides the horse through trust and respect, without force. Riding in harmony gives the horse confidence, balance, suppleness and lightness. In this partnership, the horse is obedient of his own free will. He happily and enthusiastically participates in the dance. Once the rider obtains the feeling for riding in harmony, he can never again accept anything less.

You may ask how we achieve such harmony. Is this the realm of a few "naturally born" horsemen and horses, a state with doors barred against all but the anointed? In fact, it is an achievable goal for those who choose to study, work and care. It is imperative that the rider understands and shares the emotions of the horse, respects the horse's nature, and has the commitment to riding in harmony and lightness, working with the horse as a true partner. Beyond this, however, also lies the requirement of knowing how to proceed: technical details of how and when to give the aids, how to structure the training, how to evaluate the progress of horse and rider.

Throughout history, there have always been "new" and "modern" ways of riding, short-cuts to achieve a momentary success. But when such so-called improvements work against nature, they are inevitably doomed to failure. A trainer who has had apparent success with one or two horses can gather a large following of supporters, but how does he weigh in the scales of hundreds of years of classical training, and millions of hours of experience passed from one generation to the next? Although not everything that is old is good, everything that is good has come from ages of experience, passed through the grand masters of the art.

If you say "I am just a normal person and 'classical' riding is too fancy and too difficult for me—I just love my horse," I would reply that if you love horses, then riding in harmony is the only way to proceed. Do not concern yourself that it is "classical." Think instead of the benefits of lightness, balance, kindness, and self-confidence. You can find out later that what you are doing is classical. The validity of this way is grounded in the experience of centuries of horsemen.

Through a true understanding of and respect for the horse's nature, the equestrian artist can evoke the highest level of athletic performance from each horse. For it is only when the horse works in total relaxation and confidence, without any tension or tightness, that it is capable of displaying itself with the greatest brilliance. Winning the horses' trust and relaxation takes the greatest patience and self-discipline, a lesson that riders can learn only if they are made aware of the necessity of learning it.

Any horse can be ridden in harmony. Can there be a horse who resents going in balance or who hates a giving hand? Some horses may accept a strong hand and rough kick and use of the whip, but riders who use such aids are of course limited to riding these few unfortunate horses. With lightness, sensitivity and tact, any horse will respond, from the heavier built warmblood horses through the sensitive thoroughbreds.

Now some may say that one needs to drive the horse in order to develop the horse's strength, and that if that requires a strong spur or harsh whip, so be it. They say if the rider consequently needs a strong bit or special reins to control the horse, this is just the horse's problem. But these things are never necessary for the rider who knows the right way. To enable the horse to perform, we must of course provide gymnastic, strengthening work, enabling the hindquarters to carry more weight and to lift and lighten the forehand. Yet the work and exercise required must also remain in harmony, and new movements and exercises have to be introduced in a way that enables the horse to understand and eagerly accept the work. Enlightened training is the result when we energize, strengthen and engage the horse through gymnastic exercises that fully express the horse's nature while keeping him supple, balanced, and happy. As Herr von Neindorff has said, "one's goal should be to achieve great things playfully."

I will later set forth technical details of how movements are to be performed, how the aids are given, how the horse should react. But I will also discuss how to introduce new movements to the horse in very gradual and progressive ways. For example, after becoming used to a slight positioning on a 20 meter circle, the horse thinks nothing of being asked for shoulder-in on the circle. When this is familiar, the circle is flattened on the long side of the arena, becoming shoulder-in along the track, with the horse never confronted with something new or disturbing. Does this take longer than the direct approach of bringing the horse around the corner and trying to shove and pull him into his first shoulder-in? Perhaps the direct approach can achieve a shoulder-in like movement somewhat sooner, but how long will it then take to overcome the horse's suspicion and lack of confidence that was created at the very outset? Riding and training horses is difficult enough without creating more obstacles to success.

Others may say that without strong discipline and hard work we can not prepare a horse for the top levels of competition, that "classical" and competitive riding are mutually exclusive. This is nonsense. If you want to ride a test that is rough and forced, then by all means practice rough and forced riding at home. The competitions that I know of are called "shows." People bring their horses to *show* what they have mastered, to feel proud of their horse and accomplishment. Everyone wants to perform (and/or see) elegant, fluid, athletic tests. If this is your goal, I recommend that you practice elegant, fluid and athletic riding at home. People don't want to see your spurs in the horse's side, the mouth open, unnatural movements, or ears pinned back. As my old friend Willi Schultheis, one of the best trainers in the world, said years ago: "That which is beautiful must also be good!"

On the other hand, don't confuse harmony with sleeping! I think of Fred Astaire's dancing as harmony, not the sleeping "couch potato." We don't have to use force to make the horse powerful, athletic and elegant. These he gets from nature. It is our responsibility to maintain and nurture this athleticism while keeping a clear sense of cooperation and joy. As anyone who has ever tried to imitate Fred Astaire quickly finds out, it takes a great deal of strength, power and body control to make it look so effortless!

There has recently been in North America an explosion of interest in dressage. Although prior American experience with horsemanship has been long, deep, and rooted in a fundamental love of the horse, it has been primarily a utilitarian relationship. Horses were for so many years relied upon in so many ways: by the frontiersman, the cowboy and the cavalry. On the other hand, we have not had a long tradition of riding as art. Around the world, the situation is not much different. Until very recently, horses were almost exclusively used for transport, and occasionally for sport (such as hunting and racing). Only a handful of institutions and people had the money and/or interest in riding as an artistic endeavor. (Fortunately, these few institutions have managed to preserve a thread of knowledge through the centuries.) With the advent of the automobile, we now have a great growth in interest in riding for sport and art. Freed from the requirement that the horse do work, we have been able to focus on riding for fun. The explosion in sport horse breeding is one clear indication of this trend.

This history presents the American dressage enthusiast with a particular problem: the lack of qualified instruction and experienced horses from which riders can learn (schoolmasters). While I hope you will find my book (and others) helpful, one can not learn to ride without riding, and you will need an instructor. In Germany, even the top Olympic riders have instructors who work with them constantly. There are certainly many good teachers out there, but this is such a big country that they are quite often too far away, too busy and too often traveling here and there giving clinics. A very real problem then for the student is knowing how to find the right instructor. My advice is to be firm in your adherence to riding in harmony. Find the instructor that knows how to bring out the best in you and your horse's performance, without resorting to force and short-cuts. Be especially wary of comments like "I know this is not classically correct, but...."

As I hope to make clear, "classically correct" is a standard that holds up very well indeed for virtually every situation. The masters over the centuries have seen your problem before, have probably made the same mistakes you are about to make. By communicating their experiences over centuries and millennia, through schools and books, they have built a basis for all of us.

You may notice that the more experienced the horseman, the more strongly he or she believes that careful, patient work is necessary. All the great masters have gone through all the mistakes, and would like so much to help others avoid them. If they thought that beginners *should* make these mistakes, or that there was some benefit to them, they would not so uniformly and vehemently plead to others to avoid them. I have written this book for beginners as well as advanced riders. It is not written in secret code only known to the initiated. My advice to beginners is no different from my advice to advanced riders, other than to encourage the beginners to believe that they can accomplish great things, and to remind the advanced riders not to believe too much that they have accomplished everything.

Chapter 2

The Goals of Dressage Riding

2.1 Harmony

The goal of all dressage riding should be to bring the horse and rider together in harmony. By harmony, I mean a oneness of balance, purpose, and athletic expression. From the unison of a calm, square halt to the athletic movement of extended gaits, harmony requires sensitive communication through a sympathetic seat, invisible aids and the absence of force. This goal persists from the earliest handling of the foal to the highest achievements of the Grand Prix. As we ask the horse for more demanding work, we must become more tactful and intelligent in our guidance so as to maintain harmony throughout. Dressage training is not just the means to participate in the sport we call Dressage, but is the fundamental basis for all riding. Harmony between horse and rider should be the goal whether in the dressage arena or over fences, whether on a cross-country course or when carriage driving. There is no situation I can imagine where the horse's natural kindness and noble nature should be insulted or abused by dissonance, rough treatment or unbalanced riding.

The most obvious sign of harmony between horse and rider is the horse's relaxation in his work, whether on a loose rein at the walk or in a calm, controlled canter pirouette. Relaxation is both mental and physical. Physical relaxation comes from development of strength and power sufficient for the tasks at hand and the maintenance of balance that gives the horse confidence to swing freely forward. Mental relaxation comes through familiarity and trust that is born out of a respect for the rider. Horses are by nature herd animals, and will easily accept the guidance of a leader. It is the rider's job to earn the horse's trust and respect without fear.

Harmonious training of the dressage horse therefore requires study of the horse: how the horse is built, his temperament, the gaits, how he reacts to the aids. It also requires strengthening and suppling exercises which must be used in a proper and logical sequence through the seven fundamental elements of rhythm, relaxation, contact, impulsion, straightness, suppleness and collection.

Development of the dressage horse further requires that the rider learn the proper use of the aids: how to maintain and assist the horse's balance and when to give the aids. As we will discuss at length through the remainder of the book, there is a precise moment for giving each aid, and without proper timing the most subtle and elegant aid becomes clumsy, and the strongest aid becomes useless and ineffective.

In all of this study, the central focus of our attention must be the horse. While this is obvious in the study of gaits, it is also true of the process of learning the aids. Under the guidance of an experienced teacher, the rider attempts to learn the aids by paying close attention to the horse. Although the instructor and student must focus some attention on (important) details of the rider's position, in the end, the horse teaches the rider by showing his reaction to the aids. Whether this takes a year or a decade depends on how closely the rider pays attention and listens to what the horse is communicating to him. Throughout his career, the rider must learn to alter and refine the aids so the horse more clearly understands what is desired.

We must also come to know the mental and psychological nature of the horse. Many of us acquire our first experience in animal training through our relationship with our dogs. However, the differences in a predatory, hunting animal like a dog and a grazing animal like the horse must be reflected in a fundamentally different training approach between the two. The horse evolved on open prairies and steppes with wide vistas. Instinctively an easily frightened animal and highly sensitive to sound, his basic defense against attack is flight. Fighting through rearing and kicking is primarily herd and breeding behavior, and only secondarily a defense used when the horse feels trapped and unable to flee. Too often, the rider's aids form the trap and confinement. At worst, this can lead to rearing, bucking, and other dangerous situations; at best, it creates anxiety and resistance in the horse—destroying the relaxation fundamental to harmony.

The rider must also pay close attention to the horse in the physical conditioning and strengthening work. At each stage of work the horse must be taken to his limit, but never over. This limit will change as the horse becomes stronger and fitter, but the rider must be constantly mindful of its presence.

2.2 Why Dressage is Difficult

Before we get to the practical work, I would like to make one very important point, which we must constantly remember: the reason dressage is so difficult is that in this sport two fundamentally different living beings come together. On one side is the horse, which for me is the most beautiful of all animals, naturally good-natured, willing and faithful, but not very courageous. On the other side is the human being, the rider, who, unfortunately, is often impatient, ambitious and quick to resort to the use of the hands.

Almost all types of bad equine behavior are in some way created by demanding too much, using force and sometimes outright cruelty. "Anyone who can be cruel to animals cannot be a good person." (A. Schopenhauer[1]) Unfortunately, good intentions are not enough, and often inexperience and lack of knowledge lead riders to ask for more than the horse can do at the time.

The horse depends on us. The rider's trust in his horse and the horse's trust in his rider are the most important prerequisites for the success of the partnership. In competition the horse will use all his strength to prove his trustworthiness. For example, I could ride my jumpers toward any obstacle, because they knew that they could trust me not to ask more than they could do. And they would jump anything for me—a Volkswagen, a small horse, in and out of a garden restaurant, and so on.

Always remember in working a horse never to demand something that he does not understand. However, as I said earlier, in order to train a horse successfully, you must challenge the horse and come close to his limit, physically and mentally. But at the same time you have the enormous responsibility never to push him beyond this limit! Without approaching the horse's limit, you will teach him nothing new or the process will take much too long. If you push the horse beyond his ability, he will become frightened and lose confidence in the rider. You will destroy more of the training than you build up.

A good rider is sensitive to the moods of the horse. He recognizes the horse's feelings of trust, contentment, and joy in his own development of strength. The rider should also recognize the horse's feelings of excitement and fear and adjust his way of dealing with the horse accordingly. The horse expresses his emotions through his body. The eyes and movement of the ears and tail often indicate clearly the mood of the horse. Even such small details as good care in grooming and quiet handling will always be appreciated by the horse and reflected in his friendliness and attachment to us.

Thus man and horse should try to become a single entity. I know it is difficult, but it can be accomplished, and when it is, there is nothing more beautiful on earth! If one reaches this only now and then, it has been worth the effort. As Goethe (1749-1832) said, "The greatest joy on earth is found on the back of a horse."

2.3 How the Horse Learns

In comparison with other animals the horse is not very intelligent. We can be glad about this. If the horse were a cleverer creature, we would be afraid to get near him. How else would the horse have let us do to him all the things that we do? Riding, jumping, racing, eventing, pulling, farming, work in mines, etc., etc. I had to laugh when a student told me how the horse had done something wrong on purpose. A horse will never do anything on purpose. This requires deductive reasoning, which horses simply do not

---

[1] A. Schopenhauer (1788-1860) was one of the great philosophers and authors of German literature in the 19th century.

have. Only highly intelligent beings do things on purpose and with planning. But the horse has a quick instinct for self preservation, an unbelievably good memory for good things and even more capacity for remembering bad things.

I compare the horse with a small child. If one demanded total obedience from a child in kindergarten, he would become frightened and would no longer enjoy going to school. It is the same with horses.[1] One should remember never to lose one's patience, never to demand of the horse something that he cannot understand. Can one demand third or fourth grade work from a child in kindergarten? You can make yourself understood verbally with a child. You can give the child homework, show him specific exercises. In children there are differences in learning—some learn fast, some a little slower. The same differences apply to our horses (but don't expect too much from the homework).

Other significant factors in the training are the horse's conformation, breeding and temperament. Warmbloods are usually more lethargic and quieter and need to be more assertively handled and ridden. Thoroughbreds are somewhat more difficult in temperament, but when their trust is won they are wonderful to ride and require hardly any effort from the rider.

2.4 The Nature of the Rider

Now I will speak about the second living being in our partnership—the human. He should be able to work with his head better than with just his seat, legs and hands. Unfortunately, we are hand-oriented creatures. What does a baby do first? It tries to hold things in its hands. We do this into our advanced years. Therefore, we do much too much with our hands when it comes to riding. This in turn causes us to focus too much on the front of the horse instead of the more important hindquarters (the engine). I have known very few riders who do not try to force the horse into a frame with their hands. But the biggest enemy to the partnership of dressage is impatience and the human nature to dominate other creatures. To reach a good partnership, the rider must control himself before controlling his horse. Don't we always find fault with other people in life? Aren't we quite forgiving of our own mistakes? When our horse makes a small one, how quick we are with punishment! Shouldn't we be more generous and have more

---

[1] In starting young horses, I am always struck with the thought of how hard it must be for many foals being weaned from the mare. After frolicking in the pasture with other young horses for two years, he then experiences a tremendous shock when the maternal and herd bonds are broken and he is taken away. The young horse is then often forced into a dark van or trailer and is thrown around inside, eventually being put in a stall that shall be his home for many months or even years. It is only because of their trusting and accepting nature that they tolerate this upheaval in their young lives – another reason we should take care never to violate their trust.

understanding for our horse too? On the other hand, when the horse does well, we should not take this for granted, but show the horse our approval.

Short cuts will always be noticeable in the future training. When the horse does something wrong or doesn't understand the aids, the rider should ask himself if the foundation of the training was correct or did he try to take a short cut. You can never put back what you leave out of the horse's basic training and that which is done wrong at the beginning can never be completely undone—you can only make one beginning. Therefore, it cannot be said often enough that the initial foundation in training the horse is the most important.

Truly the hardest part of good riding is the foundation. One must take enough time. If the foundation is correct, the so-called harder exercises of upper levels will come easily to the horse. But if a horse's basic schooling was incorrect, he will look cramped and antagonistic.

At a minimum, it will take four years of training to take a young horse to the point where he is doing all the Grand Prix movements, and another year to bring these all together so he is ready for showing at that level. This is only possible with the best and most experienced riders and most talented horses, under the guidance of an expert trainer. Don't think of this as a timetable to be followed! Instead, think of this as an absolute minimum. Anything quicker must involve short-cuts and mistakes. These can be seen in poor or pacing walks, open mouths, tongues hanging out, four-beat canter, loss of rhythm, a passage-like trot, and so on.

So many talented horses are ruined by a rush to Grand Prix. The more talented the horse, the more they give, and the more they get pushed. Once over the limit, they lose the fun and the brilliance, and are quickly soured or even made lame or sick from the stress.

I know that beginning riders are anxious to progress, and feel that careful, progressive work is leaving them "behind" their friends, who are quickly winning ribbons at lower levels in shows. The wisdom of patient, consistent work is most clearly felt by the riders who start to ride the upper level tests, and come upon real difficulties–the open mouth, the lack of a forward, swinging back, and so on. They will try all sorts of "expert" advice, or try to resort to force (such as cranking the mouths shut), or simply blame the horses as being unfit for the Grand Prix. With a bit more help (or luck) they come to see that the mistakes were introduced very early in the training. If they are really lucky, these riders can simply go all the way back to the basics and work very carefully to bring these horses back through, although this is *much* more difficult. More likely, hopefully, these riders will learn from this mistake and their next horses will reap the reward of this experience.

2.5 Trust and Respect

Trust and respect are two-way streets. We want the horse to accept us as leaders of the herd, to guide them safely and to provide protection and comfort. In return, they will give us their respect, and willing submission to our ideas about what to do next, and when and where. But this respect can only be based on well-deserved trust. Fear should never be part of the relationship.

Our actions and attitudes around the horse must continually be guided by a desire to earn the trust of the horse. Such trust is a delicate and precious treasure. The rider who knows the pleasure and results of such trust will always go out of his way to cultivate and renew this trust at every opportunity. It is far too easy to crush and destroy this trust, and once lost, far, far more difficult to rebuild. Col. A. Podhajsky once said: "To bring the horse to his perfect expression of his abilities, one can never do this with force. It can only be done with a very fine balance between pleading and firm handling, with very frequent praise, and very infrequent punishment." The attitude that "you *will* listen and obey..." must never be found around horses.

If at times, it seems that a bit of force is necessary, it can only be a valid approach if the rider: 1) knows exactly why he is using such force, and what will happen immediately afterwards, and 2) abandons the attempt if it is unsuccessful. By this I mean that, if with experience the rider (thinks he) knows that a brief use of force will solve a problem, and he (thinks he) knows just what will happen, then it is reasonable to try. For example, a more forceful kick with a spur may be an appropriate response to a horse who kicks out at the rider's leg in an attempt to assert dominance. If what he **expects** to happen does **not**, then he must stop using force immediately, and find another way to solve his problem, otherwise the continued use of the force deteriorates into senseless punishment from which the horse learns nothing.

Chapter 3
The Foundation of All Riding

3.1 Calm, Forward and Straight

What is most important in training? Throughout the history of horse training, the answer has been Gustaf Steinbrecht's dictum: "Ride your horse forward and make him straight."[1] Reitmeister Festerling[2] had the end of his arena inscribed in a large font: "Ride your horse calm, forward and make him straight." I liked this slight re-wording so much that I adopted it in my teaching.

On the race track, the cross-country course, or over stadium jumps, we don't often forget the importance of forward movement, but within the confines of the dressage arena, it is sometimes more difficult to remember that the art of dressage is also an expression of *movement.* The basic nature of horseback riding is progression forward, and throughout training, we must remember this fundamental purpose. It is not posed or static, and we can not form the horse into beautiful images without movement. Too often, riders can be seen trying to hold their horses into a "round frame" or otherwise inhibit their horses' desire to move forward. This usually comes from learning by imitating or otherwise confusing the end (a supple, engaged, round horse) with the means.

In German, we use the word *Schwung* to describe the proper forward movement of the horse. It is like a swing arcing forward. The concept includes swinging through the back and a powerful elasticity of the steps. This swing and elasticity can only come from riding energetically forward, but is lost when the horse rushes. It requires a soft, giving hand that keeps connection with the mouth.

We will talk a good deal about the necessity for energy from the hind leg. It is the fundamental source of all power for the movement of the horse. But the power of the hind leg should be a "carrying" power, not a "pushing" power. If you want to sit in a heavy wagon behind a horse, you

---

[1] Gustaf Steinbrecht (1808 - 1885) *Das Gymnasium des Pferdes.* Col. Hans von Heydebrecht (1866-1935) was one of the organizers for the German *Reitvorschrift* (Rule Book) in 1912, based on the work of Steinbrecht. This book was written for the army, and still forms the basics of the current rule book.

[2] Guenter Festerling is one of only 15 Reitmeisters (Riding Masters) in Germany and was very successful in both dressage and jumping, and was the head of the German Reitschule in Warendorf, where all Bereiter (Apprentice Instructors and Trainers) and Reitlehrer (Riding Instructors) examinations are given.

will want him to push with his hind legs. If you want to sit on top, you will need the hind leg to carry you forward.

The apparently simple command to "make him straight" hides a world of balance, obedience, control, finesse and careful observation, and the admonition "Ride your horse calm..." means that nothing can be gained by force, and that the horse must remain in balance and rhythm, with relaxation.

3.2 The Seven Elements of Training

The requirements for riding your horse calm, forward and straight are embodied in the seven key elements of training[3]:

1. **Rhythm**. As in music, rhythm refers to the temporal sequence of beats—the four-beat pattern of the walk, the two-beat pattern of the trot, and the three-beat pattern of the canter. The rhythm of the gaits must be regular and even. Rhythm is closely related to relaxation in that lack of regularity is a sure sign of loss of relaxation. The rate at which the rhythm of each gait is repeated is the tempo. The rider must seek out and find the proper tempo for each gait for each horse. When the rhythm is rushed, the horse loses his balance and relaxation. We seek out a clear rhythm early in a horse's training yet have to pay constant attention to the regularity of the rhythm all the way through the training.

2. **Relaxation**. A relaxed horse is not stiff, not tight, not frightened. There is the obvious relaxation of the free walk on a long rein or a long, stretching trot, but there is also relaxation in action: a pirouette, passage or piaffe can either be tense or relaxed. Only when relaxed will the horse show brilliance in the movement. Muscles are found in extensor-flexor pairs and a relaxed horse tends to contract one or the other to achieve the desired movement of the limbs. A tense, nervous horse contracts both extensor and flexor muscles at the same time, thereby tightening and stiffening the joints through the action of the opposing forces. A truly relaxed horse will have every muscle relaxed from the poll to the tail, moving in regular rhythm and responding easily to all aids, and the hoofprints are light. The rider can take up the reins or give the reins, and the horse will maintain his rhythm without running away. This must be true of all three gaits.

3. **Contact**. Contact is the connection between the rider's hand and the horse's mouth. It lies at the center of our ability to control and

---

[3] The six elements of rhythm, relaxation, contact, *schwung*, straightness and collection form the basis of Steinbrecht's theory, as set forth by Redwitz, Heydebreck and Bürkner in the 1912, 1926 and 1937 German *Reitvorschrift* (Rule Book). We add the element suppleness to emphasize the meanings inherent in the German words which may otherwise be lost in translation.

communicate with the horse. For training we need very precise and responsive controls. It requires that the reins remain straight so they can instantaneously transmit increases or decreases in tension in the rider or the horse, and it requires that the horse's mouth remain soft, closed, and relaxed. The must go confidently to the bit, seeking the rider's hand contact. Contact is needed to balance the horse, keep him supple, regulate the impulsion, straighten the horse, guide the turns, and to collect. True contact must come from the activating and allowing seat and leg aids, not a pulling with the hand. The horse will readily pull back against a pulling hand, and the communication is lost when the horse locks the jaw and ignores any subtlety the rider may be trying to achieve through the hand. "Chewing the bit" is a common expression used to describe the soft connection desired in the horse's mouth. It does not mean gnashing with the teeth or opening the mouth. A proper contact does not require a flash or dropped noseband to hold the mouth closed.

4. ***Schwung***[4]. describes the power of the hindquarters that carries the horse forward ***and its transmission*** over the back. Expression of this power requires an engaged, active hind leg and the release of the propulsive energy over the back, withers, neck, poll, mouth, and back to the receiving influence of the rider's hands. The closely related term, engagement of the hind leg, refers to the articulation of the joints of the hind leg, and like a spring gives more energy the more it is compressed. As relaxation and rhythm are the mental prerequisites for work, *Schwung* is the physical prerequisite. Only when the horse has *Schwung* can one ride in relaxed rhythm, with contact, supple, straight, and collected. There can be *Schwung* without collection, but never collection without *Schwung*.

5. **Straightness**. The concept of straightness refers to the evenness of the horse from side to side. Although the horse's skeleton is symmetric, the horse is by nature one-sided (as people are right- or left-handed). The asymmetric development of muscles leads to a crookedness that inhibits the full performance of the horse. We see this in the typical situation where one side of the horse is much stiffer than the other. Thus movements such as canter, travers, half pass are easier to one side than the other. Through our training we aim to gradually bring the horse into more and more evenness on both sides. Only when the horse is straight is he able to perform every movement and figure correctly.

---

[4] The German word *Schwung* is unfortunately difficult to translate into English, but I think that its usual translation, *impulsion*, is misleading, since *Schwung* implies a good deal of "swing" and movement over the back, while many students seem to equate impulsion to engagement of the hind leg.

6. **Suppleness**. The power of the hind leg and control through the weight, legs, and hand will come to work against the rider's aims unless the horse is willing and able to flex and to readily follow the directives of the rider. Elastic, obedient fluidity of movement is the essence of suppleness, whether expressed through a supple back that transmits the power of the hind leg forward, or a softness to lateral bending that allows the horse to effortlessly flow from one small figure to another. The horse must be always ready to go forward, sideways or backward and all turns must be made without resistance. In other words, the horse should respond easily to all the rider's aids.

7. **Collection**. Collection is the highest step in our staircase of training. It must be built squarely on the foundations of the previous six elements, since to a major extent it represents the distillation of the previous elements into a concentrated expression of the greatest harmony between horse and rider. It involves the lowering and increased engagement of the hindquarters that allow them to come more forward and under the weight of the rider. This elevates and lightens the forehand and makes possible the seemingly effortless execution of the smallest school figures or the brilliant extended movements. While the rider will have the feeling of riding more and more uphill, the end result will be both horse and rider truly in heaven.

   These elements can be thought of in terms of the three pairs (rhythm-relaxation, impulsion-contact, straightness-suppleness) leading to collection. Rhythm and relaxation go together throughout the horse's training. *Schwung* is the "go," for which contact provides the control. Suppleness is the softness and flexibility which is needed for straightness. Collection is the embodiment of them all.

   Different writers may present these elements in a slightly different order, but that is because they are really quite strongly intertwined. As we develop contact and *Schwung*, the horse gains balance and confidence, and the rhythm and relaxation will improve, as we develop better suppleness, the contact will become more sure and the rhythm clearer, as we develop better straightness, suppleness and *Schwung* will improve. But the order is not entirely arbitrary. It is clearly wrong to demand straightness from a young horse without first establishing rhythm and relaxation, and it is not wise to ask for too much contact without relaxation.

Figure 1: *The scales of training*

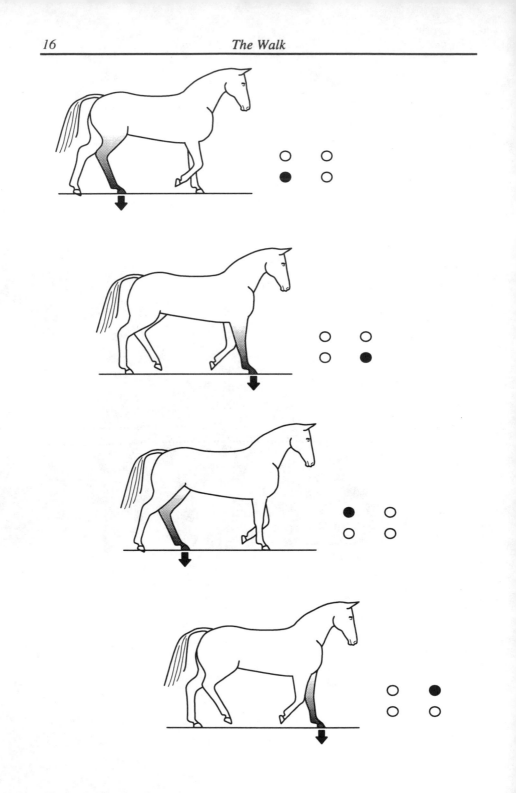

Figure 2: *The four beats of the walk.*

Chapter 4

The Gaits

The three gaits of the horse are the walk, trot and canter. Within each gait, we can ride free, working, medium, extended and collected paces.

4.1 The Walk

The walk is for me the most difficult gait and is given the least attention. Of the three gaits, it is the one with the least natural swing, which is why it needs to be ridden with good impulsion and engagement. The walk is the one gait used at all levels of training, from starting the unbroken horse through Grand Prix. It presents different and interesting problems at all levels. First I will describe the different types of walk, then return to a discussion of how to school the horse at the walk.

The walk is a striding movement of four beats. The beats come from the same side but not in the same rhythm interval: right hind, right front, left hind, left front. This is how it should always continue. If the horse moves the legs on the same side forward and together, he is doing a so-called "pace."

4.1.1 Free Walk on Long Reins

The natural walk of a horse in freedom we call the "free walk" in dressage. In the free walk the hind hoof should step two or three hoof lengths over the hoof print made by the front hoof, and the frame of the horse should be long and low with light rein contact. The nose of the horse must remain in front of the vertical. The free walk is used as the basis for the work with the young horse, as a warm-up to the schooling of a well-trained horse and as a final loosening after a working session. The quality of the free walk comes from nature.

4.1.2 Working Walk

The working walk is ridden lightly on the bit. It is similar to the medium walk but is used in the training of younger horses. The overstride should be one to two hoof lengths. Young horses should not be ridden on the bit in the walk except briefly before the transition to the trot.

4.1.3 Extended Walk

In the extended walk the hind hoof should step clearly two or three hoof lengths over the hoof print of the front hoof. The frame of the horse should be clearly lengthened, the neck becoming somewhat longer and the face of the horse in silhouette should be somewhat in front of the vertical, but clearly still on the aids, and not so long and low as in the free walk.

In the extended walk the contact between the rider's hand and the horse's mouth should be maintained. Under no circumstances should the horse get quicker. Rather, the horse should take longer strides.

4.1.4 Medium Walk

The medium walk is between the extended and working walk and is performed by more advanced horses, clearly showing some lengthening and overstride of one and a half to two and a half hoof lengths. The neck of the horse should be a little bit longer than in collected walk, but the poll should be the highest point. There should be a good connection from the rider's hand to the horse's mouth.

4.1.5 Collected Walk

In the collected walk the hind hoof should land slightly behind the hoof print of the front hoof. The hindquarters should carry more weight, and the forehand is thus lightened and elevated with the poll the highest point. The frame becomes shorter and higher in elevation, looking prouder. The nose comes close to the vertical, but never behind. At the very earliest the young horse will be able to do the collected walk after a year's training, and only when he has learned to willingly engage his hindquarters.

4.1.6 Walk on Loose Reins

In the free walk on loose reins the rider gives the horse total freedom from rein contact and allows him to fully stretch his neck. The horse strides out with a pleased expression in his eyes. The free walk is a refreshing treat for the horse after he has worked hard and accomplished something good in the daily workout. At the beginning and end of every training session, the rider should let the horse walk freely on loose reins. The walk should be well forward, but without rushing. The difference between free walk on long reins and free walk on loose reins is in the contact. On long reins, the contact is light, and the horse is asked to pay attention to the work, while allowing him maximum stretching under control. In walk on loose reins, the horse is free to look around and otherwise relax mentally.

4.1.7 Working the Horse at the Walk

As I mentioned above, I find the walk particularly difficult. This is primarily because the walk does not naturally create impulsion or *schwung*. The rider must drive the horse forward without rushing. This can easily lead to too much tightness in the rein. As riders try to get the horse in a frame, without enough energy, the walk gets poorer and poorer until it results in a loss of rhythm, and pacing. For this reason one seldom sees a good walk in higher level dressage.

Figure 3: *Walk on long reins, walk on loose reins. On long reins, the contact is light, and the horse is asked to pay attention to the work, while allowing him maximum stretching under control. In walk on loose reins, the horse is free to look around and otherwise relax mentally.*

Young horses must be started out only in free walk. With very green horses, the rider must be alert for any sudden shying, jumping and bucking, so one needs to maintain sufficient control for safety's sake. But this is a point where one can start to lose the quality of the walk. The more you can trust the horse and the more the horse trusts you, the more you should make him go long and free at the walk. When riding for my mentor, Col. Aust, we were never allowed to have more than the slightest rein contact with the mouth on the young horses.

With more advanced horses, the transition from a free walk or loose rein walk to a working walk is made from the hind end first. The rider generates engagement from the hind leg, which naturally leads to a shorter frame from which the reins are picked up. So it is with young horses. We ask for more liveliness in the free walk and more power without tightening the front end. This increased *schwung* comes before rein contact—not by the few strides as in a trained horse's transition—but by a few months! During this work, pay particular attention to rhythm and relaxation and developing the horse's balance and power.

When the horse is prepared in the walk in this way, he develops confidence that he can go forward without interference from the hand. This confidence and trust are essential for avoiding problems such as jogging, pacing, stopping, taking short steps, and "Spanish walk."

When the horse is ready to accept contact, one has to be careful to maintain engagement and to always think forward. The walk must be ridden energetically enough so that the next step can be a trot, canter, or halt, and ridden with enough softness that the next step can be on a small circle. Every gait should not be ridden for itself, but should be ridden for the next transition or movement. In dressage tests, the transitions come at letters in the arena. When schooling one should always be ready for a transition at any point.[1]

As the horse is moved up in the training, and accepts more collection at the walk, the above rule must still apply. As in all gaits, but especially in walk, the horse must not be ridden too long in collection. After collection, always lengthen the horse in a calm, forward walk.

4.1.8 Walk Corrections

The major problems that arise in connection with the walk are:

1. Steps that are too short
2. Pacing
3. Strides with too long an overstride
4. Jogging
5. "Spanish walk"

Short Walk. A short walk can come from nature or poor early work. If the horse is born with a straight shoulder and short back, the rider can improve the length of the stride slightly by working over ground poles. I space them 80cm (30-32") apart but then adjust the spacing so the horse has to stretch slightly. Start out first with one pole, then two, three and four and keep the reins long and the horse active behind. When the steps go better, the spacing can be slightly widened. While it is not possible to improve this walk a great deal, one can make a small difference—but it takes years. It is important to ride horses with a short walk on long reins whenever possible. When horses have been started with too much early contact, the only solution is to go back to the beginning and work only on long reins.

Pacing and Overstride. One of the difficulties presented in the walk is pacing, mentioned earlier, in which the right front and right hind leg step forward at the same time and then the left front and left hind leg step forward. This results in a two-beat rhythm instead of the correct four-beat rhythm. The pace-like walk is very rarely born into the horse; it is usually the product of incorrect training. It comes from tenseness, and the movement is more mechanical than flowing.

Horses with a tremendous overstride of four to five hoof lengths in the free walk and in general having a very big walk are more likely to have a pace-like walk when collected than horses with a shorter walk stride. When the long strides of the walk are shortened too much by the rider's hands the horse often responds either by a sort of goose-stepping or Spanish walk or by pacing.

---

[1] Early in the training, the transitions should be made only when the horse and rider are ready and in balance.

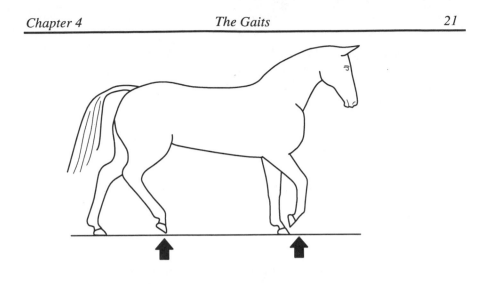

Figure 4: *Pacing walk. The right front and right hind leg step forward at the same time and then the left front and left hind leg step forward. This results in a two-beat rhythm instead of the correct four-beat rhythm.*

The best correction for these walk-related problems is to work the horse at the walk in a shoulder-in or haunches-in position, choosing the one to which the horse reacts best. The rein contact must not overwhelm the horse. It must be kept soft, yet not completely released. The goal is to activate the hind legs of the horse without holding the reins too tightly. Excessive rein contact is what produces the goose-stepping or pacing. After correct shoulder-in work, the horse will often give up the pacing, but unfortunately the problem will resurface immediately when the hand of the rider overpowers even slightly the driving aids. One should always drive more than restrain. A good recipe to follow: Hold—1/2 lb.; Drive—1 1/2 lb.

Jogging. Another problem in the walk is jogging, seen most often in high-strung horses. Jogging usually comes from fright and lack of relaxation. Again, if the rider tries to control this with the hand, the horse will jog even more. In my experience the use of the shoulder-in or haunches-in is again the best solution. It is important for the rider to sit deeply with his *Kreuz* (seat bones), not allowing the horse to free himself by dropping his back. Full halts are also helpful, as are voltes followed by shoulder-in on the long side. It is a bit of a game of patience to work with these horses but the only solution is to teach them to carry weight regularly on their hind legs and thus give up the short jogging, irregular steps.

Spanish Walk. The Spanish walk is a very bad habit that is not natural, but acquired through mistakes in the training. It is created by too much driving and too strong a restraining hand. These horse always exhibit lack of acceptance of the bit, such as open mouths, and tongues over the bit or hanging out. The horse gets tense and stiff because his back hollows and he cannot move freely in the shoulder. As a result, the movement of the stiff, constrained forelegs goes extremely high up and bounces straight down. This walk is a circus movement, and is often applauded by observers who lack knowledge and understanding of its deleterious effects on the horse. Correcting this habit once it has been acquired by the horse is very difficult. The rider must be very careful in balancing the driving and restraining aids. It will take some time and patience to win back the horse's confidence and willingness to go over the back and into the correct contact in the walk. Again, work in the shoulder-in or haunches-in, which encourages the hind leg to step under, will be of help in this process.

4.2 The Trot

In the trot the two diagonal pairs of legs move alternately forward and land as pairs. This gives the trot its two-beat rhythm. Between the changing of the pairs there is a moment of suspension in which none of the four feet are touching the ground.

The horse's conformation is of great significance in the trot, as in all gaits. The harmonious build including the length of the neck, a sloping shoulder, the length of the back, the length of the croup, and the angulation of the joints of the hindquarters will tell much about the desirable qualities of the trot movement. These qualities are relaxed impulsion, light-footedness, elasticity and length of stride.

If a rider possesses skill in the art of riding, the quality of a mediocre trot can be improved, especially through the gymnasticizing of the hindquarters, because this improves impulsion in the horse. The trot should be energetic but not rushed. In all paces within the trot (working, lengthened, medium, extended and collected) the rhythm and tempo should remain the same. The differences lie in the length of stride, the length of the neck, and the length of the base, which is the distance between the pair of hind legs and the pair of front legs.

4.2.1 Working Trot

First comes the "working trot." The length of stride of the working trot is between the "medium" and the "collected" trot. The working trot should be energetic and full of impulsion without rushing. There must be rhythm and suspension appropriate for each individual. Tracking up—the hind hoof landing in the front hoof print—is a sign of the correctness of the working trot. Of course, extremes in conformation may alter the tracking up slightly.

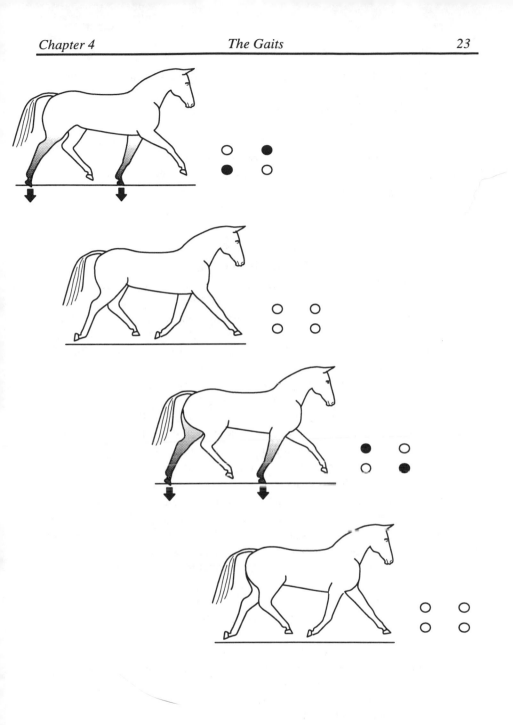

Figure 5: *The beats of the trot.*

The working trot is used for the training of the young or green horse and for warming up horses at every level. It serves also to relax the horse. Only when the working trot is confirmed, with the horse on the aids, in balance and the haunches sufficiently engaged can the lengthening of stride, or extension, and collection be started. But the working trot should still be used at the beginning of the daily workout for all horses. Also, at the end of the work use the working trot, then let the horse "chew the reins out"—as you give more and more rein length, the horse must seek the contact, without jerking the reins.

4.2.2 Rising or Posting Trot

The purpose of posting is to spare the horse's back and joints. Young horses should be ridden at the rising trot. Trained horses should be started in the daily work at the rising trot (after walking on loose reins) in order to get them feeling loose and supple as soon as possible. The rider rises to the trot only in the working trot and medium trot. In general, when trotting during a hack, the rising trot is appropriate. When the rider is stiff and the horse is not giving enough with his back, it is better to use rising trot to make it more inviting for the horse.

In the rising trot the rider does not sit every stride, but rather stays up out of the saddle, supporting himself on the knees, inner calves, and stirrups for one stride before gliding back into the saddle with the next stride. The horse lifts the rider into the posting, and the rider should remain relaxed and supple to follow the natural rhythm of the horse.

In the riding arena the rider should sit in the rising trot on the inside hind leg of the horse. This means that when the horse's inside hind leg is under his body and on the ground, the rider's seat should be in the saddle. To simplify finding the correct diagonal, the rider should check that he is sitting when the horse's outside shoulder goes back. Rising on the wrong diagonal will feel uncomfortable for both the horse and rider. When changing the rein, the rider should sit an uneven number of strides—preferably just one—and then rise again. When hacking at the trot, the rider should change diagonals occasionally in order to exercise both sides of the horse equally.

It is important when riding the posting trot not to stand up too high, looking as if standing almost erect. Also, when sitting down, the rider should merely touch, not fall heavily back into the saddle. It should look elegant with the rider's lower leg well centered under his body and his upper body inclined forward very slightly, yet not leaning over. The rider should be ready to sit, and to use his seat at any moment.

The correct technique in beginning to rise to the trot is very important. The rider should take care not to begin posting in a rough, jerky fashion. Many sensitive horses will break into the canter immediately if ridden this way.

4.2.3 Lengthening Stride at the Trot

The lengthening of stride at the trot describes itself well. The strides should become longer without losing the rhythm or getting faster in tempo. In fact the rhythm and tempo should stay the same. The lengthening comes out of the working trot, not out of a collected trot. The horse does not yet need to have the carrying power of collection, but must have sufficient impulsion to increase the propulsive power of each step. As the trot lengthens, the horse's neck should get a little longer.

The addition of lengthening of stride to U.S. dressage tests and its incorporation in training was an excellent idea. In Germany there is only working, medium, extended and collected trot. Lengthening for young horses and riders is better so that neither are overstressed and so the rider does not ask for too much at first.

4.2.4 Medium Trot

In the medium trot the steps should be longer than in the working trot, but not more hurried. The frame and neck of the horse should be somewhat longer. The nose should be slightly in front of the vertical and the poll must remain the highest point.

The medium trot is distinguished from the lengthened trot in several ways. The impulsion from the energetic hindquarters should be clearly expressed. The horse should carry himself—that means he should not lean on the reins. The hind legs should not widen in the medium trot and should land somewhat in front of the hoof prints of the front feet. The medium trot must come from the collected trot. It can only be as good as the collected trot that precedes it, because it expresses the carrying power that the horse is now developing in its collected work.

4.2.5 Extended Trot

In the extended trot there should be a clear increase in extension qualities from the medium trot. this means increased impulsion, increased length of stride, increased suspension and very energetic use of the hind legs. The frame of the horse should be distinctly expanded, meaning that the neck should stretch and become somewhat longer, but the poll must remain the highest point and the horse should carry himself.

The development and use of strength in the horse's movement is at its maximum at the extended trot, and yet this trot must also clearly demonstrate the maintenance of suppleness with no stiffening or cramping of muscles. The front hooves should land where they point. The nose should be slightly more in front of the vertical than at medium trot. In order to allow a full expression and correct reach of the legs a line extended along the face of the horse should meet the ground at the point where the front foot lands. These qualities assure that the horse will have maximum freedom and reach of the shoulders, and that the hind leg has the freedom to come under and

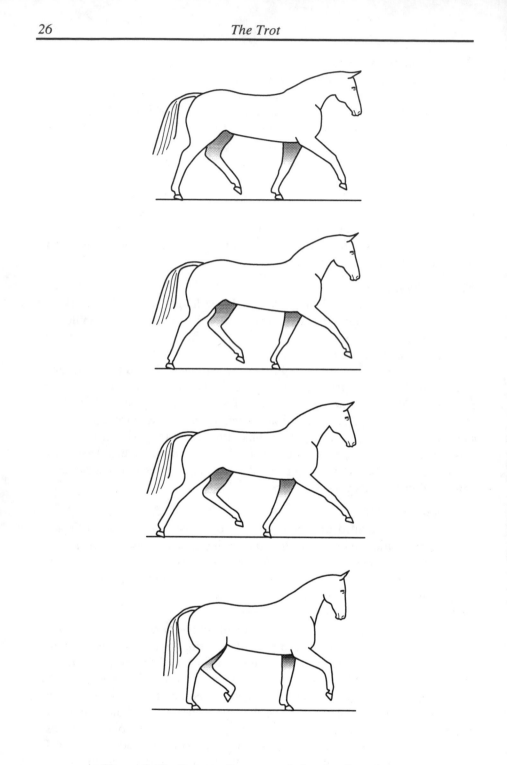

Figure 6. Working, medium, extended and collected trot.

carry the horse forward. Only then does the horse achieve the length of stride that is required in this exercise.

Because we are asking the horse to extend the gait beyond what he is used to, it is essential to maintain the horse's balance through the gait. The balance is disturbed when the rider holds the front too much, or when he drops the reins. If the hand holds the nose behind the vertical, the action of the hind leg is stopped, and the front hoof will end up coming down backwards, no matter how far forward and upward it might reach. The balance is also disturbed when the front legs extend too far, but the hind legs remain short. This results from the horse hollowing the back, and he has to step shorter behind to keep himself in balance. The profile of the horse's face should stay a little in front of the vertical. The power should come from the hind leg and needs to be metered out through the hand with the shoulder swinging freely forward to make room for the hind leg to step up and under the center of the horse.

When studying a picture of the horse at the extended trot, taken from profile, the diagonal pair of legs extending forward should be exactly parallel. This means that if the front leg is higher than the diagonal hind leg, the extension is not correct. It is interesting to check this in photos with a ruler. The rider should be at first satisfied with a very few steps that are in balance and with the power coming from the hind leg. The amount of extension should be no more than that which the rider can bring back to collection without force and without losing balance.

The horse whose diagonal pairs are is parallel and correct is a "back mover" (*Rueckengaenger*). The impulsion circulates from the haunches through the back, neck, and poll, mouth and hand correctly. The front hoof lands where it points.

The horse whose pairs are incorrect, is a "leg mover" (*Schenkelgaenger*). This horse throws his front leg much higher than the diagonal hind leg can reach. He does not use his back, but actually drops his back. The hindquarters and forehand are divided and work separately. The front hoof does not land where it points. These horses are tight and cramped and travel wide behind as they throw their front ankles and hoofs in the air. This goes against nature. Col. Aust always described these horses as "A General out in front, but with no army following behind." This happens because the horse is forced too much with driving aids and holding aids. The driving aid sends the foreleg forward, but the holding hands limit this forward movement. The only response is for the leg to swing higher and get stiff, falling back to the ground without achieving much real forward movement. With so much holding, the back is hollow, the shoulder is restricted and the hind leg can not follow enough and has to take a much shorter step than the front legs are showing.

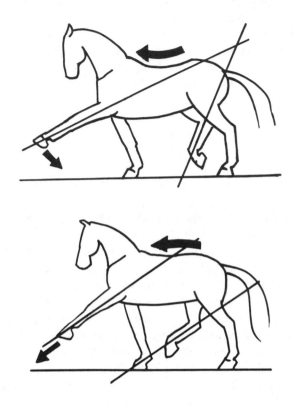

Figure 7: *"Back mover" and "leg mover." The back mover allows energy to flow from the hindquarter over the back, neck, poll and mouth back though the hand to the hindquarter. The leg mover does not use his back, and the hindquarters and forehand are divided and work separately.*

Similarly, the tendency to widen behind in the medium and extended trots usually comes from being pushed in these paces before the horse is really capable of balancing himself. When the rider prematurely decides to attempt the medium or extended trot by "chasing" the horse with his aids, the horse compensates for his lack of development by widening his hind legs in an effort to stay in balance. Therefore, one should never begin with the extensions when the horse is not comfortably in balance.

The extended trot is developed from a confirmed medium trot, which should likewise come from the confirmed lengthening of stride, which in turn comes from a confirmed working trot. Thus, the confirmed working trot is the basis for all extensions. This order is essential to maintain. The rider should not ask for too much too soon, especially when the horse shows a natural talent for the extension. These horses just need to develop confidence and familiarity with the movement in a correct balance.

It is extremely important when riding trot extensions to do them only to the degree and for as long as the rider has the horse completely under control. Do not force the horse into extensions to the point that it is difficult to collect the trot again. Never start the extension at the same place; the horse should always wait until his rider gives him the aids to start. He should not start by himself! For example, when riding on the diagonal, one should keep the collected trot as long as it takes to be sure that the horse is completely obedient. It is better to ride the whole diagonal in the collected trot, if necessary, than ever to let the horse take off disobediently in an extension. The horse should never know at what point the rider will ask for the medium or extended trot. Otherwise, he may develop the frequently observed bad habit of some horses to take off in an extension when ridden onto the diagonal. Whose fault is this? The trainer who taught the horse. One should avoid this at all costs. If it happens, the rider should collect the trot and put the horse in a shoulder-in which will engage the inside hind leg. An even better solution is to never let the situation go so far!

The medium and extended trot can be only as good as the collection from which the extension proceeds. The collected trot should be ridden so that an extension can be executed anywhere—on the short side, out of the corner, on the diagonal, centerline, etc. As in all riding, every movement should not be ridden just for itself, but rather as the preparation for the next exercise. A favorite exercise of mine is to ride shoulder-in approximately half-way down the long side and then go onto the diagonal and ride medium or extended trot. This exercise collects, engages and supples the horse in good preparation for an extension.

4.2.6 Collected Trot

The collected trot has very special characteristics: the elevation of the steps, the increased flexion in the joints of the haunches (hip, stifle, hock and ankle) and the lowering of the haunches. The haunches take on more of the horse's weight, and the forehand is lightened, which results in the elevation of the forehand. The degree of elevation of the forehand corresponds to the degree of flexion of the hindquarter joints. Thus, the correct elevation is relative to the horse's ability to flex and lower the haunches. The neck of the horse will get a little bit shorter, with more elevation, but he must give in the jaw. The poll must remain the highest point and the nose must remain slightly ahead of the vertical. The expression of the horse should get proud, but still relaxed in full concentration. In collection, the horse gets the most power and thrust from the hind leg over the back into the rider's hand, without leaning on the hand.

In contrast unfortunately, there exists also something called "the absolute elevation" which has been forced by the hands of the rider and always leads to an overly shortened frame. The hind legs are not sufficiently

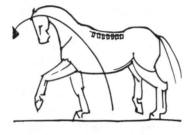

Figure 8: *Absolute elevation (top), absolute flexion (middle) and proper flexion (bottom). Only with natural elevation and flexion can the energy be carried through a round back from the hind leg to the poll.*

engaged in this situation. The elasticity and natural purity of the movement are diminished. This "absolute elevation" is unethical among good riders and therefore to be avoided.

In developing the collected trot, it is essential to engage the hindquarters over and over again without driving the horse into leaning on the rider's hands. The rider must balance the effect of the aids between driving and restraining. The hind legs should be engaged repeatedly through increased leg and back aids, with the energy directed up and over the back and neck into the rider's rein contact. The contact should be soft and steady—receiving, not restricting. This contact sends the aids back to the hindquarters, which in turn catch this flow of impulsion, increasing the carrying power and the reach of the hind legs under the horse's body. The use of collecting half steps is a very good exercise to engage the hind legs for the collected trot, and later will help explain the piaffe to the horse and rider.

The collected trot should be ridden energetically but not too freely or it will become the working trot. Nor should it be too restrained into a passage-like trot. In order to get the right amount of engagement in the collected trot, it helps to think of the piaffe, but only to a certain point. If the strides become too suspended and passage-like, the rider has gone too far. This is a big mistake, yet often seen in competition. To avoid this, clever riders sometimes simply perform the working trot with an artificial elevation of frame, instead of the collected trot. This is elevation without proper collection.

The rider must take care not to ride in collection too long. There should be frequent working, medium or extended trot periods to re-establish a swinging hind leg and elastic back. When a horse gets tired in the collected work, he may try to avoid the work by becoming "stuck" and/or crooked, and may try to lean on the hand. In making the transition into medium or extended trot, the rider should not drive too hard, nor should the rider increase the driving during the extension. The collected trot should have such strength that by giving slightly with the hand and driving just a little with the seat bones, the extension is immediately there—we should just *let* the horse go into extended trot. One should think of a coiled spring that has been pushed together. The tighter the spring is coiled, the more energy there is available to be released. If less tightly coiled, there is less energy when released. When riding forward, pay attention that the horse moves straight.

4.3 The Canter

The canter is the gait with the most movement and requires the most strength of the horse because of its jumping aspect. The rhythm of the canter is three-beat, plus a moment of suspension. The order of footfall is first the outside hind, then the diagonal pair, and finally the inside front. After the third beat, the inside front, comes the moment of suspension, in which none of the horse's feet are touching the ground.

The main source of thrust comes from the horse's outside hind leg at the canter, which is why when making a transition to the canter the rider must give the aids when the outside hind is on the ground. The canter should be

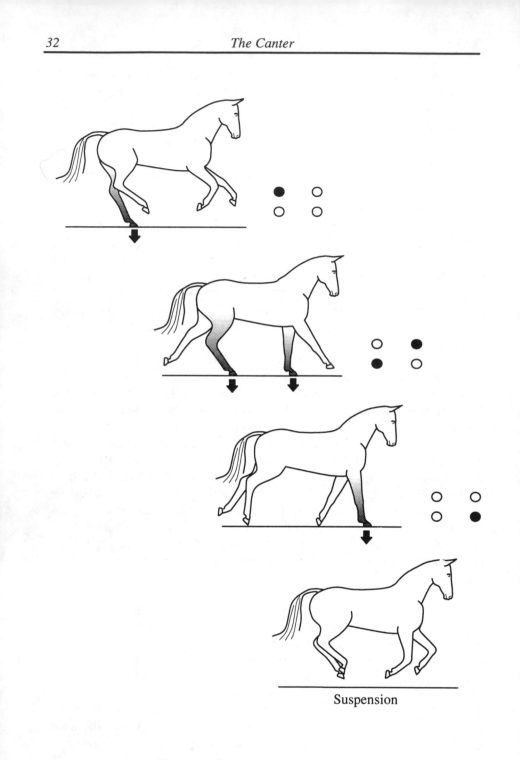

Suspension

Figure 9: The three beats of the canter.

supple, energetic, and have a definite "jumping" quality. Every jump should be ridden as though it were a new canter depart, with similar but appropriately muted aids, always inviting the horse forward by giving slightly with the hand.

4.3.1 Working Canter

In the canter, as in the other gaits, the horse can exhibit the various paces. The "working canter" has a length of stride between the medium canter and the collected canter. The working canter is characterized by its freshness and energy. The training of the horse really begins when he can perform a working canter that is balanced, engaged and supple. The extensions and collection should be started only when the working canter is confirmed. Fully trained horses should start the daily canter work at the working canter.

4.3.2 Medium Canter

In the medium canter, the strides should become longer but not faster in rhythm or tempo. The horse should gain ground, the frame should become slightly longer by the neck stretching with the horse showing more self-carriage than in the working canter. The powerful strides of the hind legs should come well under the horse's body.

4.3.3 Extended Canter

In the extended canter we see the highest development of impulsion in this gait. The strides should be very forward and ground-covering, even more so than in the medium canter, and the frame of the horse should be lengthened visibly. The neck of the horse should stretch significantly, and the horse should demonstrate good self-carriage. The rein contact between the horse's mouth and the rider's hands should be maintained, but the hands should always be giving forward to let the jump come through. The hind legs of the horse should produce the maximum power in this movement— with full relaxation.

When you want to extend the canter, be careful to think, "Longer— not quicker!" and "under control." Do not allow the correct rhythm of the strides to be lost or the tempo to become more rapid. Keep the horse on your seat and in good contact with your hands without keeping the reins too tight. Keep him round. He can get longer in the frame, but he must stay round over the back. The body of the rider should remain quiet, and should not get "faster," trying to move the horse with the rider's torso. Don't turn your toes to the outside, turn them a little to the inside.

If the horse tries to get away from you by speeding up, shorten the reins a tiny little bit and sit "against your hands" (against the rein contact). Drive with your seat and legs against this quiet hand. Don't neglect to shorten your reins. A LONG REIN IS A HARD REIN. With long reins, the rider's hands come back into his lap. The arms become loose and the

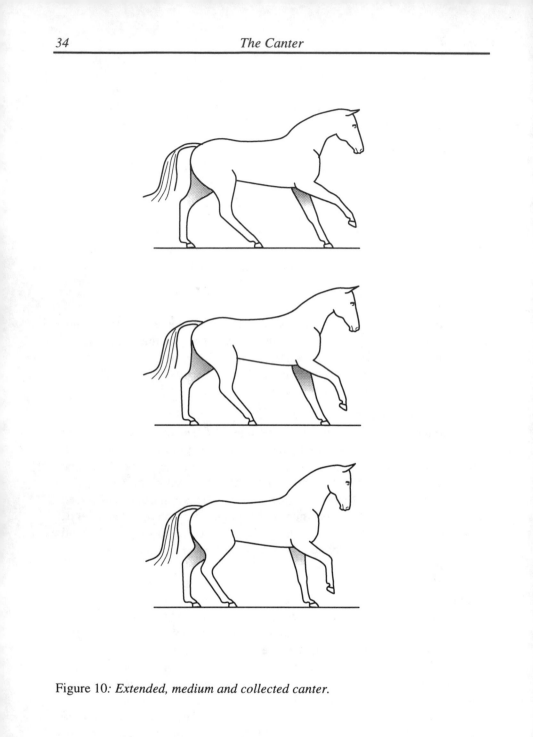

Figure 10: *Extended, medium and collected canter.*

precision of the aids is lost. The aids are no longer given with the wrist, as they should be, but with the whole arm. Don't pull backwards or to the left and right repeatedly. In German we call this *riegeln* (sawing).

To collect the canter again, put your heels down even more and be soft on the inside rein to help the inside hind leg continue to canter. Do not forget to activate the hind legs. The slower the tempo, the more the rider should drive the hind legs, especially in transitions between or within gaits. If the horse should fall into the trot, correct the trot before putting the horse back into the canter. Otherwise, we would make too many mistakes at once.

It is a good sign when the horse "high blows" with every stride of the canter. This is a fairly loud snuffling noise the horse makes through his nostrils with each exhale and is together with every stride. It means the horse has relaxed completely. My teacher always said that we should praise the horse immediately so the horse will know that the rider wants him to feel good. When a horse does this during a dressage test, the judge should be impressed with the horse's relaxation and confidence. Now you can be softer in the rein contact. Don't miss the moment when the horse gives in; then the rider should give, too.

4.3.4 Collected Canter

The collected canter is characterized by the increased flexion of the joints of the hindquarters and the lowering of the croup. The hindquarters take on more of the horse's weight, consequently lightening the forehand. The elevation of the forehand, including the neck of the horse, should be the result of the collection of the canter, and the horse should look and feel as if he is cantering uphill. I am fond of saying, "Jump up into Heaven!" In practicing the collected canter, one should always insist on a clear three-beat rhythm. The collection will be accomplished only when the horse, in self-carriage, light, straight, and with expression, confidently and willingly accepts the rider's aids correctly.

Again, I advise not to ride the collected canter too long, especially when the horse is not yet physically or mentally able to maintain the collection. Otherwise the horse's back will become stiff, and the canter may go into four-beats. The hock may also develop a snapping, upwards movement, not the forward, smooth movement which is needed. Without softness, the hooves can impact the ground sharply, leading to lameness from overloading the ankles and tendons. A sign of correct work is that the horse remains relaxed and able to go out from, and back to, collection in harmony.

Chapter 5

Preparations

Before proceeding to discuss riding technique, movements and corrections in the training of horses, I wish to discuss the general topic of preparation: equipment, the arena, and the rider's attitude.

5.1 Equipment

The equipment, the stable and the horses should always be kept "show ready." You should be ready for visitors at any time, and ready to take your horse immediately to a show. Horses easily sense when special preparations are being made for shows, and can become excited—just when we need to call on a calm, reliable performance. Most important, a neat and tidy environment is far safer and more conducive to learning.

Before every ride, the rider should check the horse and equipment. He should also find out if the horse has eaten and had water or if he has been acting strangely in any way. The horse should be clean. A clean horse feels good. If the snaffle bridle, saddle, and bandages are properly fitted, then the rider can be confident that there will be no problem during the training because of ill-fitting equipment.

The rider's clothing is also important. It should be clean, well-fitting, and comfortable. The fit of the breeches is essential. They should not be too tight in the knee, and there can be no wrinkles inside the boots. This is most uncomfortable and can create sores. The breeches should feel good to walk in; they must be long enough that while walking one does not feel a pull, but on the other hand, not so long that they hang.

The riding boots should have long shafts. They should be a little softer on the inside of the rider's leg in order to feel the horse better. The outside of the shaft should be hard. If the boots are too short, they will catch on the edge of the saddle flap which is extremely disturbing. Keeping boots clean and well-polished does more than improve one's looks; it makes them last far longer. The dirt and dust around a stable are so acidic and salty that they quickly disintegrate even the finest leather. Although you often see riders busily cleaning boots and tack just before shows and clinics, the best time to clean boots and tack is right *after* riding, while the leather is still warm. It does not do much good to clean the acid off boots 5 minutes before putting them back on. With the price of boots and equipment so high, a few minutes of care will save money.

It is best to ride and longe with gloves. The rider will not hurt or toughen his or her hands if wearing gloves, which could happen without them. The rider's sensitivity with gloves is exactly the same as without. It is just a matter of becoming used to them in the event a rider has already ridden for months without them and might be reluctant to try wearing them. There are all types and materials. Most riders prefer soft, strong, yet fairly thin leather. It is important that the gloves are big enough with the fingers long enough. If the fingers are too short, the stitching will tear soon.

The dressage whip measures between one meter and one meter and 20 centimeters, or 40 to 46 inches. For young horses, for jumping and for riding cross-country, the whip should be around 70 centimeters or 28 inches in length.

The spurs should be worn just below the ankle seam of the boot, parallel with the sole of the boot. Sharp spurs are unethical and injure the horse. If the spurs have a little wheel, called a rowel, it should turn easily to avoid cutting the horse. The rowel should be cleaned and checked manually every day to make sure that it is free of hair and sweat and will spin freely. Spurs should always be selected for each horse individually.

Spurs should be earned by the rider. Permission is given by the instructor when a rider's leg is good enough to wear spurs and the rider is not likely to use them haphazardly. It is rarely appropriate to wear spurs when riding a very young horse. The consistent use of spurs on all horses is a sign of inefficiency of the forward-driving aids of legs and seat or an excessive holding and blocking with the hand. In advanced classical riding the spurs were intended to add a bit more engagement, elevation, impulsion and brilliance. Some very good riders wear them most of the time but have the self-discipline not to use them on all horses they ride. This self discipline is hard to possess!

5.2 Care of the Riding Arena

The right kind of riding arena is of great importance in the training of a dressage horse. The arena is also a rider's calling card. For example, when I visit a stable and see that the arena has no letters, then I can be quite sure that there is not much accuracy in that rider's training. Dressage is correct riding and requires accuracy.

It is important to have mirrors in the arena. The first mirrors should be put in the four corners of the arena, so the rider can see the angles of the shoulder-in, travers, and leg-yielding along the wall. By having mirrors completely across the short side of the arena, the rider will also be able to check centerlines, leg-yielding across the arena, half pass, lengthening across the diagonal, pirouettes, etc. A mirror in the middle of the long side will allow the rider to see if the horse halts correctly and stays on all four legs. While mirrors are very helpful for checking out your progress and monitoring the work, the rider should be careful not to twist his body to look into the mirror, thereby bringing himself out of balance, especially in difficult situations. Mirrors must of course be kept clean so we can easily see the reflections.

There are many types of footing available for arenas, with advantages and disadvantages of each. Regardless of the type of footing, all arenas require regular maintenance—watering, dragging, leveling, etc. If I see an arena with a large oval path trodden on the track, then I know immediately that the rider never rides into the corners properly and that the standard must be quite low. It is also a bad sign when I see a small hill in the center of one or two large circles where the horses have been longed continuously. This is very bad. It doesn't cost much to paint letters on the walls and to rake the arena in order to have it be flat and without trodden paths!

Dust is another problem that must be dealt with. It is very bad for the horses to have to breathe the dust, as it is for the rider and teacher. It is sad to see someone emerge from a dusty riding arena looking as if they just came out of a coal mine, covered with dust or soot!

Be sure that the arena walls are checked for protruding sharp nails and large splinters or broken kick boards. Safety for both horse and rider demand that harrows, tractors, or anything dangerous be removed from the arena.

5.3 Stabling

Horses spend so much time in their stalls that it is essential that we provide them with a healthful, safe and pleasant stable, where they can feel comfortable and secure, able to completely relax. The quality of the stabling is also a direct measure of our respect for our horse. The stables should be quiet and calm.

Stalls should be roomy and light, with good air circulation but not drafty. They should be carefully checked for any hazards like protruding or loosening nails, or broken boards. It is often amazing how much destruction a horse can to do to ordinary construction, so special care needs to be taken to ensure that all structures are strong and secure.

Stalls should be cleaned often to keep manure and urine from causing unhealthy conditions. Manure lying about attracts flies and harbors worm larvae, while urine can cause high levels of toxic ammonia fumes. When we walk into a stall, our heads are often well above the level of the fumes, but consider the horse with his head down, nibbling hay or feed. The bedding, hay and feed should also be dust free.

Keep the aisle and walkways clean and not slippery. All forks, rakes and other implements should be kept safely out of the way. Since we rarely plan accidents, it is hard to schedule a good time to leave hazardous materials around!

One can never be too careful to avoid fire in a stable. Horses lack the instinct to flee from their stalls and run through the flames to safety, preferring to stay where they have always felt safe. Since we have provided them this trusted haven, it is our ultimate responsibility to make it truly safe. Halters and leads should be always kept readily at hand to enable rapid evacuation of the barn. Smoking is never to be allowed anywhere near the barn, and all electrical work must be to the highest standards. Be especially wary of any heaters or equipment which can fail while no one is around.

5.4 Riding with a Plan

I recommend that every training session follow a plan. It is often terrible to watch riders "schooling" their horses when they have not made a plan. Without a systematic approach, one never reaches a goal. If a rider takes the time to really study his horse he can design a program to suit his horse's particular needs. The plan must follow the classical principles, but one must leave room for small differences in technique that will be needed for the horse's individual characteristics. What is good for one horse can be wrong for another. This is what makes dressage so interesting.

Although we make careful plans, we need to be able to recognize when these plans must be abandoned. The first principle must be that we have all the time in the world, and that we are never rushed to reach our goal. If the horse comes out of the stable tense or tight, we may need to spend the entire session just suppling and loosening, forgetting our day's plan. This is especially true if some other appointment or commitment limits the time we can spend with the horse. Don't try to do in 30 minutes that which you know would take an hour or 45 minutes. Work on just the first part of your daily routine—rhythm and relaxation. This work is never wasted!

5.5 On the Subject of Clinics

When I gave my first clinics, I was asked to give my opinion of clinics in general. I believe they are very important for the riders in this enormous land—the U. S. and Canada—because there is no central training facility. Hans Pracht had a good idea. He wanted to build a training facility in Canada similar to Warendorf in Germany. But in giving my first clinics there in Ottawa, it became clear that the riders' basics in dressage were not yet established and real "pioneer" work was necessary to bring riders to a level at which they could then make use of such a facility.

After giving several clinics it seemed more important for me to travel and hold clinics in order to do the most good. The people of North America seem more idealistic and enthusiastic and willing to go to great lengths to get instruction here than we in Germany would be! But even if there were training centers, who could afford to stay away from work and family for months in order to train?

The journeys these riders make with their horses are incredible! Around the time of the 1984 Olympics in Los Angeles, I gave a clinic.

Riders came all the way from Texas, having to drive for days. In Germany we would not do this, because every city, town and even villages have riding clubs with nice indoor facilities and stabling and a permanent professional instructor who is always there to help. The riders are under his watchful eye all the time. This makes it much easier to make progress.

It is important for the rider to stay with one clinician rather than taking clinics from many different people. Unfortunately, every instructor seems to have his own system. If a rider is not yet sure enough of the basics and goes from one clinician to the next, trying different techniques, nothing much is gained. The horse and rider gradually become unsure of what they are doing. The recent efforts of the U.S. and Canadian dressage associations to standardize instruction and to institute examinations of instructors is a sign that the situation will improve. I can not over-emphasize the need for steady, consistent teaching across the country, based firmly in the established principles of classical riding.

Clinics are most helpful for good riders, because these riders know what advice to take with them that helps them and their horse. Less experienced riders who go to several instructors will become completely confused. It is better to have a regular instructor, whether good or not so good, than to change instructors frequently.

Another problem in North America is the lack of school horses— the "old professors." In Germany we have old Grand Prix horses in the riding clubs. Young or inexperienced riders can learn half passes, flying changes, piaffe and passage on these horses. It is very difficult for us here, because the horses and riders are often at the same level. Here the riders and horses need to learn the same things at the same time. It is extremely difficult for a rider and his horse to learn shoulder-in when neither has ever felt it before! It is possible to make progress under these circumstances, but it requires unbelievable work and patience from the horse, the rider and the trainer. It is very good in these instances to use video tape to see clearly what is happening and to explain what is going on.

5.6 Attitude Adjustment

I would like to emphasize that in order to develop a horse, the rider and horse must work hard. One cannot proceed with an overly cautious style of training. As I said earlier, the rider should frequently push the horse to his limit to make progress, and yet be careful never to push him beyond it. Under or beyond the horse's limit is wrong. We have no right to harm these beautiful animals. But if one never approaches the horse's limit, one will never make progress!

One must have a strong will, and a determination to train successfully. "Willpower can overcome mountains," they say. "The gods placed sweat in the path before success." "No sweat—no prize!" Riders should not think they are at a spa when attending a clinic!

On the other hand, we must not confuse our strength of will with a willingness to use force. A new student said to me recently, "I didn't realize that riding a horse on the bit could be done without fighting. I thought that force was the only way. Driving with seat and leg into a quiet hand until the horse trusts the hand and stays round without a fight is a brand-new idea!"

When you make a mistake, do not dwell too long on the mistake. Try it again. The rider must ask himself "what different aids must I give in order for the horse to understand?" If the correction doesn't work today, it will work tomorrow. If not tomorrow, then maybe the next day, or next week, or next month. But we have to take time to understand and get together with the horse in a partnership. We must learn to accept that achieving true partnership and understanding with the horse is a lifelong project.

I will never forget Riding Master Eggert, the trainer of the horses from the Countess von Hessen in Schloss Kronberg in Taunus. When he was 82 years old he still rode two Grand Prix horses every day. He had three. He let me ride one, because as he said, "I am no longer as strong as I used to be!" When he was in the hospital and we knew he was dying, he called me once more to his bedside. He said, "Walter, now I start to understand what riding is, and now I must die."

5.7 The Good Ride Danger

When you have had a good ride one day, it is wonderful, but it is also very dangerous. On the next day, as soon as you mount, you tell yourself, "I hope it will be as good as yesterday...." And the rider expects the same performance from the horse immediately. I remember Dr. Reiner Klimke, after his team ride in the Olympics at Los Angeles said, "Only once in a lifetime does it happen that everything comes out perfectly! Tomorrow I am sure that I will do 25 percent less than I did today." If the rider tries to get the feeling he had yesterday right away, then he will start to get tight. I cannot expect to start my search for a butterfly with him already in the net! I have to wait for him.

Not long ago I took my first golf lesson. After a terrific drive, I tried very hard to do even better on my next stroke. It was a disaster. My instructor asked immediately, "Did you feel how tense and tight you were, trying to hit the ball?" Then he said, "Let the club work more for you!" It is exactly the same in riding. We force the horse with excessively strong aids. But we should let the horse do more, and not become tense and tight ourselves. A good rider prepares and shows the horse what is desired, and then the rider allows the horse to do the exercise more by himself. The rider must always be ready, however, to show the horse again. In practice the rider shows the horse and then allows him to work in a pleasant way, then shows again, then allows again, *et cetera, et cetera.* "ANYTHING THAT IS FORCED CAN NEVER BE BEAUTIFUL" (Xenophon).

5.8 Positive and Negative Thought Influence on the Horse

I can influence my horse with my thinking, positively or negatively. For example, the surest way to success in competition is to have trust in ourselves and in our horses that comes from a solid foundation of correct work at home.

As an example of negatively influencing the horse, I will tell you of an experience I had at a show in Stuttgart, Germany. I had a great ride the day before. In walking the stadium jumping course on this day, I came to a triple combination and thought how careful I would have to be at the second element because the ground was uneven. Then again before riding the course, as I waited my turn and went over the course in my mind, I thought briefly how careful I would have to be in the combination. Later, as I rode into the combination, my horse stopped and I landed almost on his ears. Even though my horse had been perfect the day before, on this day I let my concern affect my confidence and tried to be too cautions. My horse got the message and lost his confidence too. Every day the rider must find the partnership again with his horse. We cannot take his trust and willingness for granted.

5.9 Communication with the Horse – Part I

The first step in communicating with the horse is listening— understanding his meaning as expressed through his eyes, ears, tail, voice, sweating, gaits, and even manure.

Eyes. The soul of the horse can be seen in his eyes. Are the eyes quiet or frightened? A quiet, clear and calm eye shows confidence and acceptance. A squinting eye is usually associated with aggression or meanness. An overly open eye (showing the white) is a sign of too much energy, and a horse who is not very easy to deal with. Very un-quiet eyes and a frightened look show too much fear. These horses must be handled with lots of love in order to win their confidence. These horses are almost always the victims of poor handling, although it may also be a sign of illness or pain.

Ears. The ears are a very important sign of the condition of the horse. The horse will carry his ears forward when he is well in balance and confident in his footfalls. Ears up and twisted to the back shows he is alert and listening to what is happening behind. Ears pinned back is a sign of mistrust or aggression. In the training, the ears going back is a clear sign that the horse feels mistreated.

Tail. The tail snapping to the left and right is a sign of not feeling well, too much spurs or pain in the back from a poorly fitting saddle. When the horse presses the tail between the legs, it shows fear and tightness. The same is found when the tail is carried straight up. As long as the horse keeps the tail between his legs, he will not listen to any aids, and the rider must try to get the horse to relax. Sometimes the rider can only work on relaxation with such a horse. A nicely quiet tail, gently swing from left to right is a sign of relaxation and well-being.

Voice. The voice of the horse can be a calling to his partners, an excited snorting, or a calm and deep exhalation. The low, relaxed blowing should be music to the ears of every good rider. It is a sign that the horse is not holding back his breath or is otherwise tense.

Sweating. When a horse sweats within a very short time in training, it usually comes from cruel treatment and the fear which such treatment instills. It can also come from the horse being out of condition or from some other pain. Long hair in the winter can also lead to faster than normal sweating. Horses that are out of condition should be worked carefully, with many rest periods, and not worked into a lather of sweat. If the horse is sweating in the stable, it is always a sign of sickness or of being ridden "over the limit." The rider must know how much he can ask of his horse and stop before going too far in the work.

Gaits. In the gaits, we can see if the horse is tense. He can show short and quick jogging steps in walk. In the trot, the horse holds his back tight, and the footfalls are hard. The horse rushes forward, and the movements are stiff. In the canter, the gait is jerky and tight, also hard on the landing, and more up and down than forward. These are all signs of insufficient relaxation in the horse. A nice long rein walk, a good trot out of a free shoulder, and a good springing and light canter are signs of a very well-ridden and relaxed horse that is responding very easily to the aids of his rider.

Manure. When a horse is not dropping manure during the work, it is usually a sign that he is not relaxed. This can lead to colic. Thin manure is a sign that the horse is frightened, or has gotten bad food, or too much grass or sweet food, or a sign of worms.

5.10 Mounting

The final preparation for work is also the start of the work. Leading the horse to the arena and mounting set a tone and an attitude that the rider and horse embrace and which influence the working session. The horse should be trained to stand quietly while being mounted, and should wait until the rider is settled in the saddle and gives the aids to move forward. With young horses, this is the first training under saddle, with older horses it should be constantly reinforced.

The girth should be tightened after leaving the stable. Some horses need to be walked a little before tightening the girth. It is common to have to tighten the girth two or three times. When the rider has led the horse to the place in the arena where he wishes to mount, the horse should stand straight and quiet. First be sure that the stirrups are adjusted correctly, both with the same length, and appropriate for the rider and horse. By twisting the bottom of the stirrup leathers before mounting, the stirrups can be made to hang perpendicular to the horse's side.

When preparing to mount, the rider turns and stands with his left shoulder next to the horse's shoulder. The left hand of the rider collects the reins above the horse's withers. The left rein is held between the rider's ring finger and little finger of the left hand. The right rein is laid over the full hand on top of the left rein. The right rein should be adjusted a little shorter than the left rein, thus positioning the horse slightly to the outside. This way, there is no chance the horse will bite the rider while he is trying to mount. Both reins should have light contact, so the horse will not run away. The reins should not be tightened too much or else the horse might back up.

At this point the rider steps back enough to enable himself to place his left foot in the stirrup. Then the rider holds some of the horse's mane with his left hand. Or the rider can use a strap that can be attached to the two metal rings at the front of the pommel of the saddle. The rider grasps the stirrup with his right hand and turns the back edge of the stirrup toward him. The left foot of the rider is placed in the stirrup just behind the ball of the foot. The rider's left knee should be placed on the saddle in order to prevent the rider's toe from sticking into the horse. Then the rider lifts himself onto the ball of his right foot and makes a small jump to the side with this foot, reaches for the cantle of the saddle with the right hand, still holding the mane or strap with the left hand, and steps with the left foot onto the stirrup. The rider then pushes off with the right foot, raising his body in a forward-

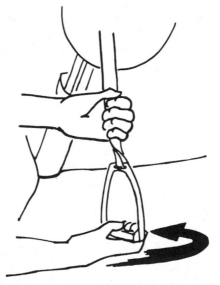

Figure 11: *By twisting the bottom of the stirrup leathers before mounting, the stirrups can be made to hang perpendicular to the horse's side.*

leaning position, up over the horse. The right hand moves to the front of the saddle into a position of support for the upper body. The rider's right leg is lifted clear over the croup of the horse and glides smoothly into the saddle. The rider's right foot is placed in the stirrup and the reins are organized. The rider should do these things quickly and quietly, while encouraging the horse to stand perfectly still until given the signal to go on. The rider then should praise the horse. This has a calming effect. Then he should ride off straight on long reins at the free walk.

The above description applies to mounting from the ground or from a mounting block. However, it is always better to mount from a mounting block, so that the rider's weight is easily and evenly let into the saddle, and the twisting and slipping of the saddle is avoided.

5.11 Warm-Up Procedure

When the horse first comes from the stable, the rider should ride a good free walk on long reins, going on both reins two or three times around the arena. The rider must remember that the horse needs time to become accustomed to the rider's weight and to find his balance again, carrying a rider.

After the free walk, the rider shortens the reins, taking light contact and starts with the working trot rising at a good, energetic tempo. The tempo must be exactly suitable for the horse. One horse requires a fresher tempo; the other a quieter one. With the stronger horses the rider will need to stay longer on a 20 meter circle. The lazier horse does better ridden straight ahead. The rider should change the rein frequently and make several transitions to the working canter from the trot. This trot and canter work will take approximately fifteen to twenty minutes, depending on the horse's needs.

The length of time required to relax and supple the horse and to begin to soften and lighten the tight and heavy side depends on the individual. Young horses and heavier horses need a little longer. The rider shouldn't work a lazy horse too long and on circles. It is better to ride briefer exercises and more straight lines with such horses.

If it is cold weather and the horse has been in a warm stall with a blanket, and even led to the arena with the blanket over the saddle, then once mounted the rider should spend a short time at the walk with the blanket still on. As soon as he takes the blanket off, he should proceed to the working trot to help warm the horse up. From the beginning the horse will tighten his tail between the legs and might jump around to make himself warm. In other words, the horse will hold the muscles of the back tight, and one needs a longer time until the muscles of the back loosen and the horse lets go of his tail and rounds his back. When the muscles of the horse seem warm and soft, then the rider can do some leg-yielding at the walk. This should be done on both reins. Turns on the forehand should also be ridden. These exercises make the horse nicely obedient.

What I see too often is a horse brought with a blanket from a warm stall to the cleaning stall (often a drafty place). After removing the blanket, the rider heads off in search of grooming tools, the saddle and bridle. In the meantime, he finds a friend and has a long conversation, perhaps a visit to the rest room, a retreat to the lounge to warm up, only to re-appear at the horse when his hair is puffed out against the cold and the muscles are tightened against the draft. Once the grooming and tacking preparations are complete, the horse is led to the arena, and the rider expects a brilliant horse, perhaps better than the one he dismounted at the end of yesterday's session! In cold weather, try to keep the horse covered all the time (or under heat lamps if possible), until ready to begin the work.

Chapter 6
Use of the Aids

The effective use of the aids depends on the rider's success in finding their harmonious coordination. When harmony in the use of the aids is reached, the horse will develop the desirable frame for dressage. This frame allows the horse to develop his maximum strength. Good riding requires the following formula: recognize the problem, analyze it, correct it, and remember the process. This shows how you must ride more with your head than with your seat, as my instructor used to say!

6.1 Communication with the Horse – Part II

How can we make ourselves understood by the horse? Only with our aids! The horse is like a very sensitive instrument such as a violin. Harmony comes from a delicate and precise balance between the bow, the string and the musician's fingers, which must have enough muscle tone to control the string and the bow, but be relaxed enough to follow the rapid passages. So must be the connection between the rider and horse through the aids. The clumsy aid, the miscue, the heavy hand lead to dissonance—expressed in the horse as tightness and stiffness.

I hear so often from students, "I definitely gave the right aids!" That may be. But the best aids will produce nothing correct if not given in the right moment. Aids that were appropriate a few meters back might need to be altered slightly because the situation has changed in this short length of time. This is what makes riding so difficult. It may take many repetitions before the horse comes to understand and remember new aids. In the process of teaching the horse, we also learn by remembering the aids that were good and those that were less than effective.

If we think we are the teachers, that is only close. We are taught by the horse. He informs us when he does something wrong that we have given the wrong aids. He couldn't understand us, or we gave the aids in the wrong moment. The rider develops feel for the right aids by listening to the horse's reaction. The right aids in the right moment provide the intended effect and the student associates the reaction with the aid. But the student must also learn from unsuccessful attempts: "that was too strong, this was not enough."

I need to mention the importance of knowing with one hundred percent certainty when each hind leg of the horse is stepping forward. Only then can the rider be effective in the correct moment. In the piaffe to passage to piaffe transitions, the need for this knowledge is especially important. The rider needs to know with which hind leg he should ride the horse forward. Only when the hind leg is in the air can the rider influence the stride to either lengthen, shorten, go sideways or backwards. This reminds us of how essential it is to be able to feel when each hind leg is leaving the ground.

Finally, the rider must learn to balance the forward driving aids and the restraining or receiving aids. It is easy to hold the front too tight and thereby lose all power and engagement in the hind end. It is also easy to over-drive the horse forward, beyond the amount that we can gently receive in the hand. We need to adjust the aids as if on a balance scale.

6.2 The Rider's Position

Only with a correct position can correct aids be given. The elegant, calm and quiet position is rooted in function, not only in a sense of aesthetics. The beautiful position is really beautiful because it is effective. Of course, you sometimes see riders who have a "precious" seat—riders who try to always look pretty, but never communicate with the horse—nice looks, but quite ineffective. Then you hear those who proclaim "I know I have a few position faults, but my position is *effective*!" Neither is right.

Often, the horse is tighter on the left side, and the rider sits crooked to this side, having been pushed over by the right hind leg. Without a correct and balanced position, the rider reinforces this imbalance by sitting to the left, and develops preferentially the left hind leg. Our "effective" rider above then brags to his friends how skillful he is to continually re-bend the horse to the left, and how strong he is with the left spur to straighten the horse out. What I see is a rider who created a problem where none needed to exist, then invented a "correction" which is based on force. He will later be able to brag that he is strong enough to keep this reluctant horse moving! This may last for a short while. Our "precious" rider may find himself quite uncomfortable, pronounce the horse unrideable or lame, and seek out another horse (hopefully he is riding in a lesson barn where he can switch horses without going bankrupt!)

I know that one can never have a truly perfect seat and position, but we must always strive to be as close to the ideal as possible. Little mistakes will always creep in, and it is very important to be watched by one who has a knowledgeable eye.

The Seat. The seat is the basis for all position and aids. The legs, back, and arms have their foundation in the seat. The seat transfers the rider's weight to the horse, and how it does this is the single most important factor in influencing how the horse will move. The rider's seat should be deep and elastic, and should follow easily the movement of the horse. His weight should be carried on the back third of his pelvic bones, in the deepest part of the saddle. The rider must *allow* his weight to rest on both seat bones. So many position problems are associated with the rider trying to avoid this

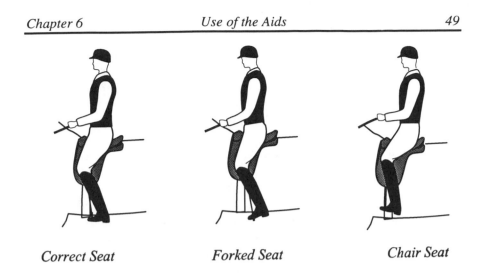

Correct Seat   Forked Seat   Chair Seat

Figure 12: *Correct seat, forked seat, and chair seats. In the forked seat, the rider over-exaggerates a long, straight leg, but the pelvis is rotated forward, bringing the back part of the seat bones out of the saddle. In the chair seat, the rider brings the knees too high and the lower leg too far forward, sometimes from rotating too far back on the pelvis.*

basic principle: they will pinch with the thighs and stand on the stirrups, or rotate the pelvis forward, lifting the seat bones off the saddle. A hollow back or shoulders too far forward are common signs of this. Even the position fault of elbows coming out from the rider's side is usually an attempt to avoid sitting deep—the rounded arms tie into a tight shoulder and rib cage that is trying to keep the rider off the saddle. In any of these strategies to avoid sitting, the rider inevitably bounces and disrupts the horse's gaits. Of course, this becomes a vicious circle, because the bouncing and disrupted gaits make it more difficult to relax and sit deep.

From the deep seat, the lower body stretches downwards, and the upper body is stretched upwards.

In the correct seat, the pelvis is tipped slightly back, allowing the back part of the seat bones to contact the deepest part of the saddle, while still allowing the leg to hang quite vertically. If the rider tries to over-exaggerate a long straight leg, he can obtain a "forked" seat, where the knees and lower leg are too far back, and (more importantly) the pelvis is rotated forward, bringing the back part of the seat bones out of the saddle.

The rider that rotates too far back on his pelvis sits in a "chair" seat. In this position, the backward rotation of the pelvis prevents the legs from hanging down, and the knees are too high, and the lower leg comes too far forward.

One should pay much attention to one's seat and be frequently reminded of mistakes that might creep in. When necessary, one should be longed to do exercises to improve the seat. Ideally, a rider should be longed once a week to maintain a correct seat, even when that rider has started competing.

The Legs. The legs should hang in a relaxed manner. The thighs should be flat against the side of the horse. The side of the knee should lie flat against the saddle with the kneecap pointing forward, not outward, which results in a gap between the knee and saddle. When the knee turns out, the thigh rotates similarly, and the rider is no longer able to sit quietly. The knee should always have a light contact with the saddle. It should never grip when either sitting or posting. In fact, when posting the trot, the knee will slide downward along the saddle as the rider rises. The inside of the rider's calf should lie flat along the side of the horse and should always have contact. The ankles should be loose and supple, not stiff. The ball of the foot should rest in the stirrups, and the heel should be the lowest point. The foot should be pointed forward, not out toward the sides. The proper positioning of the foot will ensure that the knee is pointed forward and lying on the saddle, and will ensure that the side (not the back) of the calf contacts the horse. One way to consider the proper alignment of the foot is to think of riding with very long spurs on an overly sensitive horse: if the foot is correct, the spurs will never touch the horse's side. This also means that whenever we ride with spurs, it will be necessary to consciously move the foot in order to use the spur. The proper alignment of the knee and foot enables the fine control needed for combining the forward and sideways driving aids. I sometimes see riders trying to keep their whole leg on the horse—all the way down to the ankle. Either they turn the toe out to draw the heel in, or they roll the ankles and/or pull the heels up. The legs should hang without gripping, and the point where they leave the side of the horse is determined by the conformation of the horse and rider.

The Back and Upper Body. The upper body must be balanced and carried by the seat bones. The back is the fundamental element of this balance. From the pelvis, the lower back must rise in an erect, but supple fashion. The small of the back should be flat, not hollow, not rolled outwards, and not stiff. It should be always able to go gently with the movement. The chest should be open so the shoulder blades automatically become close to each other.

The neck should be free and the head should be carried naturally upright, without being stiff. The head should not hang forward. This interferes with the correct aids of the seat. If the head tilts to the left or right, the shoulder will lower, and the hip on that side will hollow, shifting the weight to the opposite side.

The arms hang down easily out of a lightly drawn back shoulder. The arms lie along the body, with the forearm lifted lightly up so as to make a straight line from the rider's elbow through the hand to the horse's mouth.

I should remind riders to pay attention to their breathing. Sometimes riders tighten up so much that they forget to breathe regularly.

6.3 Weight Aids

As the name implies, the weight aids influence the horse through his back, the all-important bridge between the haunches and the forehand. The rider can push the horse forward to a degree with his weight aids, supported then by the leg aids. It is important here to keep the rider's center of gravity as close as possible to that of the horse's. This allows the horse to stay in balance.

The distinguishing aid in the weight aids is the use of the *Kreuz* (the cross, pronounced "kroyts"), the seat bones and pelvis. The actual effect of the *Kreuz* is delivered through the seat bones, but one speaks of the *Kreuz* in total, because it is through the musculature and angle of this lower back anatomy that the seat bones are made more effective.

To make the seat bones felt by the horse, the *Kreuz* is pushed forward. The movement is like one sitting on a swing, trying to bring the swing forward without moving the legs or upper body. The effect of the *Kreuz* is profoundly influenced by the angle of the rider's upper body. The rider cannot afford to lean either forward or backward even slightly. Again, one is reminded that the best results come from invisible aids. Perhaps this is why it has been traditionally very difficult for non-German speaking people to learn to use this indispensable aid. They could not see it being used, and the translation for the *Kreuz* has been the "lower back" or the "small of the back." And although the translation is not incorrect, what was really intended was that the seat bones be used, not merely the lower back. After all, the lower back itself is not touching the saddle. The seat bones are! In order to apply correct *Kreuz* aids, the saddle must fit correctly and not have excessive padding. Incorrect fit and thick foam padding make it impossible for the horse to feel the *Kreuz* aids.

In riding curved figures, the weight of the rider should be slightly on the inside seat bone. In changes of direction and in turns, the rider's weight should shift slightly and imperceptibly in the direction of the horse's new bend, accompanied by driving leg aids. This is done to promote increased engagement of the new inside hind leg. Changing the weight by rocking the hips and breaking at the waist is over-aiding the horse and causes him to lose his balance, instead of helping him find it.

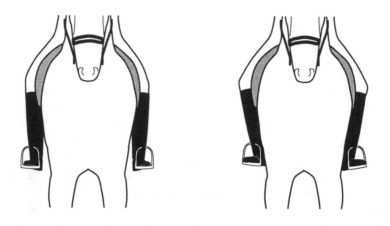

Figure 13. The rider's toes should point forward, not to the outside. When the toes turn to the outside, the knee opens, and the calf no longer lies along the side of the horse, and the quiet leg is lost.

I am often asked "where should I keep my weight?" Simply recall that where you flex or bend your horse, there must your weight be. This is true in circles, leg-yielding, shoulder-in, travers, renvers, half pass, pirouettes, and so on.

6.4 Leg Aids

The rider's legs lie flat against the body of the horse, always quiet and not constantly bouncing against the horse. The toes should point forward, not to the outside. When the toes turn to the outside, the knee opens, the calf no longer lies along the side of the horse, and the quiet leg is lost. The heel should be slightly lower than the toe, but the ankle should remain loose and springy. We want to ride with a long leg, but one often sees riders with stirrups that are too long or too short. In order to find the proper stirrup length, let the leg hang straight down, with an almost straight knee. The stirrup leathers should be adjusted two holes shorter than this position would require. Alternatively, adjust the stirrup so that distance from the saddle to the base of the stirrup is equal to the distance from the rider's fingertips to his armpit. (For jumping, adjust the length to equal the distance from a closed fist to the armpit).

Each leg influences the hind leg of the horse on the same side as the rider's leg. Depending on the position of the rider's leg, the aid is either a driving aid or a holding (containing) aid.

The driving aid position of the rider's leg is at the girth. The front of the shaft of the boot almost touches the back edge of the girth. The driving effect of the legs is accomplished through increased pressure of the leg by using either one leg at a time or both legs together. To use the leg aids in the right moment is of utmost importance. Therefore, the driving push is to be given when the horse's hind hoof on the same side is leaving the ground. Only then can the aids influence the hind leg to move forward, sideways or backwards.

The holding (containing) leg aid position is slightly behind the girth. The purpose of this type of leg aid is to prevent the horse from drifting off a desired path or a straight line, especially with the hindquarters. These aids are used in the exercises of rein back, turns on the forehand, leg-yielding and turns on the haunches.

The sideways driving aids are also given with the rider's leg in a position behind the girth. However, these aids are always given with one leg at a time, the leg needed to push the horse in one sideways direction. The other leg of the rider stays at the girth and regulates the forward movement of the horse. Occasionally in lateral work, both legs aids need to be applied simultaneously because the horse has lost impulsion, and must be driven

Figure 14. Leg "at the girth" and "behind the girth."

forward.

One often sees a rider using rapid leg squeezes or even kicks. This is always unsuccessful. The hind leg can be stimulated to move sideways (as well as forward or backward) ONLY when the hoof is about to leave the ground. Therefore, the leg aids must be given in this moment. The rider has plenty of time between these moments to prepare to use the leg again and should not feel in a hurry.

The amount of pressure used in the leg aids should always be limited to the least possible. In other words, a horse should be trained so that he reacts to the slightest change in position and pressure of the rider's legs. Then one can say that the horse is finely tuned to the leg, not numb to the leg! If the rider's legs drive or press constantly, the horse will become dull to the pressure, and eventually he will respond to almost nothing. In addition, a rider cannot use the leg muscles with greatest strength constantly. He would soon tire and would no longer be able to ride the horse well. The rider should be active with the leg, but then when the desired reaction is achieved, be briefly passive and ready to be active again. The rider's leg aids must always be given so that the rider can stay with the movement of the horse while using the appropriate intensity of aids to achieve the desired reaction from the horse. The rider should strive to remain comfortable and not have to use the utmost strength. This is easier to say than to do. I can promise you that! One should always feel as if one has a reserve of strength. This is not possible if the rider uses all his strength all of the time.

6.5 Rein Aids

The energy and power from the hind leg flows over the back, through the withers, the poll and mouth into the rider's hand and seat, then by this same route back to the hind end. The rein aids must therefore receive the energy from the hind leg, then give it back.

They are always used in combination with the driving aids of weight and leg. If the horse is well gymnasticized, it means that his muscles and joints are strong and elastic, and that his poll and jaw are also supple and yielding. Then the haunches can be well engaged, the neck will become naturally arched, with the face of the horse on or slightly in front of the vertical when seen from the side. Now the horse is presented "on the bit." The reins and the bit of the bridle provide the means for the effect of the rein aids. The rein aids are basically restraining in nature and are used to give position and bend in the horse. The outside rein controls the tempo, flexion, bending and the outside shoulder. The inside rein supples and softens and guides in the turns. It also controls the inside shoulder. The connection between the rider's hand and the horse's mouth should be fine and consistent in order to fulfill the basic requirement of dressage training. Remember that the most sensitive part of the horse is the mouth. The reins should feel like a half-pound weight in the rider's hands, and with this connection we must

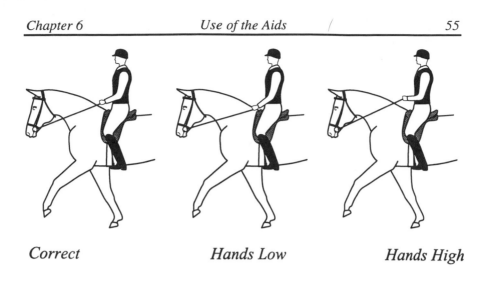

Correct   *Hands Low*   *Hands High*

Figure 15: *Proper position of the rider's arm, forming a straight line from the rider's elbow, through the hand, to the bit.*

always work forward, never backwards. The reins should act like light sticks. A stick can push the bit forward, and never loses the contact with the mouth.

The hands are carried in fists, with the thumbs as the highest point, securely holding the rein between it and the forefinger. If the rider were to hold a short crop upright in each fist, they should point almost straight up, not crossing and not pointing front or back.[1] From this position, the rider has the finesse and stillness needed for a truly soft contact with the horse's mouth. The rider's hand should be alive. That means that between giving and taking with the contact there should be a more or less constant exchange with the horse, a form of communication. The activity of the rider's hands is always used in combination with the forward-driving aids, of course. The desirable hand technique is to close the fingers into a gentle fist as though squeezing a sponge and to rotate the hand in and out. In a turn, for instance, the inside hand rotates in so that the little finger points toward the rider's other shoulder. The rider should not work with the entire arm. He should just use the wrists.

It is important that the rider's hands and arms are positioned correctly in order to maintain this fine connection to the mouth. The reins should frame the neck of the horse. The rider's hands, or fists as they are referred to in German, should be carried to the right and left of the withers and about a fist's width above the withers. Both fists are held at the same

---

[1] This is a good exercise to try on the longe, where the rider can quickly see whether the hands are correct. They will see how, often the stick rotates in all directions!

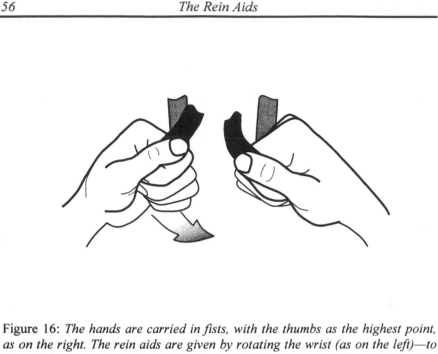

Figure 16: *The hands are carried in fists, with the thumbs as the highest point, as on the right. The rein aids are given by rotating the wrist (as on the left)—to flex the horse to the left, the rider's left little finger moves toward his right shoulder.*

height. The reins, fists and forearms form a straight line which connects the rider's elbow with the bit. This is the basic position of the hands, although there are times when it is appropriate to temporarily lower or raise them.[2] The hand holding the rein should not be moved across the withers to the other side. It is incorrect to carry your hands so far away from being centered that the rein no longer lies against the neck of the horse.[3]

It is important that the rider's hands act slowly, almost in slow motion. Both the taking and giving should be measured and deliberate. Too many times, I hear riding instructors telling their students to "give their aids quicker." The horse has gotten out of balance, or off track, and the student waits too long to fix the situation. The instructor is partially right, but he should tell the student to give their aids "sooner," not "quicker." We must learn to watch for and anticipate the need to give our aids, so that we can

---

[2] When the horse tries to go behind the bit, the hands are moved forward while keeping contact; and when the horse goes above the bit, the hands are raised very slightly with some more contact.

[3] With a young horse, however, the rider may take the inside rein away from the neck, in order to teach him to turn. This will occur with one hand and rein at a time, naturally, and the rider should never pull on this "leading" rein. As the inside rein contact is increased, the rider shows the horse the desired direction. As the rein contact is reduced—and not made loose—the horse is given the opportunity to go in that direction.

make them sooner, slower, and much less strong—and not surprising for the horse.

The hands are held as fists not to provide strength and power to be rough on the horse's mouth, but exactly the opposite—to provide the sensitivity to be softening and giving. The proper rein length is also essential for maintaining contact. My teacher, Col. Aust, always said "A loose rein is as wrong as a too tight rein." When the rein is loose, it is impossible for the rider to use the rein for any reason without bouncing the bit into the mouth. Instead of a light constant contact that becomes slightly firmer, the horse feels nothing, then a bump, then an instruction. The "soft" loose rein is perceived by the horse as a set of random bumps on the mouth. By holding the hands in fists, with the fingers closed, but the wrists soft and supple, the rider can cradle the bit in the horse's mouth, exerting only the finest pressure when needed to make half halts or other adjustments.

Too tight a rein is often seen for three main reasons: 1) the rider is frightened of a nervous horse and trying to control him; 2) the rider's balance insufficient, and he relies on his hands for balance; or 3) the rider is trying to form the horse into roundness through the use of the hand. All three are fundamentally wrong. The nervous horse will become only more nervous from the tightness of the rein, and the horse will feel that the rider is preventing him from escaping a dangerous situation. The rider is working against the horse's instinct, and will only make things worse. Col. Walzer[4] always said "The rider should hold the horse with the seat." The rider who takes his balance in the hand simply needs more longeing and work on his independent seat. The rider who tries to form the horse into roundness with the hand blocks the movement and tightens that horse's back. What is achieved in the front end comes at the expense of the hind leg. Extra driving and kicking soon degenerates into tenseness, distrust and perhaps eventually lameness.

The rider needs to continually adjust the length of the rein. It is a mistake to neglect to do this, because the horse's neck is frequently changing in length, and the reins should be adjusted accordingly. As the horse changes his frame or length of neck, the reins are adjusted so as to maintain a straight line, with light contact. This applies in the show ring as well as the school. At shows, you can see riders afraid to change anything, sure that the horse will go away from the bit or lose roundness.

---

[4] Col. Julius Walzer was the trainer of my master, Col. Aust. He was one of the most elegant riders of his time, with almost invisible aids. His horses went as well in jumping as dressage, always truly in harmony between horse and rider. He studied at the Spanish Riding School and was the trainer at the German Cavalry School in Hannover, and trainer for the Olympic team for Amsterdam in 1928. His student, Frieherr von Langen, with Draufgänger, won the first Gold medal for Germany and his riders won the team Gold medal in dressage. Frieherr von Langen also competed in the Grand Prix jumping at Amsterdam.

The holding rein aids are used when the horse resists. The rider's hands are still and unyielding for a moment while the pressure in the *Kreuz*, or seat bones and lower back, and legs are increased. The rider drives the horse into the hand. When the horse gives in the poll and jaw, the rider must immediately be passive again with the rein aids and the driving aids. Thus, in a moment of resistance, the rider maintains contact, drives, and then softens when the horse gives in. If the rider fails to recognize and handle these moments of resistance, the horse will never become sensitive to the aids and may become very dull in the mouth. All of riding involves the continual change from active to passive and back.

"Giving with the reins" is also commonly misunderstood. It is fair to ask, "When you say I should relax or soften the rein contact, should I give with my hand? What should I do specifically?" The answer is that the rider should relax in his shoulder. That will suffice completely to give the horse the feeling of softness.

The rein aids should be as invisible as possible. The tendency of many riders to do too much with the rein aids and to hang on the contact, not using weight, seat and leg aids enough must be fought all the time and from the beginning.

6.6 On the Bit

A horse on the bit is one that is connected in the circle of energy from the hind leg to seat and back. Riding a horse on the bit means driving the horse from behind, forward into a soft contact with the rider's hands. Therefore, it is essential that a definite connection exist between the hands of the rider and the horse's mouth. This we call the contact. The softness of this contact comes from the suppleness in the horse's poll.

When the horse is on the bit, the poll should be the highest point in the horse's silhouette, with the nose slightly in front of the vertical. The degree of flexion in the poll of the horse depends on the gait, the pace, and the level of training, and is different in each situation. When the horse stretches his neck as the rider lengthens the reins, the horse should maintain contact with the rider's hands.

A rider must *ride* the horse on the bit, not *put* the horse on the bit. Manipulating with the hand or trying to form the horse with the hand will either lead to unsteadiness and resistance or you will put the horse behind the bit. When the hind leg is working properly the horse comes on the bit automatically, but when the rider tries to put the horse on the bit with the hands, the hind leg will never swing through, and the hind leg will push instead of carry.

If the hind leg seems to be working energetically yet there is still a problem with the horse going on the bit, it can come from a resistance in the poll. This is usually shown as a tightness in one rein or the other, as the horse slightly tilts his head and leans into the tight rein. This is the point at which many riders succumb to the temptation to manipulate with the hand.

To be stiff in the poll, the horse uses the muscles in his neck as one against the other in a strong tension. The rider's job is to encourage him to release this tension and relax these muscles. They are not like stiff leather that can be softened by flexing them back and forth until they "break down." There must be a willing "letting go" of this tension that can only come through relaxation. To release the tension in the poll and get the horse even on both reins is one of the most important goals in all riding. This is the only way to achieve a straight, supple, balanced horse whose back swings (a *Rueckengaenger*, or back-mover).

Thus, the problem of "putting the horse on the bit," should really be thought of as getting the horse to yield in the poll. The first and foremost step is to be sure that the horse is good and relaxed. I have seen riders bring their horses from the stable into the arena and almost immediately try to put the horse on the bit by sawing left and right, before they have ever had the chance to stretch and relax. The muscles have to be first relaxed before we can work with them. Every athlete knows how important stretching and suppling are.

After relaxation, the second ingredient is a quiet hand. The hand must remain still so that the horse can have the trust to go to the contact. It is generally easier to overcome the resistance in the horse's poll when the horse is moving forward than at the halt, because the energy that exists in forward movement helps the process. The rider should remember that the flexion in the horse's poll and the arching of his neck should not and cannot be forced through the use of hands alone. Think always that when the horse is doing something wrong with his head that something is wrong in the back. The hind leg is not working enough. Rather than correct the head, we have to engage the hind leg more to round up the back and make connection between the hind leg, back, withers, poll, mouth and rider's hand. One should not forget that the back is the bridge between the hind leg and the front. Don't think very much about the position of the neck. Think first of engaging the hind leg over the back and into the hand. The "forming" of the neck will then come automatically. At first, the horse may rush and stretch the neck out. Use circles to control the horse, but in no way should you try now to force the horse into a frame. The horse will fight against the hand, and will lean more on the tight rein, and tighten the poll more, not less—or worse, will go behind the bit. You must have the patience to wait for the giving in the poll. You often see an experienced teacher get on a student's horse that is resistant in the poll, and you quickly see the horse going on the bit, but the student never sees the teacher *doing* anything. The teacher simply has the patience borne out of experience to let the horse come to the bit. It is of course a problem even for the willing student, trying to keep quiet hands, who sends the horse forward but as soon as the horse takes a bold or rushing step, takes with the hand, re-tightening the poll. This is why in order to keep the quiet hand, the rider must be able to sit independent of the rein contact. In other words the rider should not seek support for his strength or balance through the rein contact. He should have an "independent seat."

The rider should pay special attention not to hang on the rein on the side to which the horse is stiffer and heavier.[1] The horse should always seek contact with the rider's hand, and yet never try to be supported on it. Do not give the horse this opportunity. Soften the contact on this side over and over again, even when it is the outside rein, and try to achieve more contact on the naturally hollow side.

When the horse has relaxed the tension in the poll, he can work more confidently over the back, and take direction from the rein aids without resistance. We now need to add suppleness and the acceptance of our guidance for bending and turning. We don't want to upset the horse and re-lock the poll just to make a turn.

It is very helpful in this pursuit to ride the horse on a circle, bending the horse with an indirect inside rein, by rotating the fist to the inside, and by pressing the inside leg quietly against the horse at the girth. This bends the horse to the inside as he goes around the circle. At the same time, the outside rein and outside leg, which work to contain the horse and keep him from stepping to the outside, are of extreme importance. That which the rider drives with the inside aids, he must catch with the outside aids. And the effect of the rider's inside rein, must be limited through the use of the outside rein.

When the horse responds to these aids, yielding in the poll and bending in the body, the rider should soften the inside rein contact immediately while maintaining the outside rein contact and continuing to guide the horse on the circle through the outside rein contact. As soon as this submission is achieved at the walk, it is good to go into the working trot and try for the same results. In teaching the horse to yield to hand and leg, it remains important for the rider to soften the rein contact on the side that the horse is heavier or stiffer. Even if the horse is heavier on the outside rein, still the rider should be lighter on that rein, while the rider's outside leg will have to be more active and drive more.

---

[1] I have often seen riders use a draw rein on the stiffer side, trying to make the horse give on that side. When asked why the rider does this, the answer is "to make the horse give in." Then I ask, don't you realize that pulling on the draw rein will only strengthen the jaw and neck muscles that you would like to soften? What this rider is actually doing is strengthening the horse's resistance by building up his muscles on that side. In other words, the rider is increasing the problem, not solving it. It is a tragedy but often seen, even through the highest levels of dressage competition.

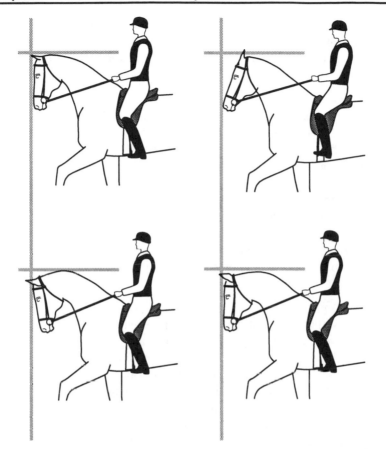

Figure 17: *"On the bit," (top, left) "above the bit," (top, right) and "behind the bit" (both lower figures). In the lower left, the horse is behind the vertical and obviously behind the bit. In the lower right, the horse's nose is "on the vertical," but the highest point is at the third or fourth vertebra. This is also "behind the bit."*

When the horse is properly soft in the poll and jaw, the horse can be easily flexed left and right. When the flexion is changed from one side to the other, the crest of the mane will snap or flip to the new direction. The horse that is tight in the poll and jaw will not show a flipping of the mane. The horse will not really flex from one side to the other, but will more or less bend the whole neck, giving at the withers, not the jaw and poll. At the halt, you can make an exercise of flexing the horse from one side to the other, verifying that the crest flips. This increases submission. This exercise can clearly show a student whether the flexion is correct, and can show them how to balance the aids. They must use the rein aids to ask for the flexion, but if they are too strong, either the jaw will lock or the whole neck will bend, and the crest will not flip. This exercise can also be done when a horse is lame and cannot be worked. He is given something to do to fight the boredom. It can also be done from the ground before mounting. It is important not to overbend the horse's neck in this exercise. It should affect just the jaw and topline, with the neck firmly anchored at the withers.

6.6.1 Above the Bit

The horse is above the bit when he resists the contact with the rider's hand, stiffens his neck and poll muscles and lifts his head and neck up, like a giraffe.[2] This is a serious problem. The forward driving aids should be the principle means for making the correction here. To start with, the rider should use leg and *Kreuz* to drive the horse forward enough to establish rein contact, paying careful attention to have lighter contact on the stiffer-feeling side of the horse's mouth. Then the horse should be ridden on a circle. Through bending, the horse will gradually begin to yield and round his frame. The rider's hand should rise a little when the horse is above the bit in order to keep the bit working on the corners of the mouth rather than on the lower jaw.

6.6.2 Behind the Bit

A horse that is behind the bit is over flexed in the third vertebra of the neck (or even further back). Usually his face is behind the vertical, possibly with his mouth open and the lower jaw moving toward his chest, or tongue over the bit or hanging out. Many riders misunderstand this silhouette to be "on the bit," although there is unsteady or no rein contact. They believe they have the horse on the bit because they have the horse flexed and very light on the hand. The problem, however, is that the energy from the hind end "escapes" at the third vertebra, which acts like a ventilator—none of the aids can complete the cycle and return to the hind leg. With every rein aid the horse comes lower and more behind, rather than accepting the gathering of energy into the hind leg.

This serious flaw shows that the rider uses his hands too strongly and does not drive sufficiently. It is oftentimes accompanied by the horse having the tongue over the bit. This is a very bad mistake and very hard to correct—the horse has lost the confidence to step to the rider's soft hand. In order to correct this, the rider should maintain light contact and drive the horse from behind until the rider's hands can be moved forward as the horse pushes his nose forward to or in front of the vertical. It cannot be accomplished with loose reins. The horse will never stretch his nose forward by the rider giving up complete contact. It should be corrected by riding as if the reins were like sticks in each hand that push the bit gently forward. The seat and legs drive the horse over the back to this contact.

---

[2] When the horse seeks support on the rein contact and leans on the rider's hands, he is "leaning" on the bit. If he resists the rein contact by pulling upward to get away from the contact, he is against the bit.

Going behind the bit is by far the more difficult fault to correct and therefore a more serious fault than going slightly above the bit. So it is far better to never allow the horse to go behind the bit. The driving aids and rein contact are in a delicate balance. The rider should not push the horse so much forward that the horse rushes and the rider is forced to catch the horse on his hands. Then the horse repeats the problem as he slows down, overflexing behind the vertical and dropping the contact. Therefore, the rider must carefully drive the horse, paying attention to a steady rhythm, moving his hands slightly forward only as he succeeds in getting the horse to stretch his neck and head forward onto or slightly in front of the vertical. The rider's hands move in the direction of the horse's mouth without giving up the contact.

6.6.3 On the Buckle

Occasionally during the work and again at the end, the rider should let the horse walk on loose reins on the buckle. Now there is no contact with the horse's mouth, and the horse is allowed to fully stretch his neck forward and down. This is a type of reward for work well done. However, the horse should not go to sleep. He should keep up an active, long stride. When stretching forward and down, the horse should not go low and behind the vertical. He should be looking for the rider's hand and stretch to it.

If the horse can trot and canter on loose reins in balance, it proves that the horse does not support himself on the rein contact. My instructor always said, "If you cut the reins, the horse must go exactly the same as if you still held the reins in your hands!"

When the rider gives on the rein or reins, the horse can stretch his neck a little. The rider should briefly open the fingers slightly. In dressage tests when the command is "free walk on long reins," the horse should respond to the careful opening of the rider's hands by stretching smoothly forward and down with his head and neck. The horse should not jerk the reins out of the rider's hands, and the rider should not throw away the contact suddenly. In German the expression is literally translated, "the rider allows the horse to chew the reins out of his hands."

6.7 Half Halts

What is the purpose of the half halt? It improves the frame and rhythm of the horse when in motion. Or it gets these back again when they have been lost! The half halt is also used to make the transition from a higher to a lower gait, or from a lower to a higher gait. Here specifically the half halt engages the hindquarters of the horse. It is used before riding a volte, before riding through a corner, etc. It is used to prepare for every exercise. It means that the horse should pay attention; something new is coming!

To give the half halt, the rider uses a holding rein aid and simultaneously drives with the leg, almost immediately softening the rein (without losing the connection). The rider should use his driving aids when the leg of the horse to which the half halt was directed is leaving the ground. The rein and the leg aids are given on the same side of the horse, most often on the outside. The holding on the reins must not be so strong or held so long, however, that the horse stops. When the horse responds to the aids, giving to the hand and engaging from the leg, the rider has asked the horse to "prepare," and the horse has responded that "he is ready!" The rider must respond with giving, forward hands that allow the horse to carry himself in his restored balance.

I had a long talk with Colonel Podhajsky once and asked him among other things how many half halts he gave during a working session with a horse. He said that he had never counted, but he was quite sure it was more than five hundred in a single training session! I will come back to the subject of half halts many times in this book.

6.8 Full Halts

As the name implies, a full halt brings our horse to a complete halt from any of the three gaits. It is executed after preparation with one or more half halts, depending on the stage of training of the horse. The rider's holding rein should be accompanied by the forward driving aids, so that the horse is driven from the haunches forward into the contact of the rider's hands. One should ride the horse *into* the transition. As soon as the horse has halted, the rider's hands should soften through relaxation in the rider's shoulders. The connection between the rider's hand and the horse's mouth must be maintained with great sensitivity, particularly in the moment the rider softens this contact. Otherwise, if the moment is missed, the horse may step backwards or to the side. It is rare to see the halt well done in dressage competitions.

In a correct halt the horse stands absolutely still with equal weight on all four feet. The aids should be as invisible as possible. The less obvious the aids, the better trained the horse and the better the rider. Then you have classical dressage!

To read this description of the full halt, it sounds simple and logical. But I must assure you that the path to the riding of a correct halt is long and full of thorns! I will try to make it a little easier for you and your horse. With young horses, think "walk then halt" to keep them from becoming afraid of the aids for halt.

6.9 Spurs and Whip

There are a few things I would like to say about the use of the whip and spurs. They are used to enhance the forward-driving leg aids and sometimes to punish the horse. They should be used as rarely as possible for punishment. When the horse does something wrong, it is usually because he did not understand the aids or the rider gave the aids in the wrong moment, or the rider demanded too much or something beyond the horse's present ability.

Col. Aust always said, "Before you strike the horse even once, you should think about it and ask yourself, 'Is this necessary? Shouldn't I, perhaps, be the one who should be whipped?'" The use of the whip and/or spurs for punishment should only be carried out when the horse is very disobedient. And in that case the rider should give the horse one strong slap with the whip and a poke with the spurs. Then the rider should promptly go on with the work, not dwelling on the punishment. It should be over quickly and forgotten.

The ancient Greek Field Marshall Xenophon asked:

"How can a horse look good and proud and show all his beauty when he always gets spurred and whipped? "

Xenophon meant that one should not arbitrarily and without plan use these instruments or use them out of anger or to abuse the horse or make the horse sore. Their role is to sharpen and refine the response of the horse to the leg aids. They should never replace the legs.

Young horses, ticklish mares, and mares in season should never be ridden with spurs. With these horses the rider should use only the whip when it is appropriate.

6.9.1 The Whip

The whip is used to get more respect for the rider's forward and sideways driving leg aids so that these can become quieter and more efficient. It is not a substitute for the feeling of the leg aids but a gentle reminder when needed.

Timing is of the utmost importance when using the dressage whip. If using the left leg, asking for more activity from the horse's left hind leg and getting little or no reaction, the rider then uses his leg together with a light tap with the whip on the barrel just behind the rider's leg, when the horse's left hind is just leaving the ground. Leg-yielding is the easiest way for the rider to learn the timing of the driving aids. Once again, the timing of the aids is essential for an harmonious, quiet effect.

The intensity of the tap with the whip is also very important. This is especially true later for piaffe and passage work and requires years of experience with the whip.

Wait until the horse is really nicely round before changing the whip from one hand to the other. Take both reins in the hand holding the whip, and with the free hand slide the whip out and replace it on the other side and then divide the reins into two hands.

Never change the whip when the horse is off the aids or running away. Also, one should not change the whip when changing across the diagonal of the arena or on the centerline. It is too difficult to maintain the

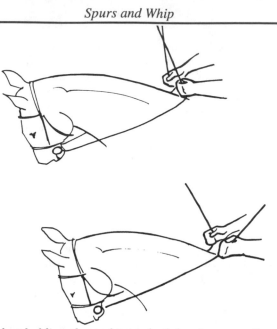

Figure 18: *A student holding short whips in both hands can easily see the proper alignment of their fists.*

horse's straightness. The ability to keep a horse straight with one hand while changing the whip is an art!

The whip is also a useful aid in working a horse in hand or on the longe, where it substitutes for the forward or sideways driving aids. As with the leg aids, it is always essential to discover how strongly or lightly to use the whip and in what moment to use it. The horse should not become afraid of the whip and yet must respect it completely.

The whip can be of help to students who have the bad habit of crossing their hands with one hand above the other or for correcting flat hands, palms down. I suggest that these riders ride with a short whip in each hand, the longer part above and holding the whips vertically. Hold the reins in the normal fashion. The whips should cross at a very small angle. When the riders start to cross or open their hands, the whips will clearly point out the error. In this way the riders will be made aware of what they are doing immediately, and they will be able to correct it.

6.9.2 Spurs

"Spurs can be like a razor blade in the hands of a monkey."

Spurs should be used with the same approach as the whip. The rider should not constantly poke the horse—one often sees horses with worn hair or even sores in the area of the rider's heel that are a clear sign of poor horsemanship. They should be used only when the horse has not reacted sufficiently to the rider's seat and legs. Different horses need different spurs. Lazy horses need sharper spurs—short, dull spurs will not work well. Mares require gentler spurs usually, because they are prone to becoming annoyed by and ticklish to spurs. The horse reacts to spurs as if they are horseflies, and will vibrate the skin and wring the tail—or even kick—to get rid of the fly.

Spurs with rowels are gentler than those without. The rolling action of the rowel prevents the spur from abrading on the side of the horse. It is important, however, to keep rowels clean and freely turning. Horse hair and sweat can easily clog and jam the rowel.

The timing of the use of the spurs is exactly the same as that of the whip: when the hind foot is leaving the ground and only when the horse doesn't react sufficiently to leg and seat. On a lazy horse the rider must use the spurs very energetically a few times to get the horse to react. It is good to use them strongly enough to make the horse actually jump forward. Then the rider will not have to repeat the strong aids with the spurs.

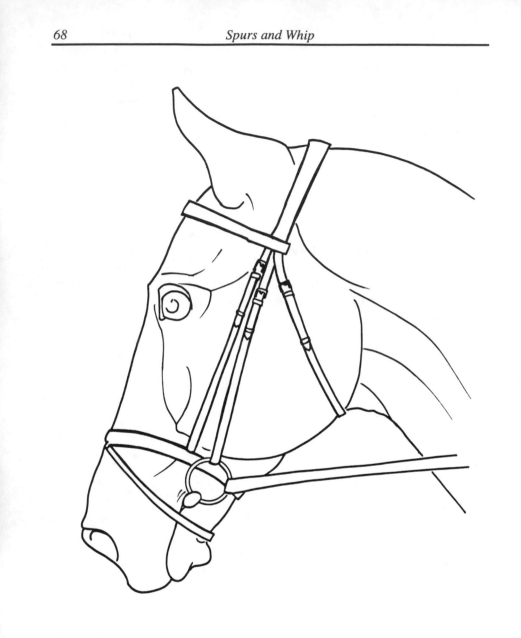

Figure 19. The snaffle bridle.

Chapter 7

The Young Horse

7.1 Initial Handling

Grand Prix dressage starts with a young horse—a foal or weanling. That which is not done correctly at the start cannot be done again. Every mistake at this stage is carried with us throughout his training, and snowballs from one mistake to another. The requirements of the advanced horse are trust, understanding, cooperation and partnership. We must work from the very outset to earn this trust and partnership in harmony. Training starts in the stable, and it is the trainer's responsibility to ensure that every human interaction is positive and correct; this includes stall cleaners, grooms, visitors.

The problem is that young horses, like the young of all species, are playful and by their size can be dangerous. We need to keep the situation safe and under control, but if we start with force and strength at this point, we will struggle throughout the rest of the training to overcome this mistake. Because horses are herd animals, they naturally take guidance from a leader. We must be very careful never to show the horse our weakness and his strength. Never try to fight with the horse, because in every fight, it is really the rider who loses. Try to arrange situations to avoid the fight in the first place. Take your time and *think*!

Foremost, the young horse has to be made to feel comfortable and safe in his new surroundings. So much has changed in his life in a short time with many moments of fear. I like the horse to feel that his stall is a calm, secure home where he can relax from outside stress. It is best to keep horses that don't get along or who kick at the walls or try to bite over the dividers separated.

7.2 Saddling the Young Horse

What should we watch for especially in the saddling of a young horse? One must have much calm and patience in putting on the saddle and bridle the first time. There will be so many times that we will saddle the horse again during his career, now is not the time to instill fear and unpleasantness. An assistant should hold the horse. Under no circumstances should the horse be tied or cross-tied. If he becomes frightened, he could break everything and in the future be very difficult to tie and to saddle.

The saddle should be carefully placed on the horse's shoulder area and then slid back, moving with the lie of the hair. Never slide it forward against the hair, instead pick the saddle up and start again from the front. Otherwise, the horse will easily get a saddle sore and become very sensitive. The helper then lets the girth down carefully. The girth should lie a hand's width behind the horse's elbow. Do not fasten the girth too tightly, because this can lead to an over-sensitivity to the girth, and the horse can jump violently forward or backwards and run right over someone, or even throw himself over backwards. The horse will not forget this experience quickly. It will take a very long time to make him relaxed again.

Do not lay the saddle too close to the withers as this can create an excruciating pain for the horse that might only be noticed when he is ridden. Many nerves run over the horse's withers, and this can set the training back significantly. The saddle pad should be attached with loops on the billet straps and girth so that it, too, cannot slide into a bad position, creating painful pressure to the horse. Even a well-fitting saddle can cause pressure on the withers if the saddle pad is not pulled well up into the throat of the saddle (at the pommel).

The saddle must fit the horse well. The horse is being introduced to something new and foreign, and we should not add pain and discomfort to his first impression of being ridden. This can stay with him for life. The saddle must sit with even contact on the entire saddle area of the horse's back. The deepest point must be in the middle. If this point is too far forward, the rider unavoidably will be forced to sit in a perched fashion—the perched seat. If this point is too far back, the rider will create pain for the horse by sitting over the kidney area, and the seat of the rider will be like that of someone sitting in a chair—the chair seat.

7.3 Bridling

We should take care when bridling the young horse. Remember that the mouth is the most sensitive part of the horse, and we must be careful not to make the horse head-shy or afraid of the bridle and bit. The bit should not be too wide, hanging to one side out of the mouth, nor should it be too narrow, as it will create an undesirable pressure on the horse's mouth. The bit should not be too thin. A thin bit is a harsh one. A medium-thick bit is gentle, and one should use this kind. A lubricant such as Vaseline applied to the corners of the horse's mouth prevents sores from developing.

The snaffle should not be buckled too high by the cheek pieces, pulling the bit up in the horse's mouth. Neither should it hang too low in the horse's mouth, because he will play with it and might get his tongue over it. The throat latch should be fastened loose enough that you can put your fist, held vertically, between the throat of the horse and the leather.

The brow band should not press or pinch on the ears or forehead. The nose band should not be so tight that it impairs breathing, yet not so loose that the horse can open his mouth, play with the bit or even put his tongue over the bit. One should give the horse sugar when bridling, so he associates bridling with a treat.

7.4 Longeing

The training of young horses should not be started before the horse is three and a half years old. (In earlier times training was not started until the horse was four years old.) The young horse is more likely to hurt himself during the early training. That why it is especially important to be careful. The horse should wear bandages or as extra protection, boots on all four legs. This is done to prevent the horse from wounding himself through a misstep with his hoof against his leg. The bandages must be put on securely so that they will not slip or unravel. The older and more advanced the horse gets, the less likely he is to hurt himself because he has attained better balance and coordination.

Longeing a horse correctly is a great art. On the longe, the trainer can see if the movements and rhythm are correct. Letting a horse run around in circles while lifting the longe over one's head and not even turning has nothing to do with longe work. This is merely exercising the horse.

The longe cavesson is placed over the snaffle bridle and fitted snugly so it will not slip or rub. A well-made cavesson has an extra strap that fits under the cheek, similar to, and in addition to the throat latch. This is fastened firmly to prevent the cheek pieces of the cavesson from going in the horse's eye. The cavesson is used so that the longeing does not hurt the horse's mouth, and the half halts are felt more on the horse's nose, not in the mouth. Through the whole training of the horse, we should remember that the mouth is the most sensitive part of the horse. We must always take care to maintain very fine and light feeling to the mouth. The longe (ideally seven meters in length) is attached to the middle ring of the cavesson. The snaffle reins will be twisted around each other and the throatlatch of the bridle opened and threaded through and refastened to secure the reins.

The stirrups are secured by knotting them with the stirrup leathers. After about two weeks the stirrups should be let down so that the horse becomes used to them.

The helper leads the horse to the working area, either a closed arena or an open area will do. First let the horse see everything by leading the horse on the track. This should be done in both directions. It is safest to build up a circle of 14 meters diameter in one corner of the arena out of cavalletti or jumps. Do this beforehand. This makes the work with the horse easier, because he cannot break away from the circle, and we do not have to pull on the mouth to keep him in.

Let the helper lead the horse behind the longe line out onto the circle and around a few times. This way the horse will get accustomed to moving on a circle. He will also get used to the helper leading him on the circle.

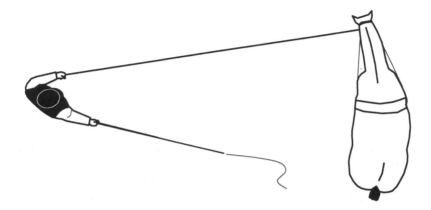

Figure 20. Longeing.

The helper must distance himself gradually from the horse. He should keep the longe line lightly in the left hand and move a little in on the circle, carefully keeping the horse out on the circle. He can then move a bit further from the horse, and so on until reaching the center. Now the person at the center of the circle holding the longe can take over, and the helper can assist with the longe whip. The whip should be long enough that the lash can easily touch the horse. We let the horse go a good free walk on the circle. If the horse is more high-strung and trots or canters off on his own, let him go in that gait for a while. All shouting or running should be avoided! Any fast move could frighten the horse.

One should use his voice according to the temperament of the horse. A sharp tone of voice should be used to drive the horse on, and a calm, quiet voice should be used to calm and slow the horse. Remember that the words have far less meaning than the tone of voice. Don't forget to praise and give a little sugar or carrots. This is very important in the work with the young horse.

One should not try to pull or to jerk strongly on the longe line to get the horse to fall back into the trot. Calm him with your voice, and generally, the horse will calm down quite soon and fall back into the trot or walk. Now let the horse continue at the trot or walk through the positive use of your voice and the driving effect of the longe whip. Do not crack the whip. Lifting the whip slightly signals the horse forward. Lowering the whip means the driving forward has ceased. The whip should be pointed toward the croup of the horse. It should never be dragged behind the trainer. The whip should be carried so that it can be used to drive the horse forward at a moment's notice without an exaggerated movement by the longeing person. The longe line should be kept taut and not twisted. (If the snap of the longe line is of the swivel type, it can easily be secured with electric or duct tape so that it will no longer twist.) Only in this way will the horse gradually become accustomed to the aids. I have recently seen longe lines with chains at the end. These should never be used—the chain is so heavy that it bounces around, and puts too much weight on the bit.

At the start one should make things easy for the horse to find his balance. For most young horses, this will mean going to the left. The longe is held in the left hand when longeing a horse on the left rein. The hand should be held at the height of the horse's mouth. The trainer's right shoulder points toward the hindquarters. To give half halts on the longe, the trainer's hand can move across his body. The longe line should be kept taut and untwisted. If it becomes loose and half halts cannot be given, shorten the longe line. The trainer should move in a very small circle when longeing a horse properly and not walk or run around. In no circumstance should the horse be jerked around, upsetting his balance and making him frightened.

If the horse falls in on the circle to the left on the longe line, the trainer should step with the right foot toward the horse, lifting the whip in the direction and height of the horse's shoulder. If this doesn't help to drive the horse back out, then the left hand, holding the longe line, flips the line in a wave like fashion toward the horse's mouth. The horse sees this "wave" in the line coming toward him, and he will move out to avoid it.

Work on the longe is like kindergarten for a child. It should be the first step toward obedience in the training. The horse should recognize our superiority in rank to him and respect us but never fear us.

The work on the longe should be limited to only 20 minutes so he does not become too tired. Later, it can be gradually lengthened, not exceed a total time of one half hour in length. The horse will get used to the work in two or three days. Once the horse has become accustomed to the work on the left rein, then the same is done on the right rein. But first let the horse go on the left rein a few minutes. If it is easier for the horse to on the right rein on the longe, then start the longe work on the right rein. After few minutes one should bring the horse quietly to a halt with a light half halt on the longe line and the use of the voice. Once he is standing still, the trainer should walk calmly toward the horse, gathering and coiling the longe as he goes. Then praise the horse and give him a little sugar. One should not let the horse walk toward him. After another two or three days the horse will get used to working in this direction, and one should be able to longe the horse without a helper.

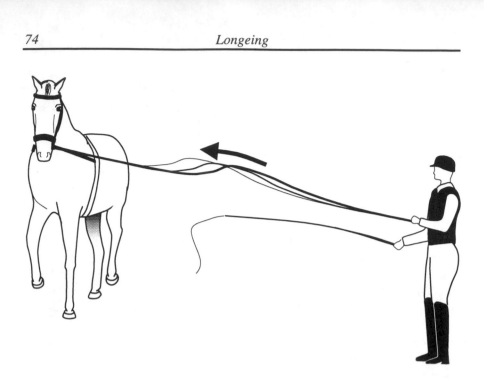

Figure 21. To help move the horse back out on the longeing circle, flip the longe line to create a "wave."

Once the horse can work daily in both directions, we can remove the boundaries we built up to form a fence. It is very important not to lose your patience in this work; it could be a great disadvantage for the future training.

After a week without side reins, they should be used and attached quite long, so the horse will not become frightened. Attach them to the girth at about the level of the bottom of the saddle flap, being careful that they can not slip too low.

It is best to attach the side reins to the rings of the snaffle first and then to the girth. This way, you can maintain a slight pressure on the bit as you bring the side reins back and attach them and the horse is not surprised by the pressure.

7.5 Free Jumping

Once a week, add free jumping to the horse's program to keep him from becoming bored. It is best to do this on the long side of an indoor hall. If there are mirrors in the arena, they must definitely be covered. Horses will not understand what the mirrors are and may think they are a continuation of the arena, jumping into them. As some who have experienced this can testify, this is not a pretty sight.

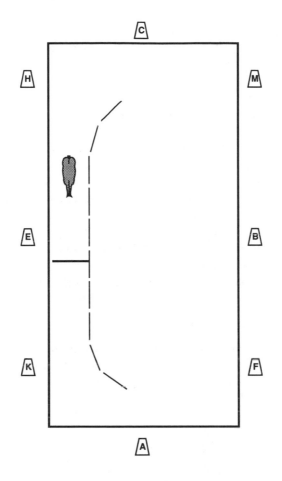

Figure 22. Using a chute for free jumping.

On one long side of the indoor hall, put up a line of rails or a rope to create a corridor just wide enough for the obstacle, so the horse cannot run out. The rope should be made as easily visible as possible by hanging something from it in many places. Then start the horse in his easier direction, left or right, but always toward his stall or "home." This is a good use of the herd instinct. Then lay a single pole on the ground half way down the corridor or lane. The helper leads the horse by the halter into the lane, always staying on the side of the wall. Another helper waits at the end of the lane with a bucket of grain.[1]

---

[1] I always gave this reward to the horse by squatting down and giving the grain almost at the ground. Whenever they were free-schooling, if I would squat down, the horses would

First the horse is led at the walk over a pole lying on the ground. On the other side the horse is given a little grain and is praised. Do this two or three times. Then put up a single cavalletti and do the same at the trot. The helper goes along also, but just before the cavalletti he lets the horse go, making no sudden movements. Then a small jump can be put up. Now the horse is led only to the entrance of the lane, quietly released and usually goes willingly over the jump, because he knows the reward is there at the end. "The path to love is through the stomach!"

When the horse has become accustomed to the single jump and is not afraid, a second element can be added to make a combination. It is essential, however, that the distance be made absolutely correct for the horse's canter stride (6.5 to 7.5 meters for a single stride, 13.5 to 14.5 meters for two strides). These jumps can also be raised gradually. This should not happen too fast. The work should be spread out over several months. Change direction when the work has gone well in the easy direction.

Free jumping should be done calmly and with no cracking of the whip and yelling. Never forget to praise and to give a reward. In just the same way that we respond well to praise, so does the horse. Free jumping should not be forgotten in the later training of the horse.

7.6 The First Mounting and Dismounting

Through the longe work the horse has been introduced to obedience and to carrying the saddle. Now we go a step further and get him used to the rider's weight. After a half hour of longeing in both directions, stand the horse in a place where he is confident of his surroundings with his right side to the wall, but not too close. Then undo the side reins, free the snaffle reins from the throat latch and check that the stirrups are the right length and twisted so they hand perpendicular to the horse's side.

Now a light but very skillful and experienced rider should mount the horse while a helper standing in front keeps the horse busy with grain or some treat. Another helper lifts the rider onto the horse so that the rider lies on his stomach across the saddle, letting the horse get used to the weight. Then the horse should be praised from all sides. The rider should stay in this position a short while before letting himself slide down carefully. Repeat this two or three times and that's enough for the first time. The next day repeat this a few times on the stomach, but then the rider can be lifted into sitting in the saddle. The rider should sit down slowly, first supporting himself on his hands and knees. Under no circumstances should the rider fall onto the horse's back. The stirrups should be taken carefully, having been let down fully beforehand and turned out so they can be easily found. It is good

---

immediately come to get their treats. Later, if the rider falls off, the horse stays close to him and does not run away, waiting for a treat!

to drop the stirrups and take them again repeatedly during the training to accustom the horse to the possibility of the rider losing his stirrup. Next, the rider can begin to mount carefully using the stirrup. The rider should hold the stirrup leather just above the stirrup iron and turn the stirrup into a position so that his foot can easily be placed inside.

The reins should be carefully taken in both hands. Again, the horse should be praised a lot and made calm by feeding some grain. If the horse is calm and not frightened, the helper can lead the horse forward carefully a few steps so that the horse gets used to carrying the rider's weight in forward movement. Again, if the horse is quiet, I would try to lead him once around the whole arena. The horse is accustomed to being led and gains confidence from this.

To dismount, first take both feet out of the stirrups, lean the upper body forward, lift the right leg slowly and carefully over the horse's back. Then slide down. While the rider is dismounting, the helper should distract the horse by feeding him something.[1]

7.7 The Lead Horse

In the first days under a rider's weight, not much more than I have described here should be done. So far, the young horse has been led around with a rider on his back. On the fourth or fifth day, the rider will take over. Now the longe and cavesson are removed and the rider receives a short whip to carry. To reassure the young horse, an older, experienced horse should be brought into the arena and ridden by an experienced rider to act as a lead horse. The young horse will take comfort from the other horse. Many times throughout the future training, a lead horse can prove valuable in calming frightened horses, showing the way over jumps and streams, past new obstacles like flowers, cars, arena letters, and so on.

At first, the young horse should be led behind the lead horse, and both stay at the walk on the track of the arena. Change the rein a few times, and if all goes well, try the first trot, but again, not for too long. One should be thankful and pleased with every small step of progress. It is important that the young horse starts to feel comfortable and safe along the track of the arena.

---

[1] With a quiet or trained horse, one can also dismount as follows: First, put the left hand on the mane and the right hand on the front of the saddle. Then take the right foot out of the stirrup. Now, the rider, by standing in the stirrup, lifts his seat out of the saddle, takes the right foot out of the stirrup, and quietly swings the right leg over the horse, and steps down lightly to the ground with the right foot, the left foot remaining in the stirrup. And as in mounting the rider turns so he is facing the hindquarters, with his left shoulder to the horse's left shoulder. This prevents the possibility of poking the horse with the rider's toe. Then the left foot is removed and placed next to the right foot on the ground. While dismounting in this fashion the left knee stays in the saddle, and the rider turns on his axis while stepping down.

The work with the lead horse should not last longer than two weeks. After the first week, one should try to ride the young horse without the lead horse after the first two thirds of the lesson. The lead horse is ridden to the center of the arena to wait. The young horse will try to follow the lead horse, and the rider must guide the young horse back to the track, working for the first time against the herd instinct of the horse.

Let us assume that we are on the left rein. We want the horse to turn to the right to return to the track. The rider takes the right rein contact and uses an "opening" or "leading" rein technique to lead the horse back to the track. The whip is in the left hand. The rider gives the horse a light tap on the left shoulder, and to yield to this tap the horse will move around to the right. Soon the young horse will be on the track where he has been used to going, and he will feel safe and comfortable there.

7.8 Use of the Whip With a Young Horse

From the beginning of mounted work, a whip should be used with the young horse. At first, use a short (about 18") whip, only applied lightly on the shoulder where the horse has become accustomed to the touch of the reins and the side reins. If you use the whip on the hindquarters or belly where the young horse has not felt anything yet, he will be frightened and possibly jump, buck, or run away.

It is important that the rider already know how to change the short whip from right to left hand skillfully. Let us assume that the rider holds the whip in the left hand and wants to put it in the right hand. To do this the rider raises both hands a little. The whip should not be lifted away from the rider's body. Now the rider moves the tip of the whip from the left hip where it was to the right hip. Then the right hand takes the whip and both hands are lowered. The whip is there only as a somewhat stronger aid, and used for punishment only when the rider is convinced that it is fair.[2]

7.9 Breaking into the Canter

If the young horse breaks into the canter for any reason, the rider should not interfere. Quite on the contrary, the rider should accept the canter and support it. The rider should sit lightly and go well with the movement. Do not drive with the legs too much. Be quiet with the legs and hands. When necessary, tap lightly with the whip on the horse's shoulder to encourage him forward. Also when the young horse falls back into the trot, by no means should the rider try to force him back into the canter. Let it be.

The formal work at the canter starts only when the young horse trots willingly and fairly well balanced on both reins. After working the horse at the trot on straight lines, 20 meter circles, and changes of rein, then we start the canter on the left rein. Again, most horses canter more easily in the left

---

[2] A good way to check your own attitude is to see if your teeth are clenched when you use the whip.

lead, but the first canter should take into account the hard and easy sides of the individual horse. On the left rein, take the whip in the right hand, the outside hand. Take a good working trot, but not rushed, on a large circle. Be careful that the horse does not drift out over the outside shoulder. The rider's outside leg behind the girth guards against this and should be ready to counteract this movement energetically. Sit the trot for approximately a half circle. Of course, this sitting trot should be kept light. Take care not to sit too heavily on the young horse, because the horse must get used to the weight, and the musculature of the back develops gradually. Consider how long it would take yourself to build muscles and carry such a weight!

The best place on the circle to give the aids for the canter is between the open side and approaching the wall. The rider should not kick with the outside leg far back, but rather, give the aids by dropping the inside heel to shift his weight to the inside. The rider also takes his outside shoulder slightly back, and the hands go slightly forward. In the moment when the outside shoulder goes back, give the horse a light tap with the whip on the outside shoulder. The horse will want to avoid the whip and will take the canter. Once in the canter the rider should go straight ahead to avoid pulling the horse around. Be careful not to throw the reins too much forward. The rider should keep a light, elastic contact with the horse's mouth, and be thinking, "forward!" If this transition doesn't work the first time, it should be repeated, but only when the horse has relaxed again. If the horse picks up the incorrect lead, stay with that lead and carefully change direction so he goes in true canter, free and without too much correction.

At first, one should ask for the canter always in the same place with a young horse. In this way we make it easier for the horse to learn and remember the aids. When this works well a few times, then try it in another location, but never between the wall and the open side of the circle or after the second corner of the short side. These places truly invite the horse to run away. Also, it is too easy for the horse to fall out over the outside shoulder when asked to canter in these places.

Most young horses learn quickly to take the canter in the right place. On the third day the rider can try for the other (right) lead canter in the same way, again being careful that the horse does not fall out over the outside shoulder or run away. When the horse is relaxed in the canter, work on circles can be introduced. With energetic horses, it is best to work on a circle. With lazy horses it is better to go straight ahead.

After six months, the horse should have gotten used to the rider's weight, leg and hand aids. Now he can be made familiar with leg and rein aids on the same side. We arrive at the suppling exercises, which will be discussed in Chapter 10.

7.10 Shying

Young horses often shy and jump away from new objects or situations or quick movements. Older, more experienced horses may also jump away from new "goblins," but usually time has accustomed them to weird blankets, shadows, flowers, sun-beams, and so on. One should never forget however that the horse evolved as a grazing animal whose main defense against predators is flight. A few months or years of training will never overcome millions of years of evolution.

To cure shying, the horse must be brought to trust his rider and himself. He must trust that the rider will let him run away if something terrible happens, and he must feel balanced and in control of his body. You often see riders trying to force their horses past a "scary" object, and the horse becomes more and more tense, and the rider resorting to more and more force. You can never beat the shying out. What is really happening in the horse's mind is that he is being trapped near this frightening thing, and that his one defense is taken away. Also, he learns to associate a whipping with an object, place or situation, and we have succeeded in teaching him that this thing is to be feared, and he becomes more and more tense.

When riding past a frightening place, the rider must become more relaxed, careful, cool and quiet. When the horse trusts that he *can* run away he will accept that he does not *need* to—yet. The rider must lightly control the horse, but always give the horse the reassurance that flight is possible. He must also keep the horse well balanced, so the horse feels that he can jump away.

By positioning the horse with a good bending away from the object (shoulder-in for those horses who understand it), the horse can not bolt away so easily through the inside shoulder. He can still escape through the front. When a horse shies from an object on his right side, he usually bends strongly right to look at the object, plants both front feet and pushes out through the left shoulder. Keeping the bend left makes this more difficult, making it easier for the rider to keep the horse going straight past the object. Making the horse bend right and pulling him towards the object makes the horse more frightened because escaping forward takes him *toward* the hazard.

Horses tend not to shy as much when they are being led or when they are with other horses. This comes from the herd instinct, trusting the leader. As mentioned above, using a lead horse can be helpful in situations where a young horse is frightened.

When horses become older and more experienced, riders often become less tolerant of shying and resort to the whip when shying occurs. He "should know better!" Like people, some horses are more frightened of certain situations than others. If we always spur or whip the horse near one "scary" corner of the arena, they will surely come to fear that area. It is

Figure 23. When riding past a frightening object, position the horse with bending away from the object (right). When the horse is positioned toward the object, he can easily spin out through the outside shoulder (left).

better to look for exercises and figures which keep the horse's mind on the work, gradually coming closer and closer to the frightening area.

As in all aspects of his training, the horse relinquishes his natural fear and becomes cooperative and responsive when he becomes familiar with the objects in his surroundings and learns that they are not a threat.

Chapter 8
Introduction to Advanced Training

8.1 Starting Advanced Work

One of the most dangerous phases of a horse's training is the beginning of advanced work. The goal is a balanced, harmonious, happy horse working in partnership with the rider, with mutual trust. As the training progresses, we develop more engagement, power and suppleness. The horse carries himself in a round, fluid, energetic fashion. The difficulty is that inexperienced riders confuse the end with the means. Too often, we see riders pulling the front end round "like a dressage horse," then having to resort to whips and spurs to kick the horse to get what they think of as "forward." By this means, they plan to "make" a dressage horse. What usually results is stopping or rearing or worse.

Advanced work is the consistent, gradual development of engagement, relaxation, impulsion, suppleness, straightness and collection. Through this work a round, forward, happy horse emerges. (A happier rider also, since nothing is nicer than to be in harmony with his horse.) We must choose our demands carefully and progressively so that the development of the horse is like grass growing: we never see anything happen, but over time things get better and more beautiful.

I am often asked how long it will take to master this or that movement. My answer is always the same, usually found to be unsatisfying to the student: "it depends." It depends on the horse, his prior handling and training, the skill and temperament of the rider. Another suitable answer might be "why do you ask?" We can not set time limits and then say "time is up, now move on to the next step!" Rushing the training according to some time limit always leads to a fiasco!

We must always pay close attention to the needs of our horse and his ability to handle any new work we ask. If by some mistake, we find that the horse objects to the work because we have pushed a step too fast, then we must immediately back off for awhile. Pushing on in the face of resistance will usually develop the resistance, not the horse. Similarly, we cannot skip any steps. Short cuts imply that something is being cut away, and this can never be taken back.

THAT WHICH IS NOT DONE CORRECTLY AT THE START CANNOT BE DONE AGAIN.

8.2 Characteristics of the Well-Trained Horse

The characteristics of the well-trained horse can be evaluated by observing first the whole horse, and then the detail. The horse's back, the bridge between the haunches and the forehand, should swing gently up and down, allowing the rider to sit with suppleness and to use leg, weight, and lower back to drive. He should be responsive to all aids, evenly connected on both reins, and move easily the same forward, sideways or backwards. He can not be stiff or tense.

The rein contact is the consistently fine connection between the rider's hand and the horse's mouth. The well-trained horse should seek this contact, and the rider with an independent seat and hand should use variation in the contact depending upon the demands on the horse. A good rider will always try to be brief in his use of increased rein contact, in order to return to a lighter contact. When the horse is working with correct contact, and chewing evenly on both sides of the mouth, he is on the bit and carries himself. If the horse goes above or behind the bit, it shows that the rider's hand dominated incorrectly and that the opportunity to use the driving aids was missed. The desired harmony of rein aids with driving aids was not achieved. The driving aids, *Kreuz* and leg, should always prevail over the restraining rein aids. "Driving comes before restraining."

A steady, strong contact is evidence of a tight poll in the horse, the result of a lack of muscular relaxation. However, if the horse allows and responds to a brief strong contact, this proves the horse is solidly on the bit. Only when the horse accepts a light and steady contact and seeks the bit can the rider make the necessary changes in the horse's frame from longer to shorter, etc. The horse should show his confidence in the harmony of the rider's aids by chewing softly with his mouth closed. This cannot be achieved by forcing the horse's mouth shut with a very tight nose band, which can seriously affect the horse's breathing. Rather, an open mouth and tongue over the bit or hanging out are always signs of too strong rein aids, and the rider must correct his aids in order to win back the horse's acceptance.

The trot and canter of the well-trained horse must have *schwung*, resulting from complete athletic relaxation: a swinging back and springy hind legs. *Schwung* can only come from the hindquarters—the motor! The best car is worthless when the engine doesn't work! The movements of the horse should be supple and graceful, effortless and powerful. The *schwung* in a horse is easily recognized by the moments of suspension in his trot and canter. Whereas a horse without *schwung* shows a lack of suspension. *Schwung* is seen both in collection and in extensions. A well-trained horse with good suspension lands and pushes off lightly from the ground. He should appear to hate to touch the ground.

8.3 Ride to the Limit - But Not Over

The characteristics of the well-trained horse include happiness and strength. We can keep the horse happy by turning him out and never working him, but that will never develop strength, or we can drive, drive, and over-drive our horses to develop strength, but quickly have a sour horse. Riding Master Eggert confided in me that he once had a horse who was resistant. He felt he had to *make* the horse obey and spent 2½ hours to "correct" the horse. Instead of getting better, the horse got worse, the rider got frustrated, and finally gave up! The next day, the horse would not go into the arena—sure that in there was a maniac![1] He came to understand that this was not the right way, and that what does not come today will come tomorrow or next week or next month. What is done in force will never be good.

The secret lies in riding "to the limit—but not over." When we are building strength, we must exercise muscles without over-stressing them, and without losing the horse's enthusiasm for work. When we are introducing new movements, we must show the horse things that are new and unfamiliar, but we must find ways to minimize the unfamiliar, and we must pay close attention to his attitude: is he just confused or is he frightened?

Riding over the limit is often too easy to see: lameness from pulled muscles, tightness and soreness from overwork, colic, cold sweat after work. What is harder to see is the loss of spirit and confidence, but to the sensitive eye of the teacher (and hopefully the student) can sense the horse's nervousness and desire to be somewhere else. We will discuss figures, transitions and movements designed to build strength and suppleness in the horse. These will allow the horse to develop strength without resorting to force. When working through these exercises, be careful to listen to the signs that we have gone over the limit:

- The horse does not understand what we want.
- The rhythm is not regular.
- There is tenseness or fright.
- The horse has lost confidence in the rider or confidence in himself.

In the following chapters, movements are presented in a gradual series of steps, starting with versions that are easy for the horse to understand. It may seem that taking the time to master each step will take far too long, but be assured it is the shortest way to overall success.

---

[1] Riding Master Eggert is certainly not alone in having such an experience. We have all had moments where our judgment has been clouded by a desire to achieve. To paraphrase an old saying: "the secret to good judgment is experience, but the source of experience is bad judgment!"

I often hear riders planning to enter dressage shows who are trying out new levels: "I'm not really confident about the shoulder-in, but I hope it will go OK" (or the judge doesn't look close enough). One should ride one level higher very well at home before entering a show at a lower level. This is not just to avoid embarrassing ourselves in the show ring, but to avoid rushing to master a new movement in order to "make it" through a show. Whenever we rush to establish a new movement, we invite work "over the limit."

On the other hand, if we never work "to the limit," we won't develop the strength needed for advanced work, or the submission and obedience required. The beauty, effortlessness and grace of a well-developed horse takes substantial strength in the hindquarters, and the higher the collection, the more strength that is required. A horse can easily be taught *how* to do a pirouette, but he will have great difficulty in performing one without proper musculature. Riding to the limit does not mean to ride the horse "into the ground," but it does mean a vigorous program of well-planned exercises, mixing collecting work with good forward stretching work.

Mentally, the horse must perform every exercise we ask without fear and with confidence. He must not have a "mind of his own," bolting and shying or galloping off, but he must not go around dull or dispirited or in constant worry of the rider, protecting himself by going behind the bit or not freely stepping forward. Again, "over the limit" is easy to spot: horses that stop and back up rather than continue on with a tough movement, horses that hide in the back corner of their stalls, or balk at going into the arena. They must trust the rider completely, from the handling in the stall, through daily work, at shows, and when we introduce new ideas.

Not working "over the limit" mentally means never trying totally new movements. This startling sounding statement is not so surprising when we remember the basic tenets of our training. We require that the horse trusts the rider. This trust comes from consistent, familiar unforced work. Doesn't a new movement violate this trust? The secret is to have a very gradual but steady path to more difficult work. For instance, before we can introduce the pirouette, we need a proper volte, shoulder-in, travers, and half pass that the horse fully understands and accepts without tension. We can then make a half pass to a volte that maintains a bit of travers position. Perhaps at first the volte will be a slightly larger circle, but the horse can easily understand what we want. The volte can gradually become smaller until the pirouette is reached. Trouble comes when the rider wants to get there "right away."

This idea of gradual development starts very early as well. We introduce leg-yielding by using the horse's natural desire to return to the track, we start shoulder-in through shoulder-fore, and so on. Maintaining the horse's trust is foremost, and minimizing his confusion is key to keeping this trust through the introduction of new movements. Relaxation throughout the work is the hallmark (and absolute requirement) of the well-trained horse.

If you visit the riding halls of the great masters who routinely produce brilliantly outstanding horses at the pinnacle of horsemanship, such as Reitinstitut von Neindorff in Karlsruhe, Germany, you will be overcome with the sense of calm and understanding on the part of horse and rider or handler. You will not see a horse who appears to have difficulty learning any new movements, and you might think that no "learning" is going on—they are just practicing what they already know. Perhaps you have visited the barn of a "hot-shot" new trainer where you can see horses pushed into new movements all the time. You might sense that the obvious signs of "learning" are happening there—the horses were being challenged and taught, and the fussing and fighting are just because the horses had not yet "learned." "As soon as they figure this out, they will be great," you are told, "Have you ever seen such movement?"

But return to those two places in two years. Still nothing much is happening at the Masters'—except that the horses that are now pleasantly exercising the Grand Prix were the very ones that were pleasantly exercising lower level movements earlier. At the "hot-shot" barn you will seldom find the same horses even there! They have developed physical problems, been sold off as "not really talented enough" or perhaps they are struggling still with the same basic problems. Those few that do advance are seldom happy and proud, confident and relaxed.

The Master achieves his highly repeatable success by staying within the horse's mental limits, and using the essential nature of the horse to learn through comfort and familiarity.

8.4 Forward

Recall the fundamental goal set forth in Chapter 3: "Ride your horse calm, forward, and make him straight." Forward is embodied in the concept of *Schwung*, the engaged, active hind leg and the release of the propulsive energy over a relaxed back, withers, neck, poll and mouth, and back to the receiving influence of the rider's hands.

Schwung is naturally developed through the working and medium gaits, but must be maintained in all turns, transitions and in collected work. Collection is not the opposite of *Schwung*; it requires *Schwung*.

The collecting movements—shoulder-in, travers, renvers, half pass, etc.—are to be ridden with *Schwung*, but the horse can easily lose the swinging power when kept too long in collection. It is therefore important to intersperse the more forward working and medium gaits with collection. One should ride no more than two lengths of the arena in collection before lengthening the stride to get back *Schwung*.

Be careful not to confuse forward with fast. We make it difficult for the horse if we exaggerate the forward riding by going too fast. Each horse should be ridden at his correct tempo.

8.5 Straight

We will be concerned about the straightness of the horse repeatedly throughout the training, and we will be kept busy trying to improve it, because without a straight horse, nothing can be correct. When straightness is achieved, everything else will be easier.

To understand the straightening of the horse, we will need to understand his natural crookedness. Just as with humans, each horse is stronger on one side than on the other. (Usually the horse's left side is stronger, so for clarity, we will assume the left side is the stronger or "stiff" side. For horses with a stiffer right side, everything is simply reversed). The muscles of the left will be slightly shorter and tighter than those of the right, where the muscles are longer and not so strong. The left hindquarter will be flexed more and carry more of the horse's weight, while the right leg will be straighter and stiffer. When at liberty, the horse will tend to go to the left, and will show a preference for cantering on the left lead.

The rider feels crookedness through uneven rein pressure, through displacement of the shoulder relative to the horse's path and through uneven hips. Thus, the rider feels a heavier left rein because the horse's entire right hind leg is naturally straighter and stiffer than the left. The horse may be described as being unlevel in his hips, also as lowering his inner (left) hip. While the right hind leg is stiffer, it provides more of the forward pushing power. He seeks to balance himself by leaning on his left side and on the rider's left rein contact. He forms an arc to the left, with its axis from the right hind leg to the left rein, and bows the shoulders out to the right and the haunches in to the left, where they carry more weight.

Viewed from the side it is easy to see which side is heavier and tighter, because the snaffle is often pulled further through the horse's mouth on that side. The horse takes more pressure in the rein on the tighter side and chews there more. If the horse trots on a straight line away from the viewer, it will be noticeable that the horse carries his haunches a little to the stiff side and not directly behind his shoulders.

Let us assume that the horse is crooked to the left. (A few horses are heavier on the right side and softer on the left side. Naturally, with these horses the technique will be the opposite.) This means that the horse bends himself too much to the left and likes to travel in a travers-like position. The shoulder of this horse is falling too much to the right and makes the hind leg go too much to the left. He takes a heavier left rein, and does not so readily accept contact on the right. Turns and lateral work for this horse will be generally easier to the left: travers, half pass, pirouettes, and canter. Leg-yielding to the left (right leg-yielding) will be easier for this horse. The

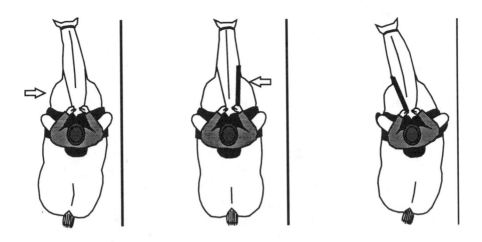

Figure 24. The crooked horse travels with the shoulder falling out (left panel). Correct the shoulder to the hind leg, using outside aids (center). If the rider tries to pull the shoulder to the inside, he will only make things worse.

exceptions are shoulder-in and renvers, which will be easier on the right rein.

8.6 How to Straighten the Horse

Remember that crookedness originates in the horse's natural preference for moving to one side, largely due to the increased strength of that hind leg[1]. Straightening must therefore be a long term process that gradually evens out the two sides. The goals are to:

1. eliminate the horse's dependence on the left rein;
2. bring the horse's shoulders to the left;
3. increase the pushing power of the engaged (left) hind leg;
4. increase the carrying power of the stiff (right) hind leg;
5. get the horse away from the tight (left) rein and get more contact on the loose or vacant (right) rein.

These objectives can be advanced all the time, even when working on other things. The sensitive and alert rider will always seek to lighten and give the taut (left) rein, and try to steady and receive more weight on the vacant (right) rein. This can be done when schooling transitions, lateral movements or on hacks and over small jumps. To produce more contact in

---

[1] Again, we will assume that the horse is stronger on the left side.

the vacant (right) rein, the rider drives more with the left leg, increasing the pushing power of the left hind.

8.6.1 Correct the Shoulder to the Hind Leg

Throughout the horse's training, straightness and alignment problems will surface—haunches leading or lagging in half pass, shoulders leading in leg-yielding, haunches swinging in at the canter, etc. A guiding principle in fixing these problems should be to adjust the shoulders to the hindquarters, and this will come up over and over throughout the remainder of this book.

When ridden on the left rein, the horse will tend to carry his haunches in as in travers. The correction should be to bring the shoulders in slightly. By closing the outside contact and bringing the shoulders to the left, the rider helps the horse find contact on the outside (right) rein, frees up the inside (left) rein, increases the carrying power of the inside (left) hind leg, and brings the rider to the left. If the rider is not skilled enough to bring the shoulders in with the outside (right) rein, it will be counter-productive to try to bring the shoulders to the left by pulling on the left rein. This will reinforce the crookedness, and make it even easier for the shoulders to fall to the outside. In this case it is perhaps better to ride in a slight renvers (haunches-out) position. This will diminish the rider's tendency to pull on the left rein too much, the rein on which the horse is heavier and tighter. Renvers will work more directly to increase the carrying power of the right hind leg; shoulder-in will decrease the leaning on the left rein. Both contribute to straightening when done properly.

On the right rein with this horse, he should be put in a slight travers position. This increases the flexion of the right hind, and encourages contact on the soft side. It stretches the whole left side and gives more bending to the right side. All of these corrections have to be without any force and with much patience. Although we are trying to get the horse to accept the contact on the right rein, the inside (right) rein must remain soft in the travers. It is the stretching and bending which helps, not a *pulling* into the travers. You can not change in a day (or a year) what nature has made over millions of years without inducing serious pain, injury and/or permanent damage to the horse.

All aids should be given so that they are almost invisible. This can be done only if the correct aids are given in the right moment. This is one of the most important things a rider must know and be able to do: the rider's aids to influence forward, sideways and backward movement, or to restrain movement in the horse will only be successful when given in the moment that the designated hind leg is about to leave the ground. In the beginning of a rider's training, it is a good idea to have a helper who can say when the left hind leg of the horse is leaving the ground until the rider can reliably feel it. Then the rider must learn the same for the right hind leg. It is very important for the rider to be always aware of the position of the hind legs, and this part of the rider's training should not be overlooked. Whether it is the need to be posting on the proper diagonal or timing the aids in a canter depart, flying changes, piaffe—in fact, all the time—it is the hind leg that determines the timing.

As we begin to straighten him, the horse will try to support the rider's added weight by increasing his engagement. He reacts much the same as we would. If a person carries a weight on his left shoulder, he lifts that shoulder higher and holds it higher in order not to lose the weight. The horse reacts exactly the same. When the horse lifts his left hind leg and hoof from the ground, we give him an increased leg pressure with our left leg. Also in this moment the rider gives or lightens (but not loses) the contact of the left rein. This gives the horse the opportunity to step forward and under the weight of the rider with his left hind leg better. This is what we call engagement.

The rider's inside (left) leg drives against the soft contact on the outside (right) rein. This outside rein is very important. It controls the tempo through the rider's use of half halts, and it controls the position in the horse. The horse feels the pressure of the rider's inside leg and he reacts by stepping more actively with his inside (left) hind leg. This action moves diagonally toward the contact of the rider's outside (right) hand, thus bringing the horse into the contact of the outside rein. It is critical at this point to remember the importance of the rider's outside leg. It has the job of guarding against the mistake of the haunches swinging to the outside in response to the rider's inside leg. If the outside leg is used well, it will encourage the horse to step more forward and under his and the rider's weights. This balances the horse.

Another very important factor in the straightening process is the horse's neck. I take for granted that every rider has observed his horse in freedom, either in the pasture or in the riding hall. In freedom, the horse uses his neck much the way a high-wire acrobat uses the balancing bar, namely he carries it to the left or the right according to his need for balance. The rider should never make the neck too short, because then balance becomes too difficult for the horse. This is so extremely important for the later training of the horse that I cannot remind the rider often enough of this. The use of the neck is of utmost importance in all forms of riding, including jumpers and 3-day event horses. Without proper use of the neck, nothing will be correct.

I have frequently had the pleasure of watching George Morris give jumping instruction. He is certainly a master! He insists that the horse's neck not be shortened too much, that the horse go straight, that he be light in the hand and that he be in balance. This has special meaning for me, because Colonel Aust taught in almost the exactly same fashion. Col. Aust and his students were overjoyed to see the American jumping team riders in Europe in the mid 1950's riding with such elegant seats: low and giving hands, deep heels, quiet legs, and good posture. There was wonderful harmony between horse and rider.

If we spend the necessary time to understand the theory, it will always be reflected in the practice.

8.7 Natural Balance

Forward, straightening and balancing go hand in hand. You might ask, "Well, isn't the horse already in balance?" Yes, in freedom the horse is in balance. But what happens when we put a snaffle bridle and a saddle on him? It is against nature. This small added weight already brings the horse out of balance. Then comes the rider with his one to two hundred pounds. You can imagine how the poor animal must feel. However, I have often experienced that a light rider can ride as if heavier, and a heavy rider can distribute his weight so well that he can ride as if lighter than he actually is. To get and keep the horse in balance the rider must develop the horse's confidence in his own ability to step further under his body and that of his rider's. The horse then carries more weight on his hindquarters than would be his natural way of going and becomes much more in balance. When the horse has learned to balance himself on his four legs and not on the hands of the˙ rider, then he is "in balance." Only when balance is achieved can the gaits and exercises be nice and harmonic.

8.8 *Durchlässigkeit*

Translated literally, *Durchlässigkeit* means the quality of combined suppleness and strength that allows the leg, *Kreuz*, and rein aids go through the horse's body. I will call it "submission," although it is more than this. One wants to see the willing submission of the horse in half halts and full halts with good engagement of the hindquarters. A supple poll in all gaits demonstrates willing submission of the jaw of the horse. The horse does not resist on either the harder or softer side. The rider must recognize which sides these are by taking the time to study the horse. In order to do this, the rider must have the ambition and patience to teach himself.

A horse lacking submission resists and avoids the aids by leaning on the reins, going behind or above the bit, tossing the head, or opening his mouth. The non-submissive horse may also avoid the position to the right or the left by tilting his head. The rider's weight gets shifted to the tighter side, reinforcing the tendency of the horse to go crooked.

Sometimes this is due to a lack of physical condition in the horse. The horse who finds it hard to carry himself and the rider may come to rely too strongly on the rider's hands for balance. These horses need simple, forward strengthening work—a project that will take time, but should not be overlooked. Such work has to be carefully measured and without force, and the rider needs the patience to let the strength develop while the horse's mind stays happy and confident. If the rider pushes the horse too fast at this point, the mistake will remain throughout all the rest of the horse's training.

A fully submissive horse permits his rider to use desirably subtle aids to enhance the beauty of the overall picture. The result is almost invisible aids. In fact, the less one sees the aids, the better the horse is reacting to them. Crude, strong aids lead to harsher and harsher aids. A horse ridden this way will become a fighter. Fighting should be avoided at all costs. The harsh use of aids ultimately may produce rearing, bucking, bolting, shying, kicking and biting and under the worst circumstances, going down and refusing to stand up. One often hears it said that these horses are not suitable for upper-level dressage or jumping. But these horses are actually the smart ones, because they refuse to be treated this way without fighting back. They might have been very good horses, had they not been ruined by mistreatment.

A student of mine once watched as a horse was brutalized with spurs, bit and whip and in a few minutes was soaked with sweat from fear, and bleeding from the mouth and sides. My student asked the owner, who was also watching, how she could tolerate this cruelty. The owner responded that if a horse cannot withstand this type of harsh training, it will never become a Grand Prix horse. My student then said that if this were the only way—and she was sure it was not—then she hoped never to have a Grand Prix horse.

I would like riders to avoid the tendency to copy others who might use extreme force. It will always lead to disaster.

8.9 Beginning Collection

One often hears that collection is the highest goal of the horse's training. Yet few understand the meaning of this truism. Riders are often frustrated by the need to ride their horses for extended periods in a longer frame. They say "When am I going to work on collection?" They fail to understand that the quality of a collected gait is less dependent on the rider's aids at a particular moment than on the past years of work and development. Collection is developed over time as strength is increased through correct training and appropriate schooling exercises, and the horse becomes more comfortable and confident carrying the weight more and more on the hindquarter. Thus, true collection becomes almost effortless, just as the human athlete develops a certain self-carriage as his training progresses. It is only when the horse has achieved this level of physical development and offers collection as his natural way of going, that the movements such as half pass, flying change, or extended gaits, can be performed with brilliance and ease. When the rider and horse are concentrating all their mental and physical energy on creating and maintaining collection, they have nothing left for anything else. Hence the crabbed and stiff movements so often seen in competition at the upper levels.

Advanced work therefore consists of a sequence of exercises and movements designed to develop and enhance natural collection.

First come the transitions, trot-walk-trot. These must be very calm and fluid. Then the rider proceeds to lengthening the strides, a few at a time, and then collecting again. These transitions should also be energetic yet fluid. The steps of lengthening should be longer but not faster. The rider should ride only as many strides of lengthening as he can control.

If this goes well, the rider can begin with smaller circles and voltes, shoulder-in exercises, travers, half passes, full halts, and from full halts to trot. Then the rider should give the horse a little break on long reins.

Then we begin the canter work. Again, make many, frequent transitions to the canter from the walk and back to the walk. Then the rider starts with smaller circles and transitions from walk-canter-walk on these circles. When the horse is comfortable and obedient with this exercise, the rider can start with lengthening and shortening the strides at the canter. Counter-canter can be introduced when the horse's transitions walk-canter-walk and the lengthening and shortening of stride are going well. This is done on the long sides of the arena from walk to right-lead canter and back to walk, and then to left-lead canter, etc. The rider would be smart not to ask for the counter canter in the corners! Ask for it either well before the corner or after.

At the walk, turns on the haunches and rein-back can now be introduced. These should be ridden at the walk and without halting before the turn. But if ridden with a halt before the turn, the first step forward should be the first step of the turn.

8.10 Collection and Elevation

Hidden in the German word for collection—*Versammlung*—is the term meaning "gather up." What does the rider gather up in collection of the horse? Energy. Energy is necessary for the upper levels in dressage. And where is the energy gathered up? In the hindquarters of the horse, in his motor.

The movement of the horse becomes more expressive when the rider's aids are able to tap the source of energy in the hindquarters. In all three gaits one speaks of cadence and elevation. The carrying power of the hindquarters is developed more and more for the purpose of lightening the horse's forehand. This is accomplished as the hip and stifle joints of the hind legs are more flexed, thus lowering the hindquarters and elevating the forehand. This elevation of the forehand, resulting from the increased flexion of the joints of the haunches, I mentioned earlier as "relative elevation." This leads to the development of a harmonious frame of the horse in which the topline of the horse's neck rises smoothly and uninterrupted (without a notch) from the withers to the poll. This gives the impression of riding slightly uphill.

The horse's ability and level of collection grows harmoniously with his training. It should be a slowly growing process, and under no circumstances should collection be started too early or forced, nor should the horse be made to maintain collection for long periods too soon. Otherwise, the suppleness and then the impulsion will deteriorate. Also, the desirable natural qualities of the gaits will deteriorate, such as the length of stride.

8.11 Collection and Self-Carriage

Collection is the highest level of dressage. The horse carries increased weight on well-flexed and active hind legs. This in turn promotes the elevation of the forehand and the lightest possible rein contact. For the more advanced exercises, the engagement of the elastic and active hind legs with the relative elevation of the forehand and a light, elastic rein contact that is not rigid, are required. These qualities allow a high level of impulsion to develop and be maintained.

Self-carriage is a goal and a result in the training. If the self-carriage is good, the horse will successfully stretch his frame in the walk, trot and canter extensions *and* shorten his frame in returning to the collected tempo. He will do this reliably.

An easy test of self-carriage is for the rider to stroke the horse's crest with one or both hands, temporarily losing contact with the horse's mouth. The horse's reaction to this stroking should be that he does not lose his balance and speed up, lifting his head. He should change nothing, except to stretch his neck very slightly, still in a rounded frame. The stroking test should not take more than one or two seconds, and should be done so as to lose and regain rein contact carefully and not suddenly. It should, nevertheless, be clearly visible.

Years ago it was required in dressage tests to show this *Überstreichen* in the medium canter. For instance the test would read, "In the middle of the long side, *Überstreichen*." One would see very interesting reactions from both horse and rider. Sometimes panic. Sometimes wonderful elegance when the exercise was successful. This requirement disappeared for a time, but has now re-appeared in AHSA tests at Second and Third Levels, for which I am grateful.

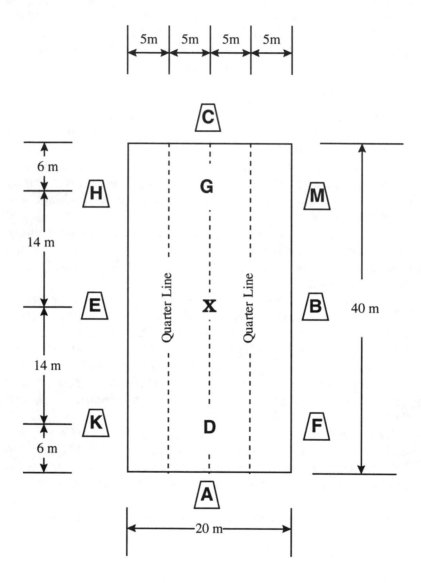

Figure 25. Small Arena.

Chapter 9
School Figures

School figures have been developed over generations of training. The demands of practicing them for competition are clear enough, but why should riders who have no desire ever to enter a competition worry about them? Because they form a basis for training the logic of which follows from the way horses learn and from their innate desire to feel comfortable with their surroundings and with the work. We start with the largest and most gradual of turns, corners and circles which are needed to get around the arena with the least disturbance to the horse's balance; in these he can always go easily and confidently forward. More complex patterns emerge as both proof of the horse's increased balance and as a means for developing engagement and balance.

Another significant benefit of well-defined school figures is that they provide a test of our precision and the horse's suppleness: a circle does not have corners, straight lines don't wave from side to side. If the horse is not supple and evenly on the aids, the rider cannot execute any figure correctly or at the prescribed letter.

Riders should not think that the whole point of school figures is to execute movements at particular points like in an army drill team. The figure is a test of the communication, and you must pay close attention to and learn from the results. You must know your horse and where and when to prepare him for a figure. Why is it always harder to execute a 10 meter circle at B on the left rein than on the right? Why can't you keep the horse straight on the centerline? The problems in executing school figures come from very basic problems with the horse's training. These problems will always come back to haunt you unless they are identified and resolved at a relatively early stage.

The school figures are performed in a prescribed arena. The show arena for lower levels usually measures 20 by 40 meters. For F.E.I. level tests, including the Prix St. Georges, Intermediaire I and II, the Grand Prix, the G. P. Special, and International 3-Day tests, an arena measuring 20 by 60 meters is used. The accuracy with which a horse and rider combination can execute the figures in a dressage test is one of the most important aspects of the judging. If the figures shown in a test are sloppy, it shows one of two things. Either the horse's training is not yet sufficient to be made accurate, or the rider's knowledge is not yet sufficient for the level.

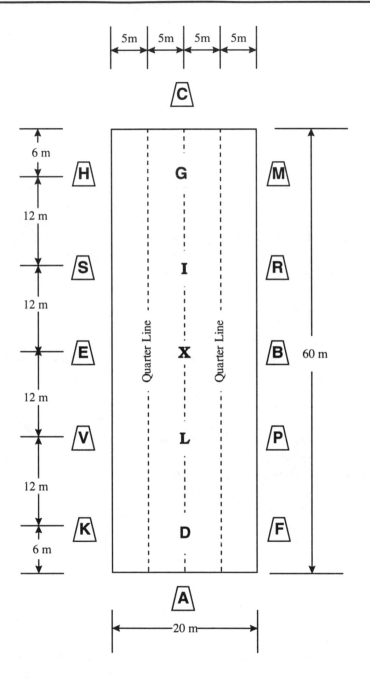

Figure 26. Standard Arena.

One frequently sees fairly good riders and horses getting low marks, because the ring figures were incorrect or inaccurate. The importance of the accuracy of these figures is enormous. If a judge sees two equally good horses, he or she will place the horse that executed even a few ring figures more accurately ahead of the other horse. "Dressage riding means to ride with precision!" said General Stecken.[1] Thus it is important to practice in an arena with letters. An arena without letters will lead to inaccurate figures and consequently inaccurate training.

The following are ring figures (described in more detail in the following sections): the whole arena is C-M-B-F-A-K-E-H, going on the right rein. Then comes the half school or arena: C-M-B-X-E-H. The long sides are M-F or K-H. The short sides, ridden on either rein, are A and C. The centerline is ridden through the length of the arena, C-X-A or A-X-C. Changing across the diagonal is M-X-K or F-X-H. Changing across the half arena is M-E or F-E or K-B or H-B. The center point of the arena is X. A circle is 20 meters in diameter. It is important to know where the three quarter lines are in order to judge the width of many figures.

To change through the circle, the rider turns onto a 10 meter half circle between the long side and the centerline, changes direction and bend and rides onto another 10 meter half circle on the other hand, with the first curve exactly the same as the second. Changes across the diagonal are ridden from points M, F, K, and H. Simple serpentines (or broken lines) go a maximum of 6 meters away from the long side starting at M and ending at F, or from H to K, in either direction. A double broken line or serpentine means to make two 3-meter loops from the long side, riding again from M to F or H to K. The rider goes for one horse's length on the track at E or B and then rides off the track again and back to the last letter. Both loops must be equal in size and shape.

Serpentines through the whole arena can be ridden with different numbers of loops. For instance, with four loops the rider arrive at the track four evenly spaced times, staying on the track for one horse's length each time.

A volte is a circle of 6 meters diameter. A double volte consists of two voltes ridden in immediate succession at the same place. A half volte out of the corner is a turn, 6 meters in diameter, which brings horse and rider back to the long side 2 meters beyond the last letter of the long side.

A figure eight is a volte on the right rein, followed immediately by a volte on the left rein, or done in reverse. This is always done in the center of the arena at X, or on the short sides. It can be done in larger sizes also, 8 or 10 meter circles, if so directed.

---

[1] General Albert Stecken, from Bonn, Germany, is one of the very best classical dressage trainers and teachers. He has helped many of Germany's top riders.

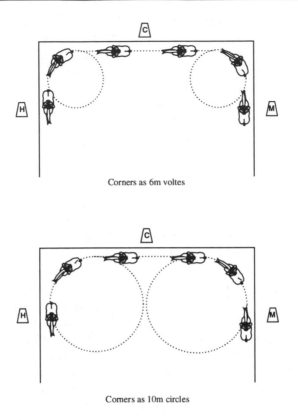

Corners as 6m voltes

Corners as 10m circles

Figure 27. Corners should be ridden as 6 meter voltes. Less developed horses should be ridden on 10 meter circles through the corner.

9.1 The Corner

The corner is the first difficult turn for the young horse. Either he goes too deep into the corner, requiring that the rider pull him out, or he cuts the corner, falling over the inside shoulder. Through the progression of the horse, the "corner" progresses from half of a 20 meter circle for the young horse into smaller and smaller quarter circles. Less developed horses should be ridden on 10 meter quarter circles through the corner, finally reaching one quarter of a 6 meter volte for the trained horse. To decide how small a circle is appropriate for each horse, the criterion is whether the horse can go freely forward in balance and harmony on the figure chosen.

Going through the corner is a turn. We give a half halt before the corner, and then after the corner. And with every step we turn. There is an open side to the outside of each corner, so be careful to use outside aids, rein and leg, so that the horse doesn't drift out in the corner. The inside rein is shortened so the little finger points in the direction of the outside shoulder and releases after every step (almost in slow motion). The outside rein and leg control or limit the bend to the inside. Because every step through the corner or on a volte or circle is a turn, the rider should give aids to turn followed by a release with every step. The use of the inside rein aid shows the horse where to go and the release of that aid allows the horse to go in this direction. The rider drives the inside hind leg forward as it is leaving the ground. Keep your hands together. Don't pull with the inside rein. The outside leg is back, watching. Keep a little more contact to encourage the horse to step into the hand. Keep his topline round (haunches, back, neck, poll).

Correct riding of corners is very important. It seems like a small thing to everyone. But riding through the corner is preparation for riding a volte, because it has the same radius.

9.2 The Circle

It is very important that you ride the line of the circle correctly. When you ride a correct circle, you do not go into the corner. To do this you should think of the four points of the circle and ride from one point to the next. The "points of the circle" are those points that the horse is to touch for one horse's length. In a 20 x 40 meter arena, the points of a circle beginning at C going on the left rein, are C, a point 10 meters from the end of the arena (4 meters after H), X,[1] and a point 10 meters from the corner (4 meters before M), and then C. The circle is ridden so that one arrives one half a horse's length before the circle point and leaves one half a horse's length after the point.[2] This way you are on the point of the circle for only one horse's length (about 3 meters). Now you ride from each point to the next.

A second circle lies between A and X in the same way. To change circles, the rider rides a full circle, finishing at X, smoothly changing and riding the second circle in the other half of the arena.

The horse's whole body should be bent around the rider's inside leg. The rider should be able to see a shimmer from the horse's inside eye and a bit of his inside nostril. It is very important that the rider drive the horse forward every step. But be careful to keep the right tempo: do not drive so much that the horse runs too fast. Just keep more contact and drive more with your seat against a fixed or stationary hand. And every step is a turn. With each step, the rider should shorten the inside rein by turning the little finger toward the outside shoulder, helping the turn and bending, followed by a release. The inside hip of the rider is lower and, therefore, the inside heel will be a little lower than the outside heel, as his weight shifts slightly to

---

[1] In a 20 x 60 arena, the point at X is replaced by a point 20 meters from C, which is 2 meters from I.

[2] For my young students, I would keep a marker painted on my arena wall at the circle points, together with two markers indicating the "landing" and "takeoff" points which were 1½ meters on each side.

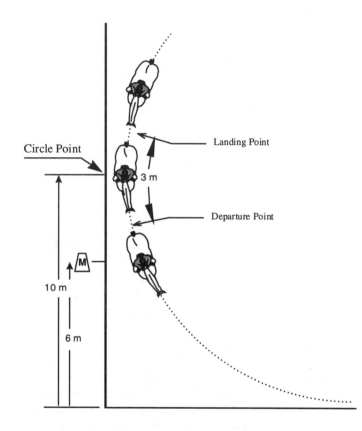

Figure 28. A 20 meter circle at C touches the track 10 meters from the end of the arena (the "point of the circle"). The horse should "land" about 1 1/2 meters before the point, and depart from the track about 1 1/2 meters after the point.

the inside. Don't hang your head to the inside. If you do, you will break at the waist on the left and then you will shift your weight to the outside.

Keep the inside rein well against the neck of the horse. Do not hold it away from the neck. The neck should be enclosed by both reins. The most common mistake is for riders to pull the horses around too much, so that the neck is overbent to the inside. When this happens the horse goes over his outside shoulder. To correct this, think of a very slight renvers position.

Be careful to keep your outside leg well against the horse so that the horse doesn't step out with his outside hind leg. Keep the horse bent and round. The left hind leg must step into the direction of the left front leg. The hoof should not step between or into the hoof print of the outside hind leg. And remember to keep riding from one circle point to the next. In order to go correctly on a circle, the exercise must be repeated many times.

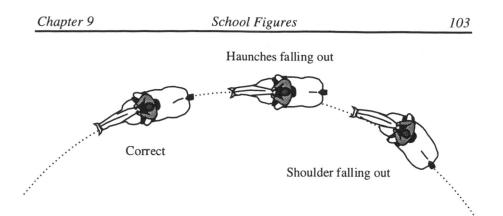

Haunches falling out

Correct

Shoulder falling out

Figure 29.   On the circle, watch that neither the haunches nor shoulders "fall out."

9.2.1 10 Meter Circle

When the 20 meter circle is correct, the horse can be brought in to an 18, 15 then 10 meter circle. Although it may seem a simple matter to make the circle smaller, it is not really easy to ride correct 10 meter circles. One has to watch the balance, the bending, and the willingness to still go forward on these small radius turns. They are very helpful for establishing the balance of the aids if the rider pays close attention to the figure of the circle and the continuous bend of the horse along the path. The coordination of the aids is similar to that required for leg-yielding or shoulder-in, but in contrast to the lateral exercises on the circle, the horse must track straight along the arc of the figure.

Although seemingly a simple figure, the 10 meter circle is one of the most important exercises in the development of the horse and of the rider. Without the finesse, balance, coordination and relaxation needed to do a proper 10 meter circle, we should not proceed to smaller turns (voltes) or shoulder-in and/or travers.

9.3 Tips on the Circle at Trot or Canter

When the horse is on the circle in the trot or canter and he drifts to the outside with his haunches or with his shoulder, it is a sign that the inside hind leg is not low and under enough. Thus the inside leg of the horse will take too short a stride, pushing everything to the outside. The rider should give half halts with the outside rein and leg when the outside hind is leaving the ground. In the same moment, the rider's outside leg drives. The inside leg of the rider continues to drive to engage the inside hind leg of the horse, yet not so strongly that the hindquarters are pushed out again.

9.4 Changing Circles

In order to change circles correctly, with X as the changing point, the horse should be straightened one half a horse's length before X and then flexed in the new direction one half a horse's length after X. The new outside leg of the rider slides back slightly to help bend the horse around the new inside leg. The new circle is, of course, the mirror image of the first circle.

Among the most common mistakes in changing circles is for the horse to be pulled or thrown from one circle to the other without proper straightening between circles. The rider uses too much inside rein and too little inside leg, as well as insufficient outside leg and rein to prevent unwanted lateral steps. This also causes the horse to throw his head up and get off the circle.

To keep the horse from falling in on the circle, another common problem, the use of half halts on the inside rein and a more active inside leg should be used against a steady outside rein and outside leg, ready to prevent drifting. The balance between inside and outside aids is the key to this and all exercises.

9.5 The Volte

A volte can only be ridden when the horse has collection. The greatest degree of bend a horse can physically achieve is the arc of a 6 meter volte.[1] An even smaller diameter is impossible and should not be attempted. To ride a volte beginning at C, give a half halt with the outside rein when approaching C. Then ride onto the volte when your leg comes to the marker, not when the horse's head comes to the marker. To do this you must give the aids early enough so that the horse turns onto the volte only half a horse's length after the marker. Otherwise, they will be late—too far past the marker. Be very careful to keep the reins taut. Keep the outside leg on the horse. If the horse drifts to the outside, don't pull on the inside rein. Be soft on the inside rein, and keep your outside leg on the horse a little better. If he drifts slightly to the inside, be softer with the outside rein. And keep both legs well on your horse. The horse should go between your legs as if on railroad tracks.

With the outside leg well behind the girth, the inside leg at the girth drives forward when the inside hind is leaving the ground. The weight of the rider is slightly to the inside, and the rider should sit more on the inside seat bone to engage the inside hind leg of the horse. It is very important to ride actively every step of the volte. If I miss turning the horse correctly for even one step, the horse cannot finish the volte accurately. "Every step is a turn."

---

[1] A 6 meter volte is almost 20 feet in diameter. (We use the metric system, because internationally this system is always used.)

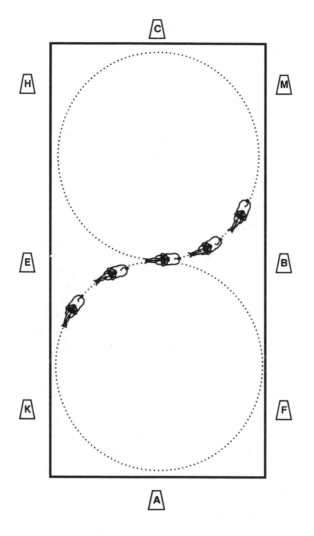

Figure 30. In changing circles, the horse is straightened just before X, then guided onto the opposite circle.

It is very worthwhile to be exact in this exercise in competition, because if two riders ride equally well, the one who does the figure with precision will win!

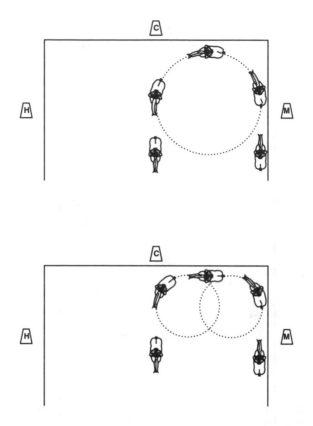

Figure 31. Turning onto the centerline.

9.6 Turn on the Centerline

One of the hardest movements is keeping the horse straight. This is why horses have such difficulty going straight on the centerline. It is very important to sit correctly on both seat bones. Keep both rein contacts the same, but always a little softer on the horse's tighter, heavier rein. Otherwise, he will drift away from this side. The horse should go evenly between the rider's two legs, seat bones and reins.

Riding often on the second track teaches how to use both legs and both reins. This makes it easier for the horse to learn to go correctly on the centerline. A half-halt on the outside rein together with a driving outside leg prevents drifting back onto the track by the wall.

Keep your head up high. Don't count the hairs in the mane! Turn your face slightly towards the horse's outside ear, in the direction you want the horse to go. This is the only way to get the horse to the exact point desired without using sudden, harsh aids. Keep your toes pointing straight ahead, not out. Enclose your horse's neck in both reins, keeping his neck straight.

The turn onto the centerline is one quarter of a volte turn. That means that the rider must turn slightly before C. In turning up the centerline, it is important to keep the outside leg well on the horse so he will not swing over the centerline. It is always better to turn onto the centerline a little too soon, and then ride to the centerline, than to go too far, thus having to ride back to the line.

A good preparation to get the feel for the correct turn onto the centerline is to ride a volte or 10 meter circle repeatedly before the centerline. This steadies the horse for the rider and prepares him to execute the turn. The centerline is one of the hardest lines to ride rectly and should be practiced many times. Ask yourself, "How many times did I ride the centerline today?" It is no wonder that in competition one usually sees riders searching for the centerline with only moderate success. This is the judge's first impression of the rider! So you can see how important it is to do this well.

When riding on the centerline, one should always ask the horse to move slightly more forward. This helps keep the horse straight, not weaving and wondering whether a turn or halt is coming.

9.7 The Serpentine

The serpentine establishes that the horse has light and supple turns to both sides, and easily bends around the new inside leg. This exercise is very valuable in finding out whether the horse is evenly on both reins, or whether one side is more difficult than the other. The serpentine movements consist of the familiar serpentines of 3, 4 or 5 loops extending across the full width of the arena, as well as the simple serpentine and double serpentine on the long side.

9.7.1 Simple Serpentine on the Long Side

On the left rein, turn off the track at F with flexion left. Just after the quarter line, even with B, the rider makes a small turn to the right. The new outside (left) leg goes back; the horse is flexed to the right. The right leg drives. When bringing the new outside leg back, be careful that the horse does not misunderstand this as an aid for the canter. The rider gives flexion to the left when back at M. At B or E in this exercise, the figure extends 6 meters away from the track.

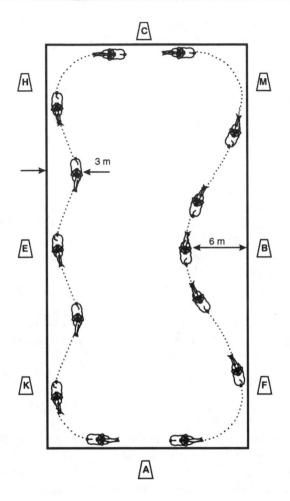

Figure 32. The simple serpentine on the long side (F to M) and the double serpentine (H to K).

9.7.2 Double Serpentine on the Long Side

On the left rein turn off the track at F, going in to a distance of 3 meters from the track, then riding back to the middle of the long side one half length before B. Stay on the track for one horse's length. Then turn off again half a horse's length after B, go in only 3 meters again. Then return to the track at M and go into the corner correctly. The purpose of this exercise is to improve the horse's turning ability. This can be done at the walk, trot and canter. In the canter, however, the horse should remain properly bent for the canter lead rather than changing flexion on the serpentine.

In this exercise it is important not to pull the horse in each new direction. If this is done, the movement of the horse is blocked by the inside rein, and then he will go over the outside shoulder. The outside rein should be released very slightly (not too much) to allow the stretching of the neck muscles to bend in the new direction. This release makes it easier for the horse to bend in each new direction. This exercise should be ridden in both directions.

9.7.3 Full Serpentines

The full serpentines are ridden across the full width of the arena, with either three, four or five loops. Again, going on the left rein, the first turn is begun at C (in the middle of the short side of the arena). The horse is not ridden deep into the corner after C, but a smooth circle is begun. The horse is bent slightly to the left, with the outside leg back. The inside rein shortens and gives. The inside leg is the drives the inside hind leg forward.

The outside rein gives a very light half halt to initiate the turn, but then is immediately ready to give so the outside neck muscles can stretch, and it is easier for the horse to bend. For a serpentine of 3 loops in a standard (60 meter) arena, the first turn at C is simply a 20 meter half-circle. The second loop is another 20 meter half-circle (to the right), and the last

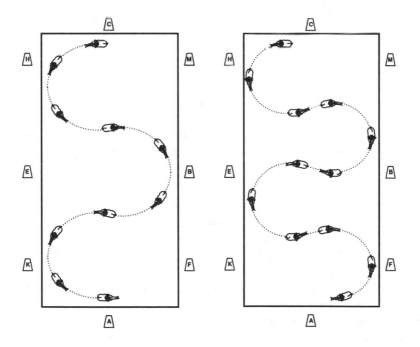

Figure 33. Serpentines of 3 and 4 loops in a small arena.

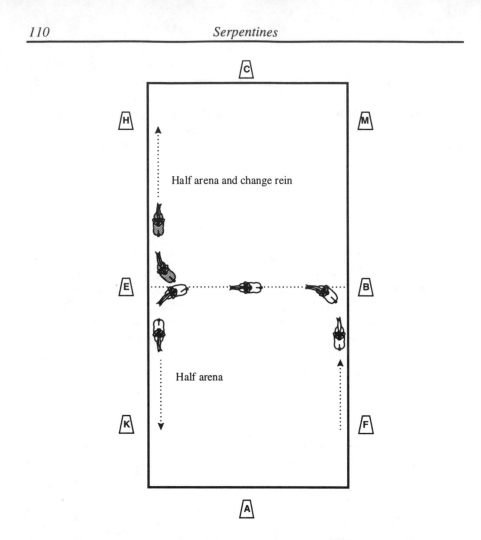

Figure 34. When riding in the half arena, make quarter volte turns at B and E. For the half arena and change of rein, turn left at B and right at E (or vice versa).

loop is the third 20 meter half-circle. The mid-point of the second loop is on the track at the letter B. In a small arena of 40 meters in length, the 3-loop serpentine is ridden with tighter loops of about 13 meters. In the 4 or 5 loop serpentine, each loop is a portion of that number of tangent circles that fit within the arena. In all cases, the rider starts onto the next loop as the centerline is crossed. There are no interconnecting straight lines. Just before reaching the centerline, heading back slightly towards C, the rider gives new bending aids, suppling with the new inside (right) rein, and half halting lightly with the new outside (left) rein, curving onto the new loop.

9.8 The Half Arena

Ride straight down the long side, but when you come to the middle of the long side at B, turn left, making a one-quarter of a volte turn—just like riding through a corner. Then turn to the left again when you arrive at the other side at E. This is working on the half arena.

9.9 The Half Arena and Change of Rein

After turning left at B from the left rein and going straight across to E, turn right at E. Don't forget the half halt on the outside rein before the turns. And the outside leg is well against the horse. If riding this exercise on the left rein, starting at F, first go correctly into the corner. Now give a half halt after the corner on the right rein. Then go straight. Now comes a quarter of a volte turn onto the line connecting B and E, and at E, turn right, go straight and go well into the corner at H.

9.10 Change Across the Diagonal

When going on the left rein after the short side at C, go correctly into the corner at H. Now give a half halt and go straight toward F, where you should be looking. Go exactly through X, and exactly to F on a really straight line. Look carefully at F. Give another half halt at F with the outside rein (left). Keep your inside rein well against the neck and drive with your inside leg (right), bending the horse to the right. Only by looking at your destination point will you get there!

One can also ride along the diagonal from H to X, but then proceed along the centerline. It is always good to vary the work so that the horse does not necessarily know what will come next.

9.11 Change Across the Half School Diagonal

This means we turn onto the diagonal connecting F and E, which is the half arena. First it is essential to ride correctly through the corner at F. Look at E. Otherwise, you will never get to E correctly. Give a half halt after the corner on the outside rein (right). Keep the neck nice and straight and land exactly at E. When riding these exercises first comes the corner, then the half halt, then the straight line, and then comes the landing at the destination point.

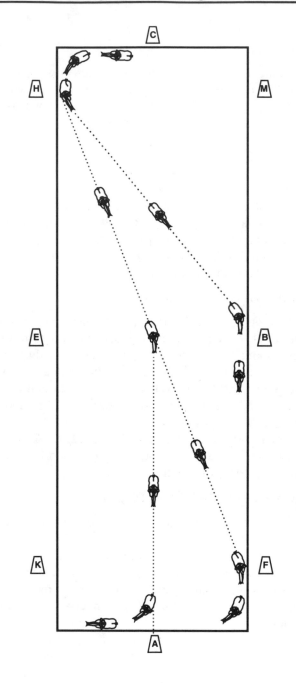

Figure 35. Changing rein on the diagonal (H-F) and half diagonal (H-B). Changing on the diagonal can be modified to proceed straight on the centerline.

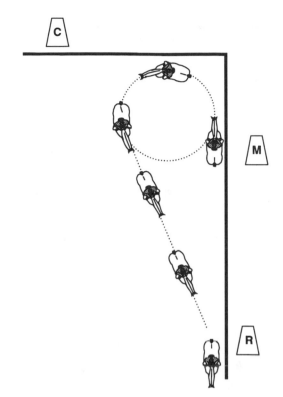

Figure 36. Half volte and change rein.

9.12 The Half Volte and Change of Rein

First ride well through the corner as part of a volte, giving a half halt on the outside before the corner. Then ride back to the track at an angle but on a straight line, arriving there 12 meters from the corner.

9.13 Change Through the Circle

This exercise is done on a 20 meter circle, always starting on the open side of the circle and riding toward the closed side (A or C) to ensure the accuracy of the figure.[1] The figure looks like an S. It is always a half turn left, then a half turn right, or vice versa, and each turn is half of a 10 meter circle.

---

[1] If it is ridden away from the end of the arena, the horse and rider can stay too long on the centerline; if ridden across the arena, the two halves can take on different diameters. Riding towards C or A makes it clear whether the middle of the figure is on the centerline, and at the center of the 20 meter circle.

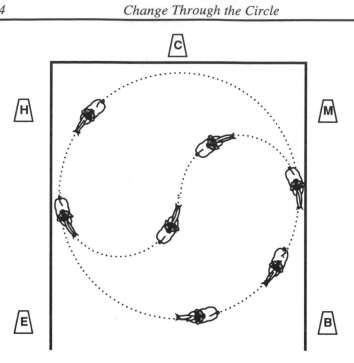

Figure 37. Changing through the circle.

Just past the circle point 10 meters out of the corner, at the beginning of the long side, turn off onto a 10 meter half circle toward the center of the 20 meter circle, driving well with the inside leg, giving slightly with the outside rein to facilitate the stretching of the neck muscles. The outside leg is behind the girth, "guarding." The rider sits on the inside seat bone. Then go straight for one horse's length and ride a half circle in the new direction. The horse should flow smoothly from bending left to bending right and then start the half circle to the right. Each half of the "S" shaped change through the circle should be exactly the same size. At the completion of the figure, the horse lands a half a horse's length before the opposite circle point.

9.14 Figure Eight

The diameter of each of the circles of the figure can be six, eight or ten meters. In the 10 meter figure eight, start this figure after the second corner of the short side. Ride a 10 meter circle in this corner and touch the centerline. In every step it is important to turn, with the inside leg driving and the outside leg back. The outside shoulder is also back. Now go straight for just a little, and then change the bend and direction to the right side. Now

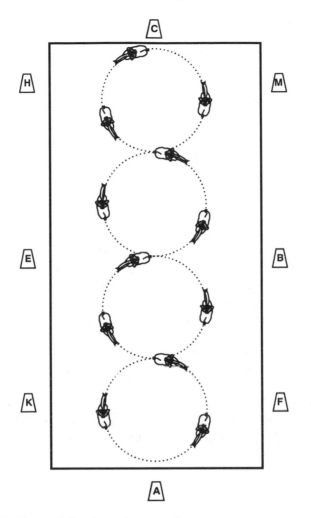

Figure 38. Figure eights down the centerline.

make a 10 meter circle on the other side. This exercise can be done in the walk, trot and canter.

The figure eight can also be started at the middle of the short side and ridden down the centerline. In this instance the centerline divides the circle across its diameter. Each 10 meter circle is ridden five meters to either side of the centerline. In a 40 meter arena you have four circles, and in a 60 meter arena, six. This is a very good exercise, because it brings you always to a new place in the arena and you have to be very attentive in order to be accurate. If even one stride of turning is missed, the horse is off his line in the exercise. It is very important to keep your hands close together and both legs on well. The horse should be between your hands and legs like the train on the railroad tracks!

If the horse is harder to ride on one of the circles, then stay on that circle two or three times. Work him somewhat longer on his difficult side. As soon as the rider feels improvement, he should change to the other side. Every horse has an easier side and a harder side.

The figure eight can also be ridden with transitions to the walk from the trot and back to the trot. Walk just before reaching the centerline. Walk one step with the old flexion, one step straight, then trot in the new flexion. Stay in the walk longer if necessary until the walk is correct and the horse is quiet. If time at the walk is needed, the rider should stay on the same circle and not change bend or direction. The quality of the walk is more important than the figure exercise!

The same can be done at the canter. Canter on the 10 meter circle until the horse is nice and round and smooth. When cantering on the circle, remember to make every stride a jump and every stride a turn. Keep the outside leg back. Keep the outside shoulder slightly back. Then make a transition to the walk and walk a half circle or as long as necessary to make the horse round again. When the horse is ready and next reaches the centerline, walk one step with the old flexion, one step straight, one step in the new direction with the new bend, and canter. Remember to turn immediately. The first stride is already a turn. Keep a soft contact on the inside. Keep the outside leg well back. Don't ride too much with the inside leg or you will drive the horse away from the circumference of the circle. It is important that the walk be correct between the canter transitions. Remain in the walk as long as necessary to make is clear and rhythmic.

Chapter 10
Suppling Exercises

The suppling exercises are extremely important, because correct work can only come from properly prepared muscles. They must be strong and relaxed at the same time. The proof of a truly supple and relaxed horse is when at the walk, trot, canter, and over cavalletti, the horse can chew the reins out of the rider's hands. This means that the as rider opens carefully his fingers the horse quietly lengthens the reins by stretching his neck forward and down. The horse should not change his rhythm or speed up. If the horse will do this, the goal of athletic relaxation has been reached.

10.1 Warm-Up

While working the horse initially at the rising trot to loosen him up, do not ride too deeply into the corners. It is essential to find the right tempo for each horse and to keep it consistently. The rider should keep a steady, light rein contact, not allowing it to become too tight. When changing the rein, do not ride sharp turns. The best methods are to change across the diagonal or from one 20 meter circle to another (called "changing out of the circle"). This is the only way the horse can find his balance. It is important here to be soft on the rein on which the horse is trying to be heavy. We are trying to bring him into a light balance on both reins. The horse works with all four of his legs unless he finds support on one or both reins, often called "the fifth leg" of the horse.

We have to get the horse away from this tight rein right from the beginning and get him to accept more solid contact on the soft rein. The rider's leg aids work simultaneously with the diagonally opposite rein. For example on a 20 meter circle to the left, the rider drives more strongly with his left leg to increase engagement of his horse's left hind leg and to increase the contact in the right rein.

In the rising trot, keep the shoulders back, sit up straight, keep the heels well down but relaxed. The rider should not post too high because it requires too much time to be seated to make a correction or to secure himself in critical situations. The rider should be only slightly in front of the vertical in the rising trot. Leaning too far forward or staying perpendicular are both incorrect.

Figure 39. Riding over cavalletti. The poles should be placed about 1.4 meters apart.

10.2 Suppling and Cavalletti Work

Cavalletti work belongs to the suppling exercises, and it is excellent for younger as well as older horses. The work here is done at the walk and trot. The poles should be between 1.5 and 2 meters in length (between 5 and 6 feet). They are wooden and should be quite substantial in width and weight. On either end blocks or crosses of wood should be attached to prevent the poles from moving if knocked by the horse's hoof.

To prepare the horse for cavalletti work, the rider rides the horse over a single pole at the walk and then at the trot. Gradually, a few poles (but not more than six) can be placed at 1.4 meter distance (5 to 6 feet) from each other on the track or on the second track. Another technique is to lay the poles out in a slight fan, with the poles 80 cm apart at one end, and 2 meters apart at the other. This puts the poles on an arc that can be ridden on a circle that allows the rider to adjust the separation of the poles to his horse's stride by riding closer to one end or the other.

A supple and elastic seat is especially important in riding cavalletti in order not to disturb the horse's movement. The rider's hands should be held low, a little bit below the withers, and contact should be maintained while allowing, in fact encouraging, the horse to stretch his neck forward and down. In the beginning the horse may want to jump through or

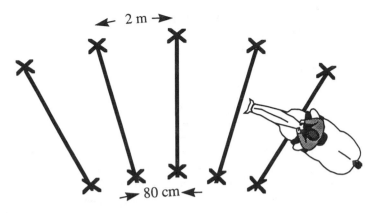

Figure 40. Cavalletti can be placed in a fan. On the inside, the poles are 80 cm apart, while on the outside they are 2 meters apart.

completely over the cavalletti. The rider should be prepared for this and not hit the horse in the mouth or back! If the horse becomes excited, or goes too fast through the cavalletti, the rider should go to a 10 meter circle until the horse is calm and quiet before re-trying the cavalletti.

Basically, cavalletti should not be mixed with jumping. Cavalletti are not jumps. They should be set at a maximum height of 20 centimeters (8 to 10 inches), and the horse should trot over them. They can be thought of as a supplement to the unevenness of cross-country riding. Their main purpose is to improve the relaxation of the horse in the trot, to improve the rhythm, and by gradually increasing the distance between poles, to stretch the length of the horse's stride at the trot. They contribute to the muscular development of the horse.

10.3 Leg-Yielding

Leg-yielding is one of the earliest and most fundamental exercises in the development of the horse and rider. It is a suppling exercise on four tracks in which the inside hind and inside fore leg step across and over the outside hind and outside fore legs. So much of what will come later in the training of the horse and rider is embodied in the leg-yield that one can not pay enough serious attention to the proper development of the leg-yield. We can think to more advanced movements only when the rider and the horse learn to do this perfectly.

For the young horse, the leg-yield introduces *acceptance* to the sideways driving leg as well as the opposite controlling leg, and *acceptance* of the straightness of the body and the neck as well as a light flexion. It also introduces travers and half pass. For advanced horses, the leg-yield loosens and supples during warm-up. It is not a collecting movement. It can also be used for correction, for instance during training of the half pass when the horse has a tendency to go too much over the inside shoulder, or when the horse shies.

For the rider, the leg-yield introduces *control* of the sideways driving aids, *control* of the outside (holding) aids and the balance between the two. By control, I mean that the rider must find out exactly how much he has to drive; he must feel for the right moment to give the sideways driving aid (when the inside hind leg is lifting up) and the half halt (in the same moment, with the same rein) and how much he has to hold without pulling with the outside rein. Here is the first time that the rider really feels how the hind leg reacts to the half halt. He also learns how important it is to keep the hands together to enclose the neck with both reins. The horse must remain straight in his body with only a slight flexion. Only when the rider gives the right aids at the right moment can the horse understand and respond properly

In order to gain the benefits of a proper leg-yield, it is necessary to maintain the same tempo through the work. The horse is not truly accepting the aids if he becomes shorter or faster in the strides, and this shows that the rider is not truly balanced with his aids. The loosening and suppling benefit can only be obtained when the horse is quiet and stretching and not too slow. The horse must go evenly in both directions. Leg-yielding is the beginning of straightening the horse. If we don't take care to keep the horse even to both sides, leg-yielding will be the beginning of the *end* of the horse's career. Do not plan on taking a month to accomplish proper leg-yielding. It will take a year or even more. Throughout his whole life, leg-yielding will be called upon as a correction.

There are many patterns and variations which can be used in leg-yielding. We will discuss a natural progression from leg-yielding:

1. on the circle;
2. from the second track;
3. from the quarter line;
4. from the centerline;
5. half school diagonal then leg-yield;
6. down the long side;
7. down the long side, turn on the forehand and return;
8. leg-yield then straight, then repeat.

10.4 Weight and Leg Aids for Leg-Yielding

A brief note on weight and direction of movement: in leg-yielding the horse should yield to the pressure of the rider's lower leg and seat bone on the same side. The rider sits slightly heavier on the *inside* seat bone and the horse moves away from the leg and the weight.[1] Both the rider's legs are back during leg-yielding. The inside leg drives, while the outside leg "catches" and controls.

---

[1] As we discussed in Chapter 6, the weight goes on the side to which the horse is flexed.

In leg-yielding from C to E on the left rein, the rider would sit slightly heavier on his left seat bone. If the rider sits to the outside (right), he sits against the sideways movement and works against the sideways driving (left) leg. On the other hand, if the rider sits too far to the inside, this will hurt the horse and cause him to lean to the left or run too fast through the outside. Think of sitting in a narrow boat. If you put your weight to the left, it would push the boat to the right. But if you put too much weight to the left and too far in that direction, you'll tip the boat over.[2] This exercise should not be confused with shoulder-in, travers, renvers or half pass. Those are collecting movements in which the horse's inside hind leg is required to carry more weight and the rider sits into the movement.

The horse should be straight through the body during leg-yielding. The inside rein gives a very slight position to the horse's head and poll. But the neck should stay straight. There will be a very slight flexion to the side the horse is moving away from. That is, when yielding from the left leg, the horse has a slight flexion left. In flexion, the horse's body and neck are straight—the flexion is in the poll, jaw and mouth. This should not be confused with bending in which the horse is on a continuous arc from the poll to tail around the inside leg.

10.5 Leg-Yielding on the Circle

This exercise is to be begun at the walk. On the left rein go on a 20 meter circle, the open side of which touches X. Here the rider makes use of the horse's tendency to return to the track to teach him the leg-yielding exercise. Ride the horse straight along the circle from the track to X. At X, start by turning the horse slightly to the left as you move him away from the left leg. This aligns him with the long side of the arena, and the last few steps of the quarter circle can be made in leg-yield. When you reach the wall, ride the horse again straight on the circle.

When leg-yielding on the 20 meter circle on the left rein, the rider's shoulders should be parallel with the horse's shoulders. Do not let your head hang to the inside. Look over the horse's outside ear slightly and in the direction you want to ride. The inside (left) leg of the rider is moved back to a position slightly behind the girth and acts as a sideways-driving leg. The right leg remains in its usual position behind the girth, ready to control excessive outward drift. Both legs are therefore behind the girth with different purposes. (There are only three exercises in which it is normal that both legs are behind the girth: the halt, the rein back, and leg-yielding.)

---

[2] These weight aids are described in German National Equestrian Federation's *Principles of Riding*, page 59. All trainers must pass written, riding and teaching exams based on this book. If an aspiring trainer answered the question wrong regarding which side to sit on in leg-yielding, he could fail the entire test because it is such a fundamental point with a clearly correct answer.

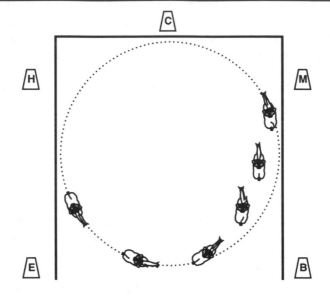

Figure 41. Leg-yielding on the circle.

To keep the horse parallel to the long side of the arena, the outside (relative to the flexion) rein has good solid contact and holds the horse's neck straight. The left (inside) rein is used in a twisting motion of the fist so that the little finger points toward the rider's right shoulder. The rider uses the described rein and leg aid in the moment that the horse's inside (left) hind hoof leaves the ground. And then the rider gives gently without losing the inside (left) rein. The outside (right) rein remains taut without pulling.

The aids should be repeated when the left hind leg leaves the ground again. In addition to the leg and rein aid, a light tap with the whip may be helpful. The tap of the whip should land just behind the rider's inside left leg and be timed together with the increased left leg pressure and left rein aid. This shows the horse that if he does not react to the rider's leg, the whip will be used. In other words, the whip should only be a strengthening of the natural aids.

The timing of the leg aid is very important in achieving success in the leg-yield without resistance. When the inside hind leg leaves the ground the rider can influence it to move upwards, forward, backwards, or sideways. This is the only moment when the horse's inside hind leg can step over the outside. When it returns to Earth, it is firmly planted and supporting the weight of the horse. At this point, it can not respond easily to the strongest leg aid, spur or whip, regardless of how willing the horse may be.

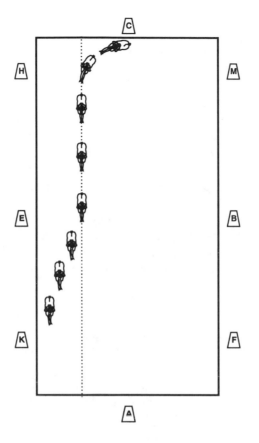

Figure 42. Leg-yielding from the quarter line.

It is very important in this exercise that the outside rein and leg maintain control. It is often necessary for a half halt to be given with the outside rein and leg pressure—for instance when he goes too close to the wall, goes too fast, or goes over the outside shoulder. Try to avoid allowing the horse to swing too much to the outside.

When leg-yield on the circle goes well in both directions, the rider can try it on straight lines, and at the trot.

10.6 Leg-Yielding From the Quarter Line

On the left rein, after turning onto the short side of the arena, turn onto the third quarter line, giving a half halt to the outside with right rein and leg, then going straight on this quarter line. The half halt prevents the horse from drifting back to the track. Later, these aids will be used repeatedly in the training.

If the horse makes the turn several times onto the quarter line and stays straight willingly, then begin to ask for some leg-yielding with the left leg. This should start about halfway down the long side, on the quarter line. It is important here that the horse stay parallel to the long side during the leg-yielding. Shift your weight very slightly to the left, and position the horse slightly to the left, having shortened the left rein a little. Then by alternately rotating the left hand in the direction of the right shoulder when the left hind is leaving the ground and using the left leg behind the girth in a sideways-driving way, then giving with that hand, the rider asks the horse to leg-yield. The right rein and leg controls the tempo and the angle. The active rein and leg aids are given in the rhythm of the left hind leg as it is just leaving the ground.

Very frequently the horse tries to go faster in order to get to the track, where he feels safest. To prevent this we must give half halts with our outside rein and leg (right) in the moment that the right hind hoof is leaving the ground. The right rein should hold the horse's neck almost straight,

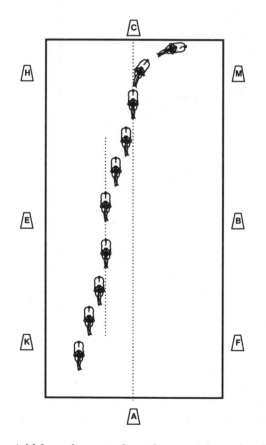

Figure 43. Leg-yield from the centerline, then straighten, then leg-yield again in the same direction.

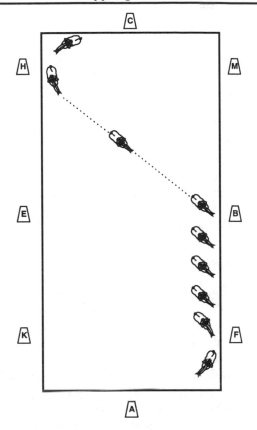

Figure 44. Half school diagonal and leg-yield down the long side.

otherwise the horse will fall out over his outside shoulder. The driving left leg aid should not be too strong. Find out just how little aid you can use—it is so common for people to use overly strong aids.

Leg-yielding from the quarter line to the track (5 meters) is too much for some horses at first. With them it is better to start the exercise only 2 or 3 meters from the track. This is called the "third track." The way is not so far and brings the same desired results. This is often a good choice for young horses and younger or less experienced riders.

When the horse understands leg-yielding from the quarter line, other leg-yielding movements can be added, such as from the centerline to the track. This is a little harder as it requires more sideways movement. A very good exercise is to ride down the centerline, leg-yield right a few steps, straighten, leg-yield left, straighten, leg-yield right, and so on. Combine this with riding down the centerline, leg-yield right a few steps, straighten, leg-yield right a few more steps, and straighten. During these patterns, it is very important to keep the horse straight with only a change in the flexion. Again, this exercise can be ridden at the trot when the work at the walk is confident and steady.

After these patterns, the horse should be supple enough so that we can start the more difficult exercise of leg-yielding down the long side of the arena. This movement brings the horse's hind leg to the inside and is the first work with his hind leg away from the security of the track. It is best introduced by crossing the arena on a short diagonal, then proceeding down the second half of the long side in leg-yield. When this is established, the horse can be asked to leg-yield down the entire length of the arena, with a turn on the forehand at the end, followed by leg-yielding off the opposite leg back down the same long side. Leg-yielding down the long side should be ridden only at the walk, and only on the second track. The horse has his head against the wall, and this takes the free forward movement away from him, something we never want to do at the trot or canter.

10.7 The Half School Diagonal and Leg-Yield

To start leg-yielding down the long side, we make it easier for the horse by coming from the short side of the arena, and changing rein across the half-school diagonal (on the left rein, from H to B, see Figure 44). This brings you to the long side (M-B-F) at B already in a 35° angle desirable for continuing the leg-yielding down the remainder of the long side (B-F). [1] Just before arriving at B from the diagonal, the rider sits a little heavier on the left seat bone and gives the leg-yielding aids with left rein and leg pressure when the horse's left hind leg is leaving the ground. The rider gives a half halt in the same moment with the left rein. It is important that the rider catch the horse with right leg and right rein so that the horse does not go at too wide an angle from the track—not more than 35°. Continue this leg-yielding down the long side. At the last letter before the corner, the rider gives a half halt left and straightens the horse onto the track with his right leg. The horse should never straighten himself.

Leg-yielding down the long side is a challenge to the horse to move the haunches away from the track. The horse is used to going along the wall in a straight manner. Now we ask that the horse go with the hind leg away from the track and the head against the wall. The horse can become somewhat frightened by the wall and feels that he can not escape. He then may either swing the haunches to be parallel to the wall or go too much sideways and backwards, getting away from the wall. This makes the movement a test for the rider to maintain a balance between the lateral and holding aids.

Thus, leg-yielding along the wall should be begun only when the horse and rider are confirmed in the other leg-yielding exercises. If the horse

---

[1] Although this can be ridden at a 45° angle (as I had to do in earlier times), I like the 35° angle better because it is not so hard for the horse or rider.

swings the haunches back to the track, riders are often tempted to drive too much with the inside leg, either sending the horse out the front, or swinging the haunches, resulting in an undesired turn on the forehand. Sometimes the horse will go backwards off the track because of too much use of the rider's hands. Then the rider should give with both hands and drive the horse forward with the left leg. The rider should take care not to drive too hard. All aids should be given with a feel for balance.

I do not recommend leg-yielding along the wall with the head to the inside because the horse will easily be confused when we later introduce shoulder-in.

10.8 Leg-Yielding on the Long Side

This leg-yielding exercise makes use of the moment when (on the left rein) the horse's right hind leg is still in the corner before the long side. Now the rider shifts his weight from left to right and changes the position of the horse from bending slightly to the left to slight flexion to the right. The leg aids also shift in the same way. This requires great skill. The shifting of aids from left to right is done with a moment of straightness between the two positions. The active left inside aids now become outside, watchful, guarding aids.

The right leg of the rider having been the outside leg now becomes active as the inside leg, driving sideways, at the moment the horse's right hind hoof leaves the ground. A very common mistake is for the rider to use too little left rein, allowing the horse's neck to bend too much. If the position in the horse is exaggerated by pulling the neck to the right, the horse will have difficulty yielding to the right leg. The horse becomes unbalanced across the shoulders, and he will fall out on his left shoulder. The left rein must have good contact, and sometimes it is necessary to give a half halt with it. The rider's left leg is also important. It must stay in good contact behind the girth so the horse does not increase his angle to the wall beyond 35°. It is essential not to ask for more than a 35° angle in this exercise If more is asked, the horse may become so frightened that he will step on himself. Limiting the angle to 35° is the job of the outside (left) rein and leg. (If the horse is narrow-chested, the rider should not insist on a full 35° angle to the track of the arena. Such horses will bang their knees together when crossing their legs in leg-yielding, and they will understandably become frightened).

10.9 Turn on the Forehand

It is best to ask for the turn on the forehand in an enclosed arena or fenced-in working area, and specifically to start on what we call "the second track"—a few feet in from the track of the arena. This gives the horse's neck and head sufficient space to move and not hit the wall or fence during the turn on the forehand. This is also a safety precaution in case the horse should

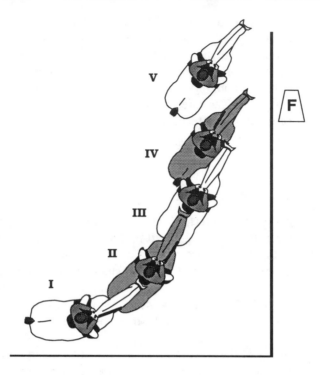

Figure 45. Starting leg-yielding down the long side. The horse at (I) is ridden to the outside (right) rein to start the corner. At (II) the outside aids straighten the horse, so he is straight at (III). At (IV) the right leg is active, driving to the left rein, proceeding down the arena (V) in leg-yield.

fall, that he not be close to the wall where he could crush the rider by accident.

Riding on the left rein, turn onto the second track from the short side and halt at P. Change the whip to the right hand. The halt should last several seconds, and the rider should not move around in the saddle or move his hands. The rider positions the horse to the right, and shortens both reins, the right slightly more. The right has now become the inside rein. In positioning the horse, the rider turns the right fist in a twisting motion so that the knuckle of the little finger points toward his left shoulder and then releases the contact slightly by straightening the hand back into the original position. The length of time between taking and giving with the rein is approximately one second for each phase.

At the same time, the rider shifts his weight slightly to the right seat bone so subtly that an observer cannot see it happening. The rider puts his right leg slightly behind the girth, pressing the haunches step by step around the forehand until 180° have been completed. The rider's left hand prevents .

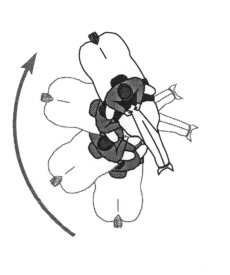

Figure 46. Turn on the forehand.

the horse from moving forward with a small half halt. Thus the horse will be made to move his right hind leg across and in front of the left hind leg.

Each step of the turn on the forehand dictates the timing of the rider's use of leg and rein aids. The aids should be given when the horse's inside (right) hind is just leaving the ground. These rein aids are usually given too quickly and too abruptly. One should be careful and sensitive.

The outside leg (left) of the rider rests behind the girth, ready to prevent excessive swinging of the haunches and ready to stop the turn on the forehand for a pause whenever necessary. During the turn on the forehand the horse should not walk forward. The inside front leg of the horse should step but stay in the same area while the outside (left) front leg moves around the inside.

It is not so easy to ride a classically correct turn on the forehand. The most common mistake is the rider pulling on the inside (right) rein thus forcing the horse to turn to the inside (right) with his forehand, while the hind legs stay still. This negates the effort at a turn on the forehand.

Other mistakes are stepping forward or backward. A slight tendency to step backwards is the lesser of the two evils! The aids have to be adjusted in either case: a slightly stronger half halt on the left rein when the horse wants to walk too much forward. Keep both legs on the horse so you can help him immediately if necessary for another correction. When the horse steps back, give stronger pressure with both legs and seat while giving with the hand—but only a little bit, so you don't lose connection with the horse's mouth.

Sometimes despite the aids, the horse stands completely still and does not want to turn. In this case first repeat the aids softly. Then be sure to have the whip in the right hand and begin giving the aids again, this time a little stronger than the first time. The rider should support the leg aid by giving a tap with the whip right behind his leg and in the same moment he gives the leg pressure. The whip aid should be used carefully and lightly at first to avoid frightening the horse. This is an example of how we need to study our horses so that we can learn exactly how strong to give the aids.

In turns on the forehand, as well as on the haunches, the importance of giving the right aids in the right moment cannot be overemphasized. The reason for the horse's failure in these exercises is clearly the rider's lack of correct aids and timing—it is almost never the horse's fault. The precise aids will always be different from horse to horse—this is what makes riding well so difficult, but also interesting.

This exercise is to be done also on the right rein, of course, with the opposite aids. It is good after doing the turn on the forehand to let the horse stand still for five to ten seconds before asking something else of him, so that the horse learns to stand still.

There are pros and cons to requiring the turn on the forehand in dressage tests. The horse's ability to execute a turn on the forehand shows that he can balance himself and give well coordinated response to the leg and hand aids of the rider. It can be disappointing and frustrating to see riders with uncoordinated and unbalanced use of the aids. On the other hand, it is good that riders should have to learn to have this elementary skill.

10.10 The Leg-Yield with Turn on the Forehand

When the horse does leg-yielding along the wall in each direction willingly and without resistance, the rider can start with a new exercise: leg-yielding, turn on the forehand, and immediately leg-yielding again with the other leg.

In this exercise, the rider rides in right leg-yielding, on the left rein, to the last point on the long side, and gives a stronger half halt with the outside (left) rein and leg pressure, bringing the horse almost but not quite to a halt. The rider activates his right leg, while his left seat, rein and leg aids stop the leg-yield, holding the horse's forehand almost on the spot, to begin the turn. Then the rider shifts weight to the right seat bone as he activates his right leg and right indirect intermittent rein and asks for a few steps of a turn on the forehand right. Half halts are given on the left rein, and the left leg controls the distance the haunches move sideways (to the right). It is essential that the timing of these aids be in the moment the horse's right hind is about to leave the ground. The horse should make only a few short steps

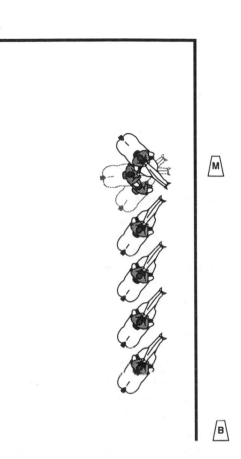

Figure 47. Leg-yield with a turn on the forehand. After turning, proceed back from M to F in left leg-yielding, where one can repeat the turn on the forehand.

of the turn on the forehand, bringing him to a position of 35° between his left side and the wall. Then the rider shifts his weight carefully back to the left seat bone, the left leg of the rider becomes active, the horse is positioned left, and left leg-yielding is begun back down the same long side of the arena.

The most common mistake in the turn on the forehand is that the horse's haunches swing all the way to the track, rather than being under control and stopping at a 35° angle from the track. This exercise will show if the horse is truly obedient to the lateral leg aids teaching the horse the correct aids for the turn on the forehand with one exercise flowing into the next.

Having leg-yielded down the long side with the left leg, again the rider comes almost to a halt at the last letter with a half halt on the right rein, and the rider's weight moves carefully to the right. Then the rider's left leg increases pressure and the left indirect rein is used, moving the horse's haunches away while the rider's right rein, leg, and seat hold the horse's forehand almost on the spot, thus performing a turn on the forehand. Again, the rider asks for a few steps in the turn, until the horse is at a 35° angle from the wall. Now the rider's right seat bone and leg ask the horse to continue back up the long side in leg-yielding to the right leg with a slight positioning right. This exercise can be done two or three times in each direction. Don't forget to praise the horse a lot!

10.11 Summary

Leg-yielding is an extremely important exercise for both the rider and the horse. For the young horse it introduces lateral aids. For the older horse it is very beneficial for loosening joints and muscles.

For the experienced horse it provides an important loosening and suppling exercise at the beginning of work, but can also be very helpful for correction, particularly in the training of the half pass. During half pass, the horse often has trouble going to one direction or the other. To make it easier for the horse, one should use the leg-yield for a while, until the horse flows confidently to the difficult side. It is important during these exercises to keep the horse very straight, without too much flexion and bending.

For the rider, the leg-yield teaches balance of the driving and holding aids. Leg-yielding on the circle introduces the feeling of sideways movement, leg-yielding from the quarter line requires the rider to maintain straightness. Leg-yielding down the long side of the arena teaches much more balance between the holding and driving aids.

As a suppling exercise, be sure not to start leg-yielding too early in a riding session. Use a walk and trot warm-up to get the muscles of the horse and rider warm before asking for leg-yield. If we ask for leg-yielding with a cold horse, it will be very hard for the horse, and he will become tense and stiffen *more*, rather than the loosening that we seek.

Although it will take a long time to perfect the leg-yield, be careful not to spend too much time on it during a session. You should not devote more than a quarter of the training session. Otherwise, one would forget to engage the horse in trot and canter, and lose the impulsion and desire of the horse to move forward in walk, trot and canter.

Chapter 11
Riding Transitions and Movements

11.1 Transitions

Transitions are some of the most important and most difficult exercises in all of riding. Although simple in concept, flowing effortlessly from one gait to the next defines the art and essence of good horsemanship. To appreciate their importance, one need only think of how many transitions are in dressage tests, and that they are scored as separate movements.

Although it is of course generally possible for any rider to pull or kick a horse from one gait to another, correct, balanced and fluid transitions must be learned by the horse through a quiet dialog with a tactful rider that may stretch over many months. In this dialog the rider must patiently explain to the horse what he expects and desires in response to his aids. The rider should not expect the horse to respond perfectly at first to even very correct aids. The rider must develop the horse mentally and physically through patient repetition. Serious and attentive study of these transitions teaches the rider how the horse is reacting to the rider's aids. They can not be repeated enough.

All transitions include a preparation phase, in which the horse is engaged and energized; giving of the aids at just the right moment; and an allowing phase where the next gait is ridden forward. In the preparation, the horse must stay engaged, with impulsion, and suppleness. The rhythm before and after the transition must be clear and constant, and all transitions must be ridden forward—the downwards as well as the upwards transitions.

One of the difficulties with all transitions is the timing of the aids, and clearly understanding how much preparation is needed. That is, how many half halts should be given, and how long before the desired transition. To develop the communication with the horse it is important to repeat transitions frequently, and to perform them at specific points throughout the arena. For example, if we wish to make a transition at B, we need to find out where we need to begin to prepare for the transition. This will vary with the horse, the rider, and the degree of warm-up or other distractions.

11.1.1 From Walk to Trot
The transition from walk to trot is the most basic upward transition. It embodies all the stages of upward transitions—preparation through improvement of the lower gait, a clearly given signal, and then allowing the horse to move freely into the new gait.

First, the walk must be engaged enough so that at any point the rider is confident that the next step can be a trot step, canter stride or halt. Only then is the horse truly responding to the forward driving aids and ready to make a fluid, correct transition. The transition can only be as good as the walk before it. Every gait should be ridden not for itself, but as preparation for the next transition. It is very difficult to get the horse to trot from a listless, lazy walk. It is far easier to *allow* the horse to trot from a walk that is engaged and energized. The aids then are a signal that "OK, now you can go."

The aids begin with both seat bones, both legs, and then with the hand allowing the horse to go into the trot. The key problem is to give forward with the hand without losing the contact. The rider must keep the reins ready to make slight adjustments and must receive the forward movement from the hind leg over the back, withers, neck, poll, and mouth into the hand. If the rider gives with the reins too much, the horse can fall onto the forehand or raise up the head and hollow the back. With loose reins, even a slight adjustment can only be made after the leather has snapped back taut, disturbing the horse's balance, rhythm, and confidence. If the hands do not give enough, or quickly pull back, the rider sends the confusing signals "Go" and "Stop!" simultaneously. Also, the thrust from the hind leg is immediately stopped. The rider should feel a 1/2 pound weight in his hands. If the tension in the rein becomes less than 1/2 pound, the contact is lost. Another way to visualize the contact is as though the reins are two light sticks that are pushing the bit forward—they are straight (because of the contact) yet encouraging the horse forward.

11.1.2 From Trot to Walk

The transition from trot to walk is the first downward transition. The downward transitions are always more difficult, because while the rider is willing to give to allow an upwards transition, he thinks he must pull back to get the downward transition. In fact, in the moment when the rider is closing and holding with the hand in the half halt, he must already be thinking of giving, and riding his horse forward into the walk.[1] Pulling on the reins without giving will cause the horse to balance on the rider's hands, resulting in either the horse diving on the forehand in an abrupt, choking walk or halt, or simply pulling more and more against the rider's hands to get away from too much pressure on his mouth.

After giving a little half halt which signals to the horse, "Something is coming. Be ready!," the rider establishes solid contact on the reins. Then he sits and drives with seat and lower legs against a steady passive hand.

---

[1] It often happens that the rider thinks he cannot give forward, but you can always go forward. I remember when my old boss said, "Give more!" And I thought, "Lord, what more can I give?" But I would give more, and much to my surprise, the situation would be better immediately. Giving is always better than taking backwards.

The half halt serves also to regain the correct frame if it was lost. To ride the transition the rider should drop his heels, thus bringing a little more weight into the saddle in a pleasant way for the horse. The rider should be careful not to lean behind the vertical with the upper body because this hurts the horse's back. Also the rider must be careful not to stretch his lower legs forward or to suddenly take them too far back. The legs should lie quietly on the horse's sides.

Just as in the upward transition, the horse must be prepared by improving the trot, with the horse engaged, rhythmic and supple, without influencing the horse too much with the hands. The signal must be clear and the horse must be allowed to move forward into the walk. In other words, we ride the horse *forward into* the walk, and do not pull the horse back out of the trot. The transition into the walk should come promptly and smoothly. Keep the rein contact. Giving the reins away too much will result in the horse continuing in the trot, or falling on the forehand in an unbalanced, non-rhythmic walk. Again, this shows the importance of giving without losing the contact.

After the transition the rider should keep the horse on the aids in the walk so that he could immediately ride a transition back to trot. Do not let the horse "escape" by jogging. As in all of riding the rider must constantly change between active and passive aids: active when the horse tries to escape from the aids and immediately passive to show the horse everything is OK.

The three most common problems that come up are transitions that are too abrupt, running through the half halt, and jogging in the walk.

When the transition is too abrupt, and the horse almost comes to the halt, or the walk steps are tight and short, the rider should not complete the transition to the walk, but engage the hind leg and go right back into the trot. Often the rider is holding too much and not giving soon enough. This means that the rider becomes stuck in the half halt. Sometimes the rider tightens his body too much, and the horse tightens too, and the transitions are not balanced. This problem also occurs when the rider loses his patience and gives the aids in an uncontrolled manner, with too much hand and too rough.

Jogging in the walk comes from either the temperament of the horse, too tight a rein, too loose rein, or giving too suddenly. When the horse jogs in the walk after the transition, it is better to ask for a little shorter walk until the balance, contact and rhythm are steady. Later the rider can ride the walk a little longer—not faster. The horse's frame can be somewhat low, but he should not hang. If he tries to hang, then the rider must drive more. This will make the horse take a longer stride with his hind leg and thus carry his forehand higher and lighter.

If the horse tries to get away from the aids by raising his head too high or carrying it too low, the rider must keep his hand quiet and drive with his seat and legs against this quiet, passive hand. In this situation the rider must be very careful not to hold the rein too long and too stiff. As soon as the horse tries to escape the contact, hold somewhat tighter and then drive with seat and legs. Finish with a slight release of the rein pressure. Keeping the reins too tight is a punishment for the horse, and does not allow him to do what you have asked.

11.1.3 From Walk to Halt

Unlike the other transitions, we will discuss the downward transition from walk to halt before discussing the upward transition from halt to walk. This is because the quality and engagement of the halt are essential for a good upward transition, and this quality is obtained through a proper downward transition to the halt.

Again it is important that the walk is lively and engaged but not quick. The horse is prepared with half halts for the complete halt. The number of half halts depends on the temperament of the horse and how advanced the horse is in his training. The half halts engage the horse and make him aware that something is coming.

When the rider has the feeling he is in harmony with the horse, then he can ask for the complete halt. The correct aids for the complete halt start with half halt, and then lowering the heels. This brings the rider's weight into the saddle and signals the halt. The steady holding (but not pulling) rein completes the halt, and then softens immediately—almost simultaneously. The number of half halts needed can be tested by making frequent halts at specific letters around the arena. To help the horse use his hind leg into the halt, the rider can think of a slight shoulder-in during the transition.[2]

The weight aids for the halt are often misunderstood. Lowering of the heels brings the correct amount of weight into the horse's back in the correct, vertical position. Leaning back drives the seat into the saddle too much and sends the horse forward because of the pain the horse feels in his back. From his natural instinct, the horse will try to flee, and not come into a balanced, calm halt.

One should not expect that the horse will come to an immediate, perfect halt. You should take the time to repeat the exercise with much patience, over and over. Soon the horse will understand what is being asked and will make very good halts. Never lose the patience. When the horse comes to a very good halt, the rider should praise the horse so the horse knows he did well. One should praise the horse a lot.

The halt should be maintained at least 10 - 12 seconds. At the beginning, the horse might try to pull the reins out of the rider's hands. In this situation, the rider holds firm the reins, tightens his seat bones and legs, and sits quietly and the horse will stay then quiet.

---

[2] Here, I assume that the rider knows the aids for the shoulder-in, but we do not require that the horse be so advanced. The shoulder-in is discussed in Chapter 12.

11.1.4 From Halt to Walk

As mentioned above, the preparation for a transition from halt to walk starts with a correct halt. The horse must be on the aids and the horse and rider in harmony. The hind leg is under the weight of the rider. The horse gives the rider weight on both hands (he is in balance and straight). He is standing square, sensitive to the legs and rein aids, round, and ready to go forward, sideways, turn, or backwards.

With the horse ready and alert, the rider drives with both seat bones and both legs and gives with both reins without losing the contact. The horse should go forward immediately in an engaged and rhythmical walk. If he does not, the rider should slightly strengthen and repeat the aids. It is better to start with soft aids and then strengthen the aids than give strong aids and then try to re-establish light aids.

One often sees riders fooling around with the hands, both at the halt, and through the transition. When the rider tries to keep the horse round at the halt with too much hand then a correct transition is not possible—the horse is afraid to go freely forward because he expects to get holding aids in his mouth. This results in the rider using too much leg to get the horse moving forward. This causes a vicious circle, because the horse will go forward too much or hollows out, causing the rider to pull back to keep control or roundness. Often the rider becomes used to this cycle and starts the transition with a pulling hand and too strong a driving leg.

I can only say again that the rider must have patience and wait and repeat the transitions carefully and correctly. If the horse does something wrong, that indicates to the rider that he must change his aids. Practice this transition so you can steady your horse and find out what aids you need to get a harmonic halt-walk transition. It is important to adjust the aids accurately to the horse.

If the rider wants the horse to move forward out of the halt with the right hind leg, the rider increases his right leg pressure to drive the horse forward while maintaining good contact with the opposite rein and leg (left) to keep the horse straight. The first stride should be as long as all that follow, the horse must step out energetically from the hindquarters.

11.1.5 From Halt to Trot

The aids from the halt to the trot are determined by the intensity that was needed to make the horse move into the walk. The aids for the trot should be the same, but slightly stronger. One must be careful not to surprise the horse. A well-trained horse need only be lightly supervised at the trot to maintain impulsion and rhythm while staying in a nice, round frame and softly chewing the bit.

11.1.6 From Trot to Halt

To develop the trot-halt transition, the horse must have a very correct trot—lively, engaged, swinging, straight, balanced, and in a clear rhythm. To maintain balance through the transition, and to keep the horse light throughout, the rider's seat and legs must perform the transition, not a pulling hand. For this, the trot must be engaged and supple with light contact.

As in the trot-walk transition, the weight aids come through a lowering of the heels. The reins hold just long enough to complete the halt, but must immediately soften while maintaining connection.

Do not expect that the horse will understand our aids immediately, nor that he will respond correctly from the outset. At the beginning, one should think of trot-walk-halt, keeping the horse's balance through both transitions. Work on this transition with lots of patience. Look for relaxation, balance, and softness. Then work for straightness and engagement through to the halt. While repetition and practice are important, be careful not to drill over and over. This would only make the horse tense. Developing a correct trot-halt transition takes many months.

Again it is very important to let the horse stay still in the halt. When he makes a correct halt, praise the horse and give him confidence to stay still. But do not let the horse sleep or lose attentiveness. He must be ready to respond immediately to the aids.

We have to be very careful with corrections within the halt. It is better to accept a slightly imperfect halt than to make the horse nervous through too much correction. Through repetition, perfect halts will come.

11.1.7 The Transition to Lengthening of Trot Stride

We can move on to lengthening and shortening the trot strides only when the transitions from walk to trot and back to walk, etc. are easy, correct and reliable. In lengthening, as with all transitions, it is essential that the transitions be smooth—not abrupt. One should see a clear transition from working trot to lengthened strides or back, but the movements should float smoothly from one into the other.

To lengthen stride the rider must compress the horse through half halts that build the impulsive power of the trot, like a compressed spring. Then the rider's hand feels forward without losing contact, thus letting the steps out. The steps should become longer and yet not quicker. The freer the tempo, the more the rider should go with it. Otherwise the rider will be left behind the movement. These transitions into the lengthening need to be practiced hundreds of times to learn the right combination of aids for each horse. In these trot transitions it is of extreme importance that the rider uses the seat (*Kreuz*) more than the legs. Only that way will the rider be ready to control the trot in the very next stride. Horses that are "kicked" through these lengthenings will fall out of balance, losing rhythm or breaking into the canter

To bring the horse back from the lengthened stride, the rider uses the same aids as for all downward transitions: heels down, hold and then give forward.

11.1.8 The Canter Depart

The aids for the canter from the walk are as follows: first the rider positions or flexes the horse slightly to the inside. The inside leg of the rider lies at the girth and activates the inside hind leg of the horse to take more energetic strides forward. The outside leg goes back a little and lies there guarding. The weight of the rider shifts to the inside seat bone by the rider moving his hip forward and sitting slightly deeper in the saddle. The horse should take the canter on one track, and the rider should pay strict attention to this. Also the rider should insist that the horse be absolutely soft in the hand. The aids just described must be given in the right moment: the rider moves his outside shoulder back when the horse's outside hind hoof is on the ground. How does the rider know then this moment is? As the horse's outside shoulder goes back, the outside hind leg is on the ground. This moment is essential, because the outside hind leg pushes the other three legs into the canter. Now is the time to give the aid. Only when the right hind leg of the horse is on the ground, for example, is the horse able to make a clean depart into the left lead canter.

If the horse is very sensitive and the rider gives the aids correctly, but in the moment the left hind leg is on the ground, the horse will take the right lead instead of the left. A less sensitive horse will take the left lead even if the aids are given in the wrong moment, but he will have to wait until his right hind is on the ground. Thus the canter depart will be delayed and a little rough. The rider will feel this delay and lack of smoothness, but usually he does not know why. It is a heavenly feeling when the rider uses the aids in the right moment and gets a prompt and correct depart. This is a good example of the necessity for the right aids in the right moment.

The preparation for the canter depart, whether from the walk or the trot, holds the secret for success. The quieter and softer the depart, the quieter and softer the horse will stay in the canter. A wrong lead, or aids given in the wrong moment, or aids given too strongly are the most common mistakes. With the young horse it is best to ask for the canter on a circle, and specifically when approaching the wall or the fence, or going into the corner. Later, when the depart is easy and reliable here, the rider can try it on the long side.

One can ask a horse to canter from the walk, trot, halt, rein back, or passage. When asking for the canter from the trot, the rider should collect the trot very slightly—almost unnoticeably. The correct moment for the depart is when the outside shoulder goes forward. The reins should not be thrown away, and the aids must be given with good coordination. Otherwise, the horse will run away at a fast trot instead of cantering.

As soon as the horse lifts himself into the canter, the rider needs to let the stride out with the hand slightly. Through the forward driving aids of weight and leg, the rider brings the canter strides into a steady flow. Each stride of the canter should be ridden as if it is a new departure stride. It is also good to imagine that every stride of the canter takes you "toward Heaven," or up hill. The rider should pay attention that the first stride is the same as the others.

The rider should move smoothly and supply with the movement of the horse in the canter in order not to disturb the submission and activity of the horse's back. This is called "going well with the movement." The upper body of the rider should not get behind the movement. Neither should the rider sit ahead of the movement, which will cause excessive rocking. The inside hip and seat bone and the outside shoulder of the rider must stay with the horse's movement. The knee and ankle joints of the rider must stay elastic. The rider's hips and pelvis must also stay elastic and move forward with the horse's movement. Otherwise the rider's seat will not stay in the saddle, which looks a little as if the rider is posting at the canter! The rider's hands should be quiet, but if the rider's seat is bouncing, it is very hard to have quiet hands.

Try not to let the horse go in a travers position (haunches in) in the canter. Every horse has a natural crookedness, which will manifest itself rather clearly in the canter. When the horse puts his inside hind leg too far into the arena, it is usually a sign that the rider has bent the horse too much to the inside, and the shoulder falls to the outside. Too much outside leg is being used and not enough inside leg to encourage the horse's inside hind to jump forward. To correct this crookedness, the rider should be softer on the inside rein and with the outside knee, the rider should try to bring the forehand into the arena a little. However, this correction cannot be given too strongly as it may cause the horse to do a flying change. If the horse is so sensitive that he does a flying change with the slightest correction of crookedness, then it is better to tolerate some crookedness at the beginning, because the flying change is the greater mistake. Exhibiting true straightness takes much longer than most people think.

Due to an ugly riding accident, I am now forced to ride sidesaddle. Yet I have had no trouble making the horses straight in their canter departs. The preparation is the key. The trot as well as the walk must be lively enough that the horse is willing to canter promptly. If this is the case the horse takes the canter with a light seat aid and goes straight. In a sidesaddle I can only work with my weight and a little with the left leg, since it is the only one on the horse, and with my whip on the right side. I recommend to my students to ride a little in a sidesaddle to experience how easily the horse responds to the seat. They are always astonished at how well the horse responds. Most horses go willingly in sidesaddle. I had horses who did pirouettes, half passes and changes to one-tempis.

11.1.9 From Canter to Walk

To make a correct transition from the canter to the walk, imagine you are sitting on a rocking horse. When the horse is coming up in front, is the moment when the hindquarters automatically are stepping under his body. This is the moment to make the transition. The rider drops his heels and gives a light half halt on the *inside* rein. I emphasize that the half halt is given on the inside rein, because the rider needs to stop the flow of the canter. In the left lead canter, for example, the rider gives the half halt left. The outside rein stays in contact, and of course the heels are deep. If given in the right moment, these aids will cleanly arrest the canter stride. If the aids are given when the horse's forehand is on the ground and the hind legs are not, the transition will be on the forehand, no matter how strong the aids are.

Note that the half halts are given on the outside rein to collect the canter, so as not to restrict the inside shoulder and hind leg of the horse in the canter. Therefore, if I want the horse to walk, not just collect, and I still give the half halt on the outside rein, the horse will not understand. The horse will collect more, getting shorter and shorter, and yet he will not walk.

The transition from the canter to trot or walk should be smooth and flowing and sure, without the rider becoming too tight with the hands. I suggest to my riders to think of the walk when they want the horse to go from the canter to the trot and to put the horses in a slight shoulder-in position that will bring the inside hind leg of the horse into a useful position under his body. Be patient. Otherwise the horse will become afraid of the transitions and of the half halts.

11.1.10 The Transition to the Extended Canter

The transition to extended canter should be soft and flowing. And just as in transitions from walk to trot, the rider should not suddenly attack the horse with the aids, but rather in a smooth way try to lengthen the strides, not make them quicker in rhythm. The rider should keep the horse on the aids, not allowing him to escape contact of rein, seat or legs. The rider will need to give half halts occasionally to let the horse know that he needs to listen to the aids.

For example, in the left lead canter the rider should keep the horse soft to the inside (left) by bending the horse slightly to the left when riding through the corner and on the short side before the long side. The outside leg of the rider should stay well connected to the horse. The outside hand gives a light half halt while the horse maintains a slight position left.

In the collected gaits the horse becomes similar to a compressed spring. Then when the rider comes to the long sides and wants to extend, the spring can be let out.

To shorten the tempo it is important to use the forward driving aids. The slower the rider wants the horse to canter, the more the rider must drive and sit into the horse. However, the rider should be careful not to drive too much or the horse will go against the hand. The rider must keep the horse "on his *Kreuz*" by keeping his heels well down. This in turn puts the right amount of weight into the saddle, engaging the hind legs.

The most common mistake is that the rider does not drive sufficiently and the half halts to collect the canter are done too much with the hand. Often the canter will become four-beat or the horse changes leads with the hindquarters, resulting in a "disunited" canter, or the horse falls into the trot. It would be better to allow a lesser mistake, such as slight haunches-in position in the transition, than a more serious mistake, such as the disunited canter.

11.1.11 The Halt-Canter or Rein Back-Canter Transition

Transitions from the halt to the canter and from the rein back to the canter are easier for the horse than most riders imagine. When I ask riders to try this exercise, they often look at me as if I were completely crazy, because their horse has never done this before. They are usually pleasantly surprised at how easily their horse can do the exercise. Later these transitions can be ridden with counter canter. Transitions from canter to halt and to halt and rein back are also good to include.

The rider must not hold the horse with too tight a rein contact nor should he throw the reins away when riding these exercises. The aids should be exactly the same as when riding a canter transition from the walk or trot.

It is a common mistake for the rider to lean forward. The horse then jumps forward, and the rider loses his balance and falls back behind the movement, pulling the horse in the mouth.

11.1.12 Canter-Halt Transition

In the transition from canter to halt, it is important that the canter is springy and correctly three-beat. The horse must be sensitive to all the rider's aids to make a good transition. The rider should feel as if he is riding uphill "to Heaven." Every rider recognizes the rocking sensation of the horse's canter, similar to a rocking horse. When the horse is up in front and the hindquarters are low and engaged, only then can the horse make a correct transition to the halt with the full halt aids.

If the aids are given when the horse is low in front, the third phase, in which in the right lead the horse lands on the right front, the transition can only end on the forehand.

The aids should be given in the moment of suspension of the canter. This moment initiates the halting process. By half halting during the moment of suspension before the full halt, the hindquarters are activated to jump more energetically under the horse, thus lowering the hindquarters.

Surely every rider has watched a Western reining horse with fascination as he makes a sliding stop. There is a similarity between this and a dressage horse making a correct full halt from the canter. The hind legs of the reining horse begin to be extremely compressed during the moment of suspension, and then continue as the horse slides with his hindquarters through the dirt, his haunches very low. With a dressage horse in collected canter, this transition is very refined. When the final full halt aids are given in the left lead, for example, the right hind is first to gain immobility, then the left hind, and finally the front legs. This is a classic halt from the canter.

11.1.13 Canter Problems

A big mistake is often made when the horse falls unexpectedly into the trot from the canter. The rider should not try to drive the horse immediately back into the canter. Instead, the rider should adjust the tempo of the trot and bring the horse back into a working trot. The horse has definitely come "off the aids" in this undesired transition from canter to trot. Therefore, the rider should first put the horse back on the aids of seat, leg, and hand. He should then wait until the horse has come back into balance. Only then can the rider give the correct aids for a new canter depart.

If the rider does not do this and tries to make the horse canter without this preparation, then the rider multiplies his mistakes! The first mistake is that the horse fell into the trot. This is a sign that the rider wasn't paying enough attention. The horse is now out of balance. The trot cannot be correct. If the rider tries to make the horse canter, such a depart cannot be correct either. When the depart is incorrect, the following canter strides cannot be good. In this way a rider would be making too many mistakes at the same time! A good rider would avoid doing this.

11.1.14 Starting Up Again After a Brief Walk on Long Reins

After strenuous work, it is essential to let the horse relax and stretch all his muscles in the free walk. But having done this, we come to another transition: picking up the contact from a walk on long reins.

As the rider takes up the rein contact again, he must try to get the horse's hind legs engaged immediately, driving with seat and legs over the back into the hand so that the horse could take the trot or canter immediately if asked. Every gait must be ridden so that any other gait could follow instantly. Only when the horse's hind legs are powerful and lively in the walk can the rider easily get the horse to trot with a slight *Kreuz* and leg combination aid. The inside hip, seat bone and leg of the rider provide the impulsion for the transition. The outside leg guards against the haunches falling out.

When a horse jogs while picking up the reins, it is a sign that the horse does not have confidence in the rider's hands. With such horses, we need to be especially careful with the reins and it is most helpful to put the horse into shoulder-in, travers, or onto a 10 meter circle (with young horses) or volte (more experienced horses).

11.2 Correcting and Perfecting the Halt

The three elements of the halt are the transition into the halt, immobility, and the transition out of the halt. The horse must be ridden forward into the halt, and not pulled into a stop. The horse should stand quietly, straight and evenly on all four legs. The transition out of the halt should be precise and immediate, without rushing. This quality of transition depends on the engagement of the hindquarter in the halt, which in turn is determined by the quality of the transition into the halt.

In the halt the rider keeps the horse on the bit by closing both legs and engaging his *Kreuz*, pushing against a light and holding rein contact. The horse remains ready to engage his hind legs, and chewing on the bit. At this time, the head and neck of the horse will move into a position relative to the horse's level of training and his conformation. When a horse is correctly on the bit, the rider will have the sensation of sitting softly on a horse that is evenly balanced on all four feet. If a hind leg begins to step sideways or backwards, it should be carefully contained by the rider's leg on the same side. Likewise, if a front leg moves, the rider's hand and rein on the same side must be ready to react.

To practice halting, the rider should halt the horse in a place from which the horse can be easily observed in a mirror without having to stretch and twist.

11.2.1 Hind Leg Correction in Halt

There is nothing more difficult than correcting a horse in the halt. I suggest to all riders first not to do it at all, especially inexperienced riders or riders with young horses. And even for experienced riders it is a work of art to do this with accurate leg, weight and rein aids successfully. It is better simply to ride forward and halt again at another place.

First, the young horse should be allowed to stand still regardless of his crookedness. The horse's nature is to be wary and ready to flee from danger. Achieving a quiet halt therefore requires the development of confidence, relaxation, and familiarity. Adjustments and nagging corrections work against your goal. You can spend a year or more practicing the halt without correcting and adjusting the horse. He will then learn to stand quietly and confidently on all four legs, and square quiet halts can come naturally, without needing special attention and correction. The rest of this chapter addresses problems that may arise with horses that have been previously trained, or who need minor tune-ups.

Let us suppose that the horse rests his left hind leg, which happens often. The horse hangs his left hip slightly. The back muscles on the left side of the horse are not stretched. One can easily feel this mistake. Even a young, inexperienced rider notices that his body hangs unevenly lower on one side in a halt when the horse rests a hind leg or stands with a hind leg away. The rider instinctively tries to straighten himself. To correct this problem, stay in the halt a few seconds, and if the horse still doesn't stand correctly, the rider should begin to use his right leg. Don't use the left leg—this will drive the horse sideways or forward or backward. When the horse feels the right leg and starts to respond, because his right hind has been stimulated, he is forced to put the left hind solidly on the ground. Then to prevent the horse from moving forward or sideways, the rider gives a very light half halt on the right rein. The left rein remains in contact, and the rider's left leg stays also in good contact with the horse's body, to prevent side stepping.

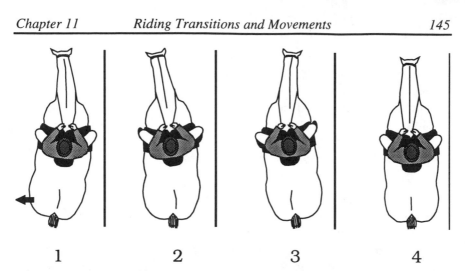

1   2   3   4

Figure 48. Correcting the crooked halt. 1) Crooked halt, hind leg falls in. 2) Correct by riding slight shoulder-in into halt. 3) For more advanced horses, a renvers position may be used. 4) Straight halt.

When riding forward to repeat the halt, the rider should try not to repeat the preceding mistake. If the horse rested his left hind in the first halt, then the rider should take care at the next halt to be lighter with the left rein, the left leg is held a little tighter, but don't forget to hold the right, opposite, rein and leg carefully in contact against the driving aid of the left leg. If the rider is fortunate and the horse rests the same hind leg, then at least the rider is prepared and knows how to make the correction.

If the horse continues to make the same mistake of resting the left hind in the halt, then the rider can ride a slight shoulder-in before and into the halt. This is a great help in driving the left hind leg under the weight of the rider.

11.2.2 Backing in the Halt

The horse may also step back with one or both hind legs in the halt. This happens either when the rider used too strong a rein aid or did not use enough leg aids. Backing in the halt is a more serious mistake than crookedness or the resting of a hind leg. It shows clearly that the rider uses too much hand with too little driving aids and how important it is to ride the horse from back to front—not front to back! Again, the same basic correction: ride forward and halt in a new place, only this time with greater and long-lasting leg and seat bone (*Kreuz*) pressure and softer hands.

11.2.3 Stepping Forward in the Halt

Stepping forward in the halt with the front legs has the same cause as when the horse steps back with the hind legs: the horse is not "together" with a rounded back. The rider has the feeling he sits in a valley because the horse is hollowing his back.

Stepping forward with the front legs very often occurs when the rider gives too much with the reins after halting. The rider should retain stronger rein contact until the horse no longer tries to step forward. In this situation, the rider should drive the horse better into the hand and then carefully retain the contact in the transition to halt. The rider should imagine riding the horse slightly backward to prevent the stepping forward, although the horse should not actually be made to step back.

11.2.4 The Crooked Halt

Sometimes the horse goes against the rider's leg in the halt, standing then with the haunches to the inside, or "crooked." In that case, halting the horse in a shoulder-in-like position is helpful. Most often if crooked, the horse will stand with his haunches to the stiff side. The rider should take the horse's shoulders a little to the inside in order to straighten him, with the opposite rein well against the neck. At this time, the rider should be softer with the inside hand to keep the horse's inside shoulder freer. The opposite rein maintains contact and gives the half halt aid for the horse to halt. Both of the rider's legs stay in good contact with the horse.

For more advanced horses, I would suggest using a slight renvers position to correct the crooked halt. This gives the horse the chance to step with the stiff hind leg under his weight and be straight.

Once again we recognize how important it is to make the horse soft on the stiff rein and to get him to accept contact on the softer rein. Above all, the horse must never have the opportunity to lean on one rein. Only when he is soft on both reins can he halt and stand evenly and balanced on all four legs. We often hear that this is one of our most important tasks in riding. It applies not only to dressage horses but also to jumpers.

"Enter and halt" is the first impression the judge receives and cannot be practiced too much. It is important to ride often on the centerline to practice straightness away from the help of the track or wall. The horse should come to feel comfortable on the centerline the way he does on the track. Riding the centerline is the real test for straightness. But when you do, halt in different places, and frequently ride the centerline with no halt. Otherwise the horse will begin to anticipate the halt.

11.3 The Rein Back

The rein back is closely related to the halt transition. One exercise leads to another. The rein back is an important exercise in suppleness and obedience. Occasionally, when the horse tries to evade collection, it is good to add some exercises in reining back. Also, if the horse tries to run away a little, the rider should make a transition to halt and rein back to put the horse better on the aids and to improve the collection. It is, however, against the horse's nature. Very seldom will you see a horse in freedom stepping backwards although it is required in dressage tests. The rider should approach this exercise with special care.

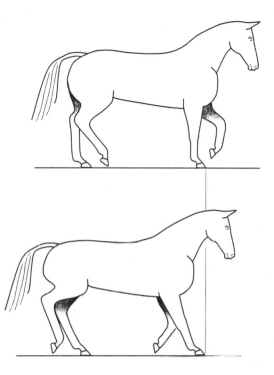

Figure 49. The rein back. The horse's legs move in diagonal pairs.

The aids for the rein back start with the horse being on the bit and straight, with the rider's legs resting quietly behind the girth on the horse's body. The rider should first drive the horse as if he would ask him to go forward. But at the moment when the hind leg lifts to step forward, the rider gives a half halt together with a driving leg (on the side that is stepping forward).[1] The forward impulse of the horse is received by the rider's direct rein aids and the hind legs are redirected backwards. This drives the horse in the rein back steps. The rider's legs control the straightness and prevent the haunches from stepping out or in, and they prevent the horse from coming off the bit. These are the aids for the classical rein back.

It is important to make clear to the horse what is expected of him. The hind leg must initiate the movement. The horse should not be pulled backwards. This only makes the horse step harder into the ground with his hind legs for support. Unfortunately, some riders at this point pull even harder on the reins, the horse throws his head up, and the next thing that happens is that the horse rears. A horse can easily learn to rear this way!

---

[1] For example, first the right leg and rein support during the activity of the left hind leg's step back, then they drive the right hind leg to step back with a half halt on the right side.

If the leg pressure is too great, it will drive the horse forward and require more rein aids to rein back. The rider's seat is important, too. If the rider sits too heavily, it will make it harder for the horse to pick up his hind feet and step back. On the other hand, the rider should not sit so lightly that he lifts his seat completely off the saddle. In the rein back, if the horse is supple, he will lift diagonal pairs of legs (as in the trot) and step back calmly, steadily and straight.

Horses starting to learn the rein back will often go crooked. We should not try immediately to fix this crookedness. The horse is already confused enough by our new aids to go back, and trying to correct and adjust at the same time will only confuse him more. Let him become a little familiar with the idea that you might want to go backwards before trying to keep him straight.

I suggest to my riders when teaching the horse the rein back for the first few times that they start with a slight turn on the forehand movement before asking the horse to step back. Assuming that the horse is on the left rein, we start on the track from the halt. The rider uses the right leg, as if starting a turn on the forehand. In the moment when the horse lifts the right hind leg, the rider should give a light half halt on the right rein. Then, in the very next moment, the rider closes the left leg, so that the horse will lift the left hind leg. Then the rider gives a light half halt on the left rein. In this way the steps of the rein back begin.

The rein back ceases when the rider stops the rein aids and increases the use of his lower legs and *Kreuz* (hips and seat bones). Remember that during the rein back the connection through the seat bones and *Kreuz* is not completely lost, just made lighter. The rider should sit and use his *Kreuz* so that he is always ready to determine the number of steps in the rein back. One should never ask for more than six steps at one time. If the rider wants to stop after the sixth step, for instance, he should not throw his upper body back or sit down so hard that the horse jumps forward. He should sit just enough more with his *Kreuz* engaged to stop the rein back and encourage the horse to walk forward. The aids to go forward should come after the fifth step if you want to go back six, by moving both legs slightly forward, riding with both legs and seat bones forward.

Horses sometimes use the rein back as a way to free themselves from the rein contact by rushing backwards. The rider then does indeed lose the rein contact, by throwing his hands forward.

In this situation I advise my riders to maintain the rein contact without pulling, but to bring their legs forward to the girth. Let the horse continue to go backwards until he realizes that he is not succeeding in losing contact. My experience is that after 5 to 10 meters or so, the horse stops by himself when he finds his plan not working. He then is ready to go forward quite willingly.

11.4 *Schaukel*

The *Schaukel* (or swing) is a rein back of a prescribed number (4 or 6) steps, followed without interruption by a forward walk of a set number of steps, then (again without interruption) another rein back of the prescribed number of steps, and then immediately into walk, trot or canter forward. It demonstrates the fine balance of the aids for forward and backwards and their precision. Its successful execution is proof of the correctness of the rein back. The aids must not be abrupt, allowing the horse to flow from one direction into the other. The horse must not drag the feet backwards, but must make the backward steps with the same lightness and precision as the forward steps.

In the rein back, the rider sits with a lighter seat, without tipping forward. The rider's legs are slightly back. As the horse takes the fifth step back, the rider starts the forward driving aids: the seat deepens and drives by tightening the seat, and the legs come to the girth and the hand gives. His momentum back will cause him to complete the sixth step back, but the driving aids will ensure that when the leg comes off the ground after the sixth step, it will travel forward. After the third step forward, we give again the new aids for the new rein back. Again, momentum makes the fourth step forward, but as the leg comes off the ground after the fourth step, it is going back.

The steps are counted as each hind leg goes back—for instance the left hind-right front pair count as 1, the right hind-left front count as 2, the left hind-right front count as 3, and so on. Since we count the hind leg, the forward steps are counted the same: left hind (1), right hind (2), left hind (3), right hind (4).

To decide whether to start with the left or right hind leg moving back, you have to know which leg you want to finish on. This primarily matters when completing the *Schaukel* into a canter. For example, to depart into the left lead canter, the last step must be with the right hind leg. Assuming an even number of steps, we must start with the left hind leg going back: *rein back*: L - R - L - R - L - R *forward*: L - R - L - R *back*: L - R - L - R *canter*: Left.

Although we have discussed the *Schaukel* here with the rein back, and before the lateral work and flying changes, it is really a movement of the highest precision which is not seen in tests until the FEI Intermediaire. There is sometimes a temptation to practice the *Schaukel* when the rein back itself is not confirmed: "See, we can do this fancy movement!" This is inadvisable. The *Schaukel* should come from the rider and horse exploring the fineness of their communication in the rein back. Only when they communicate well enough to make rein back movements of an exact number of steps followed by a halt, trot or canter should they begin. If the horse is unsure of the rein back, and one time he is brought to a halt, but the next time he is rushed right into a forward walk, the pulled back into a rein back, he may well lose confidence in the rein back, and training will be lost, not gained.

11.5 Counter Canter

The counter canter is an important exercise to make the horse sure of his balance in the canter. I do the following exercise with my riders: starting on the left rein shortly before the short side, the rider asks the horse to canter on the left lead. Then at the first letter of the long side (F), the rider asks the horse for a transition to the walk. Then the rider moves the horse off the track slightly, onto the second or even the third track. It would be hard to ask the horse for the counter canter while keeping him on the track where for months and years he has cantered on the true lead. But by bringing him into the arena a few feet, he now has room to his right-hand side to take the counter canter. Do this in both directions, and then start with the second set of exercises.

Again on the left rein and on the second or third track, the rider gives the aids for the right lead canter.[1] The rider should not use the outside (left) leg too strongly. He should use his right hip and seat bone more and give the horse a slight position to the right. The rider should take care not to overdo the position by bending the horse too much to the right, as I often see! The rider would never flex the horse to the inside so much for an ordinary canter depart. So why would the rider do this for the counter canter depart? When the flexion is overdone, the horse's inside shoulder as well as his inside hind leg are held too tightly for him to use them properly. He simply cannot canter forward under these circumstances. The rider's outside leg should stay well against the horse in these counter canter exercises. The rider should accept a little crookedness in the bargain at first in order to make it easier for the horse. It is very difficult to make the horse straight in the first counter canter exercises.

The rider should make a transition to the walk at the end of the long side, paying attention to giving the half halt to walk on the inside (right) rein and to getting the walk correctly engaged and rhythmic immediately. The outside rein and leg are used to prevent the horse from drifting more into the arena.

When the walk is good, the rider engages the horse more and asks for the left lead canter by positioning the horse to the left. The rider uses his seat (*Kreuz*) by pushing the inside (left) hip and seat bone deep and forward into the saddle to ask for the left canter. After the short side the rider makes another transition to the walk, moves the horse into the arena onto the second track and asks for the right lead canter. Moving the horse into the arena can be done by use of gradual leg-yielding. This helps the horse make

---

[1] In this discussion of the counter canter, the terms *outside* and *inside* are used in relationship to the *lead*, not to the horse's position in the arena.

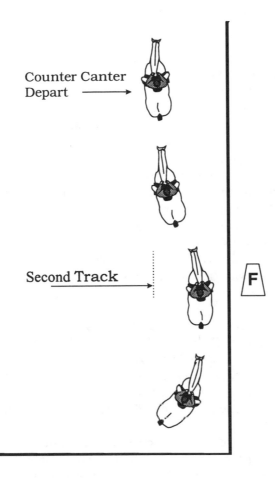

Figure 50. Counter canter depart. After walking through the corner, lead the horse to the second track, then make the transition to counter canter (right lead as shown).

straighter departs. It is important here for the rider to maintain good left leg support to avoid the horse stepping too much sideways with his left hind leg during the leg-yielding steps.

When the right and left lead canter departs are going well, the rider can ask the horse to maintain the counter canter through the short side. It is important not to ride the horse too deeply into the corners. This makes the counter canter very difficult for the horse. Horses often change or disunite in the second corner of the short side, because they lose their balance and impulsion. This is caused by the rider's inability to correctly support the horse with outside (left) leg and the rider's tendency to lean toward the inside of the arena through the corners, thus hindering the horse's balance. If the horse does a good flying change instead of maintaining the counter canter, the rider should absolutely NOT punish the horse. In fact, a smart rider will pretend he asked for it and praise the horse. Otherwise, later the horse will be afraid of flying changes when asked, which would be very unpleasant for the horse and an enormous disappointment to the rider.

To correct this and make it easier for rider and horse, the rider should make a transition to the walk before the first corner, at M, for example. Then, on the left rein, ride in a good walk well into the corner to gain ground for the following. Ride renvers as soon as possible after the first corner, leading the shoulders in with a slight flexion to the right. Then ask for the right lead canter promptly. The rider should look out over the horse's left ear, his left shoulder should go back slightly, and his right hip and seat bone are used forward for the canter depart. The rider's outside leg (left) is behind the girth and well against the horse.

This exercise should be done on each short side several times. One should not quit too soon with this counter canter correction. The horse needs weeks or months with this correction in order to become confident and strong. The rider also needs this experience to feel confident in the counter canter.

Now the rider needs to teach the horse to go from the true canter into the counter canter. The method I use is to make an 8-meter circle in the first corner of the short side. When the quality of the canter is good, the rider makes a half circle (8 meters) and gradually returns to the track in a slight travers position and continues in counter canter. It is usually easier for the horse to do this in the left lead canter first, because the left lead is easier for most horses.

When the horse feels quite comfortable with this exercise and does it reliably, the rider can start to make the half circle larger, approaching the centerline and returning to the middle of the long side. Then, with the same idea, the rider can ride from the first letter of the long side to the middle of the opposite long side, continuing in counter canter. And finally the rider can ride across the diagonal and stay in counter canter through the corner and on the short side. A useful technique in doing this latter exercise is to land about two meters before the letter, to avoid having to make too sharp a turn in the corner in counter canter. This could result in the horse changing leads.

When this is going well, it is time to start the whole process with the right lead as counter canter. To confirm the counter canter, the rider should understand that this training requires months of serious daily work. No exercise can be forced and end with a good and correct result; there is nothing different about the counter canter.

Chapter 12

On the Subject of Collection

Three things are necessary before starting to work on "collection" with your horse: 1) the sufficient development of the horse's will to go straight and forward with impulsion; 2) rein contact; and 3) a degree of suppleness and acceptance of the aids (*Durchlässigkeit*). When these elements are in place, the dressage begins to include exercises that require greater carrying power from the haunches. In other words, we begin to collect the horse.

To collect the horse means to get the hind legs to carry more of the horse's weight and to utilize their strength with complete control and accuracy for the purposes of carrying and thrusting. Increased carrying power in the hind legs is essential, because this alone allows the required "elevation of the forehand" to develop. The carrying power of the hindquarters makes it possible for the rider to shift the center of gravity farther back when the horse is supple throughout his body, thus letting the aids go through. This is called *Durchlässigkeit*, which when literally translated means "a quality of letting through." More can be demanded of the strength of the horse's hindquarters when the forehand is lightened. And to lighten the forehand, the hindquarters must be made to carry more weight.

The hind legs can only carry more weight when they are stepping well forward and under the center of gravity and the horse is straight. In this position they receive the horse's weight, and the added weight causes the joints to flex more and to push off in a spring-like fashion. This is called "the flexion of the haunches." The increased flexion of the haunches results in a powerful extension of the same joints. The gymnastic exercises depend on this alternating flexion and extension of the joints of the hind legs.

The exercises of collection should at first be less demanding and then gradually more demanding of the strength of the hindquarters and the longitudinal bending in the horse. This bending should be consistent, uniform and gradually increased as the training progresses. The strength of each hind leg is developed individually, by using exercises that require the hind leg on the inside of the bend to step farthest under the horse's weight. In this position, this hind leg will support more of the horse's weight and will be made to flex more than the outside hind leg.

The foundation of dressage is based on the concept of the gradual and progressive development of the horse's strength as reflected by the exercises he can perform. In other words, one should not take the next step until the horse can do the basic, easier exercises with ease and understanding.

12.1 Exercises in Collection

The collecting exercises include the two-track movements: shoulder-in, travers, renvers, half pass. Others are: full halts, the rein back, walking, trotting, and cantering forward from the rein back, enlarging and decreasing the circle, changes in tempo, turns on the haunches, pirouettes, piaffe and passage.

12.2 Turning

The horse must remain elastic and supple in turns, especially when working with collection. He should respond to the rider's aids without resistance and be able to bend in the direction of the movement in the poll and ribcage. In all turns the rider should bring his outside shoulder along with the movement, not leaving it back, and not hanging to the outside of the turn. In this way the rider's seat and the line of the figure will be the same.

To change across the diagonal correctly, the rider should give a half halt before the corner. The turn begins when the horse is at the first letter of the diagonal, for instance, on the left rein at H after C. The rider should give another half halt here on the outside rein when the outside hind leg is just leaving the ground, using more outside leg, position the horse to the inside, and then give immediately. By taking on the inside rein, I show my horse where I want him to go, and by giving I let him go. Now it is very important that the rider look exactly at the letter at the end of the diagonal.

By the time the horse is ready for the collecting work, the rider should be riding a half volte of 6 meters diameter in the corners. The track of a corner should be single and the hoof prints examined to check for this. Therefore, it is important to remember to keep the outside leg well on the horse and to make a new, small turn with every stride by using the inside rein lightly every stride.

The rider should remember to ride the corners in different ways, depending on the exercise. For instance, when performing an extension on the long side, preceded and followed by collection in the corners, the rider rides deep as if making a 6 meter half volte, as described before. If, however, the rider wants to perform medium trot around the whole arena, the corners should somewhat rounded to make this possible for the horse. Medium or extended gaits ridden deep into the corners are impossible and, therefore incorrect, just as when the rider goes too deep in the corner at walk or trot, and has to pull the horse out. The use of the rider's outside leg is key in riding good corners. The rider should keep the outside leg in good contact with the horse's side.

Correct Turn on Haunches

Excessive outside leg

Figure 51. Turn on the haunches.

12.3 Aids for Turns on the Haunches or Pirouette

In the turn on the haunches and pirouette, the horse makes the smallest possible volte with the inside hind leg. For the rider, they are good tests of balancing the driving leg, and the bending and holding aids. In the turn on the haunches, the inside hind leg is allowed to move slightly forward on a small circle, while in a pirouette, the circle made by the inside hind leg is so small that the foot returns to the ground in the same spot with each step. In either case, the rhythm of the walk or canter must be maintained.

Turns on the haunches in the walk are done in walk steps. In the canter they are done in canter strides. When trotting, one comes to a walk, makes the half-turn immediately, then proceeds in trot. All turns on the haunches should be done around a center point. The inside hind hoof of the horse should be as close as possible to this center point.

The horse should not halt before nor after the turn on the haunches. The inside hind hoof should not pivot in the footing, but rather step regularly

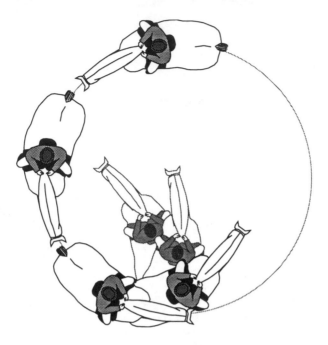

Figure 52. The schooling pirouette is begun out of a volte.

throughout the movement. The steps of the turn on the haunches in the collected walk should be in the exact same rhythm and tempo as the steps preceding the turn.

The aids are as follows: starting with the horse positioned to the inside, the rider gives a light half halt on the outside to give the horse the sign that he must almost stop. Then with the inside hip forward, the horse's shoulder is guided around. The rider's inside hip and rein guide the way, the outside knee and leg help to bring the shoulder over, while the outside rein gives slightly. The rider should think of half pass. Remember that the outside shoulder has a longer way to go than the hindquarter, so the rider must release the outside rein at the start to free the outside shoulder. The inside rein leads the front leg around the hind leg.

One should give the horse enough freedom within this exercise, so that the horse can learn to do it almost by himself. The rider is, of course, always ready with his aids to help and control.

A very successful and trouble-free way to introduce young and green horses or inexperienced riders to the pirouette is to start from a volte. After one half of the volte, the rider leads the shoulder to the inside with both hands and outside knee and leg, thinking about continuing the volte on a much smaller pattern with the horse's inside hind leg. The rider is usually astonished at how easy this approach is for the horse.

12.3.1 Mistakes and Corrections for Turns on the Haunches

Often, too much lower outside leg is used because the rider is trying to keep the haunches from swinging out. The haunches then step to the inside and cross over, resulting in a figure which is more of a small circle or leg-yielding than a turn on the haunches. If the rider concentrates on bringing the shoulders around, then haunches will be less likely to swing out or in. Therefore, ride the turn on the haunches with inside seat bone, leg and rein. The outside rein gives slightly without losing contact to allow the stretching of the outside neck muscles and allows the outside shoulder to come forward and around.

A common mistake is to try to make the turn on the haunches too precise and too small when starting to school the movement. I suggest to my riders that they ride a large volte when first teaching this exercise. The turn on the haunches can then be developed out of the smallest half circle with the inside hind leg of the horse. When ridden too small too soon, the horses sometimes step back, stop moving their hind legs altogether, and lose the desire to go forward.

If the horse steps back or stops, the rider should not continue with the turn on the haunches. He should begin again and not try to force the horse through the exercise. Horses can very quickly develop a bad habit of doing the turn the wrong way. The rider should activate the inside hind leg of the horse, going forward, and think of half pass. Then ride only one or two steps of the turn, so that the horse doesn't get a chance to swing his haunches out or to stop. Usually, the horses swing the haunches out. This shows that the rider's outside leg wasn't sufficiently on the horse and that the walk wasn't collected enough at the start. THE MISTAKE THAT IS MADE ALWAYS HAPPENED BEFORE YOU SEE IT. The desire to go forward must continue through the exercise. Therefore, ride the horse forward with inside seat bone and leg in a travers-like movement and very good flexion and bending.

The collection with good activity in the hind legs is important for the turn on the haunches. It is helpful to ride half of a half pass combined with a half volte. The rider uses the same aids as for the half pass, making the circle smaller and smaller each time the exercise is done. I ask riders to ride around me so that they have a center to concentrate on and therefore do not make the mistake of changing the center of their circle or pirouette.

Another common problem is that the half-turn or pirouette is often not finished properly. Many riders start to straighten and re-bend the horse too early—the horse is bent to the left while still taking steps to the right.

Riding the turn on the haunches from the halt is extremely difficult. There is no impulsion, and the horse almost always steps back. In any case,

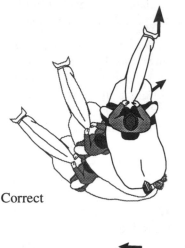

Correct

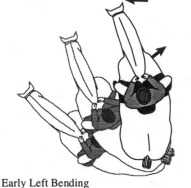

Early Left Bending

Figure 53. Finishing the pirouette. The horse should be ridden in the pirouette until the track is reached. As the horse's head reaches the track, he is straightened so he can proceed straight in the new direction. Do not anticipate the new flexion and finish the pirouette with leg-yielding-like steps.

it should never be done until after the horse has learned to do it correctly from the walk.

Riding the turn on the haunches from the halt should be done in the following way: first, establish good flexion to the inside (which must be kept through the whole turn), then ride as if you want to ride the horse forward, but with his first step, immediately start the turn. This first step forward is the first step of the turn. Again, the aids are a half halt on the outside and outside leg and knee pressure, as the inside leg drives the inside hind leg of the horse, and the inside rein leads the horse into the turn.

12.3.2 Half-Pirouette Left Followed by Half-Pirouette Right

In advanced tests, we are called on to perform a half-pirouette between G and H, followed by a half-pirouette in the opposite between G and M. This is a difficult movement primarily because the first half-pirouette often results in the loss of activity in the hind leg, so the walk between the two half-pirouettes is not lively enough to execute the second half-pirouette correctly. This is a movement which shows how important it is to keep a lively hind leg in the walk.

12.4 The Short Turn from the Trot (*Kuerzkehrt*)

The horse cannot trot around a turn on the haunches. A piaffe turn is possible but very difficult. From the trot, the turn is done in the following way: The horse should be in an energetic, active collected trot. The rider makes a transition to collected walk and slight shoulder-fore, and immediately with the first walk step starts the turn on the haunches, moving step by step around the turn. As soon as the forehand is lined up again with the haunches, the rider straightens the horse and trots on immediately, but not rushing.

This exercise can be done only when the horse is able to accept the half halt to walk correctly, remaining supple, relaxed, engaged, collected and obedient. This is one of my favorite exercises. I recommend riding it often, being careful not to rush the tempo or the transitions.

The best place to ride the short turn is on the long or short side of the arena, the long side being somewhat preferable. The fence or wall discourages the horse from stepping out or back. If ridden at the end of the long side, right before the corner, the corner helps emphasize the outside aids for the turn and the correct position.

12.5 Lateral Work

The shoulder-in, travers, renvers and half pass are lateral movements which help the horse to become flexible on both sides, help with lateral bending on both sides, and help develop and improve collection and straightness. There is a slight paradox here because the horse should have a certain degree of collection in all three gaits before we start lateral movements, yet the lateral movements are so important for developing collection without force. The horse must go in the right tempo and have sufficient engagement of the hindquarters to balance himself through the lateral movements. This can be developed through transitions, turns and rein back.

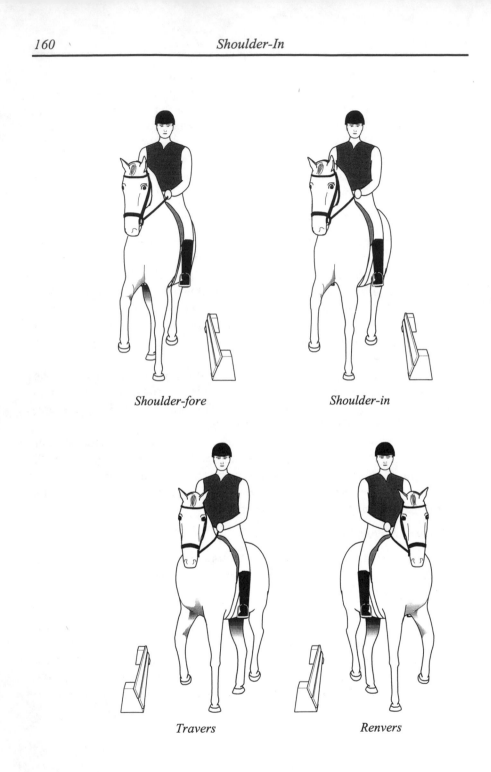

Shoulder-fore   *Shoulder-in*

Travers   *Renvers*

Figure 54. Shoulder-fore, shoulder-in, travers, and renvers.

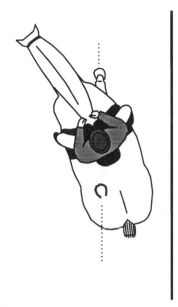

Figure 55. Shoulder-in. The inside hind leg and outside foreleg follow the same line.

It is very important not to remain in lateral exercises too long. Col. Aust never let us ride more than two or three sides of the arena in shoulder-in or travers without riding the horse well forward. We may spend a long time learning and perfecting lateral movements, but not all at once!

12.6 Shoulder-In

The shoulder-in is a lateral bending movement in which the hind legs track straight down the arena, while the shoulders are brought slightly in off the track. Commonly ridden at the trot in competition, it can be ridden in all three gaits.

The fundamental benefit of the shoulder-in comes from the establishment of the correct balance between the inside driving leg and the outside hand. This frees the inside rein (and shoulder) while engaging the inside hind leg. We introduce shoulder-in as the first lateral bending movement because it is easiest for the horse to understand. The horse is asked to bend around and move away from the inside leg. Later, in the travers renvers and half pass, we ask the horse to bend around the inside leg while bringing his hindquarters toward the inside leg—a situation which requires more trust and understanding from the horse.

Paradoxically, shoulder-in is the exercise that imparts the ability to both bend and straighten the horse. The lateral bending helps establish the proper balance which is so essential for small circles and transitions. The need to straighten the horse generally arises because the haunches fall to the inside, while the shoulders drift out. In order to make the horse straight, we "correct the shoulders to the hind leg." That is, bring the shoulders to the inside more than attempting to shove the haunches to the outside. These are the same aids as in the shoulder-in.

Another great benefit of the shoulder-in is that it helps to keep the horse obedient and supple. When the horse is bent around the inside leg, it is easier to drive the inside hind leg without losing control—we can keep a very soft inside rein even while engaging the hindquarter. This often helps when a horse shies or bolts. When a horse shys from something on his right side, ride him in shoulder-in left past the hazard. When horses shy, they always bolt out through the shoulder, so by positioning the horse to the left, it is far easier to control. In addition, the horse's head is directed away from the distraction, he knows he can move forward away from it, and it is far less likely that he will act up.

In the shoulder-in the horse moves with the forelegs displaced to the inside of the arena, while the hind legs remain on the track. This results in the horse feet creating three tracks, with the hoofprint of the inside hind leg overlying the hoofprint of the outside foreleg, as shown in Figure 54 and Figure 55. It is important that the hind legs and hips move straight down the arena (on the track). This is in distinction to the leg-yield, where both the front and hind legs cross. Such leg-yielding is a loosening exercise, while shoulder-in is a collecting exercise. Because the hind legs track straight down the track while the shoulders are to the inside, the inside hock must flex more to bring the hind foot under the center of the horse's body, while in leg-yielding the hock can remain relatively straight while the hip opens and closes laterally. In the shoulder-in, the inside foreleg moves in front of the outside fore. This opens and closes the angles of the shoulder, thereby helping to loosen and free the shoulders.

The horse should move freely forward, the steps should be lively and cadenced, and the rhythm should remain regular and clear. With a strongly swinging hind leg, the shoulder-in is easier for the horse, because he has the necessary power to carry himself. This is why it is so important to refresh the horse with straight forward work quite often during the schooling.

In the shoulder-in to the left, the horse is bent slightly left, on the arc of a 10 meter circle, and the rider sits heavier on the left seat bone. The horse is now driven with the rider's inside (left) leg forward/sideways. The outside leg (right) is slightly behind the girth and controls and limits the stepping out of the right hind leg, while helping with the bending. The outside rein helps in this control also, as it also regulates the tempo, bending and angle of the shoulder-in. The inside rein lies against the horse's neck, preventing him from falling in and gives the occasional half halt, supported by the steady contact of the outside rein. Riders starting to learn shoulder-in

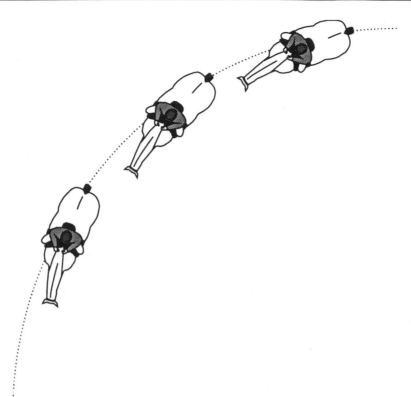

Figure 56. Shoulder-fore on the circle. Preparation for shoulder-in comes through the shoulder-fore on the circle.

often try so hard—the shoulders become stiff, the inside heel comes up, the rider leans forward and almost out of the saddle, hanging over to one side or the other. It is important to stay relaxed in the upper body and to keep the heels low. Remember that the exercise is to engage the inside hind leg, so the rider must sit up and keep the inside hip forward and lowered.

The rider should take his time with this exercise in order to truly reach his goal. If it doesn't work perfectly right away, do not get frustrated; it will improve with time, practice and patience. Remember that a well engaged, powerful gait will help the horse in the movement, so be prepared to accept only as much bending as the horse can give while maintaining impulsion. Generally, this is about that of a 10 meter circle, but less while the horse is first learning. Don't resort to force just to get footfalls in the "perfect" locations. When the rider and horse have come to understand the balance and feeling of a proper swinging shoulder-in, there will be plenty of time to ride towards mirrors and perfect the details.

12.6.1 Shoulder-Fore on the Circle

Preparation for shoulder-in comes through the shoulder-fore on the circle. In shoulder-fore, the inside hind leg steps between the paths made by the two front legs. We use the arc of the circle to naturally establish bend through the horse's body. The shoulders are then brought in slightly with both reins and the outside knee and thigh. It is very important not to exaggerate the shoulder-fore when riding on the 20 meter circle. The bend of the 20 meter circle is the proper bend for the shoulder-fore (in a shoulder-in, the horse is bent as if in a 10 meter circle). The rider should think: the inside hind leg should step between the front leg hoofprints. If the angle of the shoulder-fore becomes too exaggerated, then the outside hind leg swings too far out, and there is no longer any collection. Instead, the horse is leg-yielding.

For shoulder-fore the rider sits more on the inside. While the rider's inside leg drives the horse's inside hind leg under the weight of the rider, his outside leg stays behind the girth, guarding against the haunches stepping out too far. The outside rein is also watching. The hind legs are on the line of the circle, and the front legs come in slightly. The coordination of the aids that are learned from the shoulder-fore on the circle will carry over directly to the shoulder-in, so the rider can learn the feeling of the forward-sideways movement in a setting where the horse can remain calm and supple and relaxed.

This exercise of shoulder-fore on the circle can also be done at the canter. It is excellent preparation for walk or canter pirouettes. As in the walk, it is very important not to ride these movements with too much angle and too little engagement and activity. One should never lose the swing and rhythm.

12.6.2 Shoulder-In on the Long Side of the Arena

When the horse understands and easily accepts the shoulder-fore on the circle, the next step is shoulder-fore on the long side. This can be developed out of shoulder-fore on the circle: the rider continues the shoulder-fore while riding straight ahead on the long side. The balance from inside leg to outside rein, displacement of the shoulders, and engagement of the inside hind leg remain the same. Shoulder-in is then developed from shoulder-fore as the horse gains confidence and we ask for a bit more bending and more displacement of the shoulders to the inside.

At first the rider should not demand too much angle. Later, when the shoulder-in is fully developed, the inside hind leg will step onto the path of the outside front leg. To make it easier for the horse, I suggest riding on the second track (one half meter in from the track). This prevents the horse's tendency to "lean" on the track where he has always felt most secure. This also helps the rider realize the need to use his outside leg correctly in the shoulder-in. The hind legs should stay straight on the track. The front legs come in. Most riders make their horses do haunches-out, instead of

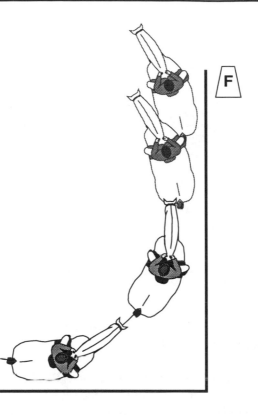

Figure 57. Starting the shoulder-in out of the corner. Ride as if you were going onto a volte. As soon as you ride the first step onto the volte, and the front leg goes in, then you give the aids for the haunches going straight ahead

shoulder-in—they use too much inside leg. The horse's hind leg should stay away from the wall.

Starting out of the corner, ride as if going onto a 10 meter circle. As soon as you ride the first step onto the circle, and the front leg goes in, then give the aids to ask the haunches to go straight ahead. This is the first step of the shoulder-in. Continue the shoulder-in, keeping the tempo and rhythm the same. The inside left hind steps in the direction of the right front foot. The horse hoofprints should create three tracks. Thus from the front one sees three legs (the two front legs and the outside hind leg). In a correct shoulder-in the outside rein is firmly against the base of the neck; and both reins *as a pair* lead the shoulders in carefully. The outside rein should never cross the mane.

The rider will have to give occasional half halts on the outside rein to prevent the horse from falling out over his outside shoulder. The rider's inside leg drives the horse's inside hind forward in the moment the hoof is leaving the ground. This timing is very important. Only in this moment can

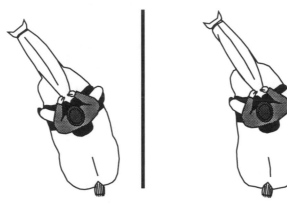

Correct Shoulder-in   Neck Overbent

Figure 58. In the correct shoulder-in, the neck is relatively straight, forming a smooth arc from poll to croup. Often one sees horses over-bent in the neck, and shoulders remain on the track.

the aid be effective. The outside leg of the rider should be well behind the girth, producing the bend around the inside leg. When necessary the rider's outside leg also is active in driving the horse's outside hind forward. The most commonly seen fault is that the horse is overbent to the inside, usually because the rider has pulled the horse into the shoulder-in with the inside rein. When ridden this way, the horse tilts his head and falls out over the outside shoulder.

If the horse comes in too far, the rider uses half halts on the outside to keep him on the track. If the horse goes too close to the track, the rider should drive with his outside leg and give slightly with both reins.

The aids for shoulder-in should be given carefully so as not to frighten the horse. One often sees excessively rough aids that disturb the movement more than help it. Such riding brings us nothing—on the contrary, it sets us back. If rough aids seem to be needed to make the horse "do" a shoulder-in, go back to shoulder-fore on the circle and re-learn the balance of the driving, holding and bending aids.

When the balance of the aids, the bending and engagement are comfortable for the horse and rider, it becomes very valuable to ride shoulder-in toward mirrors, where one can see how precise one can become while still maintaining relaxation and rhythm. One quickly learns how calm and quiet the aids must be, especially half halts with the outside rein. We can also see how little angle is needed, the same as for a 10 meter circle. Constant "fixing" and adjusting leads to a shoulder-in that progresses down

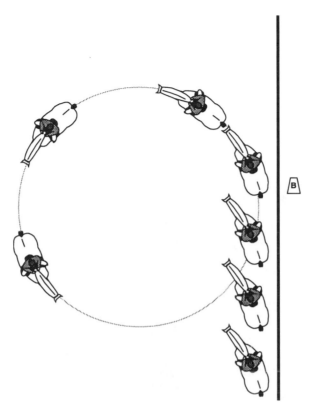

Figure 59. Shoulder-in to 10 meter circle. In going into the circle, the bend of the horse does not need to be changed, but the horse is allowed to move directly forward along the bend.

the arena like a "drunken sailor." As with all riding, we need to learn how very light and soft the aids need to be. The goal is to merely show the horse what we want and then let him do it.

12.6.3 Shoulder-In with 10 Meter Circle

If you have trouble establishing bend at the start of the shoulder-in, it is useful to ride a 10 meter circle in the corner before starting down the long side. The circle establishes the bend and the balance between inside leg and outside rein, which are then kept as you start down the long side. Stay on the circle as long as necessary to establish the bending, rhythm, relaxation, tempo and collection—a poor, unbalanced circle will not help at all with the shoulder-in.

Figure 60. Shoulder-in on the centerline. The hind legs should stay on the centerline, with the shoulders shifted to one side or the other. As in any shoulder-in, the appearance should be that the hind legs are marching along the path of the figure—in this case a straight line on the centerline.

Circles are also very useful when ridden in the middle of shoulder-in on the long side to re-establish the movement after the loss of the balance, bending or rhythm. It is far better to ride the circle than to resort to pulling on the inside rein or kicking. The circle also releases the horse from the demands of forward-sideways movement. In going into the circle, the bend of the horse does not need to be changed, but the horse is allowed to move directly forward along the bend. Upon returning to the track, the horse can be led down the long side, continuing with the shoulder-in.

12.6.4 Shoulder-In on the Centerline

The shoulder-in is introduced to the horse on the long side because the wall gives the horse support, making it easier for him to understand that he is to move sideways and forward down the track. When shoulder-in along the long side is comfortable for horse and rider, one can use the shoulder-in on the centerline to test and confirm the accuracy of the aids. On the centerline, we prove the balance of the aids where the wall is unavailable for help. This is one reason to ride shoulder-in on the second track.

As was done along the long side, one can ride a shoulder-in on the centerline to a 10 meter circle, then continue down the centerline in shoulder-in. Here, however, we have another possibility: ride shoulder-in to a 10 meter figure eight, then proceed in shoulder-in with the opposite bend. That is, if we start with shoulder-in left, ride a left circle, then a right circle, then shoulder-in right. In going from shoulder-in to 10 meter circle, we test our ability to easily shift from sideways-forward movement to straight forward movement with the same bend. The figure eight confirms that the horse is supple and that we can easily change the bend as well as changing the lateral movement. There is no benefit to be gained from roughly throwing the horse over from one circle to the other, so we need to use great care in making the change in direction. If this exercise is a bit too difficult for horse and rider, one can put a few straight steps on the centerline between the two circles.

12.6.5 Shoulder-In to Lengthening

I was very glad to see when the dressage tests began to include a transition from shoulder-in to a lengthening across the diagonal. Riding under Col. Aust, we had to do this all the time. It shows that the horse is immediately ready to go forward, and that the shoulder-in is not mechanical. As with any transition to lengthening, it can only succeed if the immediately preceding trot is engaged, powerful, relaxed and strong, with a clear rhythm in balance. Often these are sacrificed in order to achieve the shoulder-in, so it is very difficult to make the transition to lengthening.

There are two problems to be mastered. The first is simply the transition from shoulder-in to a straight line on the diagonal. Then we add the transition to lengthening. With the horse bent in the shoulder-in, his shoulders are already pointed on the diagonal. By straightening the horse to follow the shoulders, the horse proceeds straight across the diagonal:

Release the bending aid with the outside leg, and give a gentle half halt with the outside, then with both seat bones and both legs ride the horse straight onto the diagonal. Note the difference in going from shoulder-in to circle, where we maintain the bend and allow the horse to go directly forward. Here, we allow the horse to go forward and simultaneously straighten him.

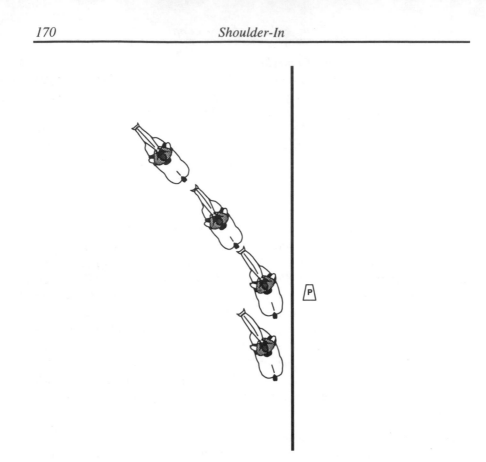

Figure 61. Shoulder-in to the diagonal.

Ask for the lengthening after the horse is moving straight. As with all transitions to lengthening, the transition should not be rough, and should come from a release of the power and energy of the hind leg by a slight lengthening of the neck. When the aids are too rough, one will surely get a canter instead of lengthening—the bend and engagement are just the right preparation for the canter transition. At first, one can take a few steps in working trot before lengthening, to clearly separate the requests you are making of the horse. As the work progresses, riding out of the shoulder-in onto the diagonal becomes almost second-nature, and we can make the transition to lengthening sooner and sooner.

While I am glad to see this movement in the dressage tests, I think that the inclusion of this movement at Second Level is more difficult than many riders appreciate. As in all training, the difficulty usually starts when the rider is anxious to achieve "results" and pushes the horse into the lengthening without paying careful attention to the balance, power, rhythm, relaxation and suppleness. Instead of developing confidence and quiet harmony between rider and horse, we make the horse (at best) confused and worried. There are many parts to this transition, and doing any one part badly will ruin all the others. Riders should take care to observe the progression from the 10 meter circle to riding the diagonal, to making the lengthening, so that we never have to confuse the horse with many new requirements at once.

12.6.6 Shoulder-In Entwickeln

One of the most difficult aspects of the shoulder-in is the beginning. Like most exercises, mistakes happen in the first steps of the movement. Riders can come out of 10 meter circles and slide into shoulder-in, but it is a more difficult proposition to ride into shoulder-in from a straight line. One of the best movements for refining the aids for starting shoulder-in is shoulder-in *entwickeln*.

I was first introduced to shoulder-in *entwickeln* by Col. Aust. In attempting to translate from the German, I find that I am unable to come up with a satisfactory term. *Entwickeln* means "developing," but "shoulder-in developing" or "developing shoulder-in" give very different images than what I consider the movement to be. Therefore, I will stick with the German phrase and ask your indulgence. As we will see later, one can perform similar movements in travers and renvers, and the movement can be done at all three gaits.

Again describing the movement on the left rein, start the long side in shoulder-in left. After a couple of steps of shoulder-in, straighten the horse as though to ride on the diagonal. Proceed straight on the diagonal for two steps only, then re-position the horse in shoulder-in and ride shoulder-in position back to the wall. When arriving on the track with the outside hind leg, proceed again straight on the diagonal for two steps, and so forth down the track.

As one can see, the movement involves repeated bending and straightening, forward, then lateral movement, and requires the finest coordination of the lateral bending and straightening aids. The *entwickeln* term refers to the repeated starting of the shoulder-in. At first, the horse and rider can straighten two or three times down the long side of the arena. When the aids become coordinated, one can straighten even as much as ten times along one side of the arena.

It is very important that the movement be floating and without resistance or rough aids. The aim is not to train the horse to jump away from the leg or become frightened from the hands, but to develop rapport and communication between rider and horse.

When making the transition from shoulder-in to straight on the diagonal, it is important to keep the shoulders at a constant angle from the wall. The horse is straightened to the shoulders (not the haunches), by straightening with the outside (right) rein and leg, while giving with the inside (left) hand. After the second step straight, re-start the aids for shoulder-in: give a

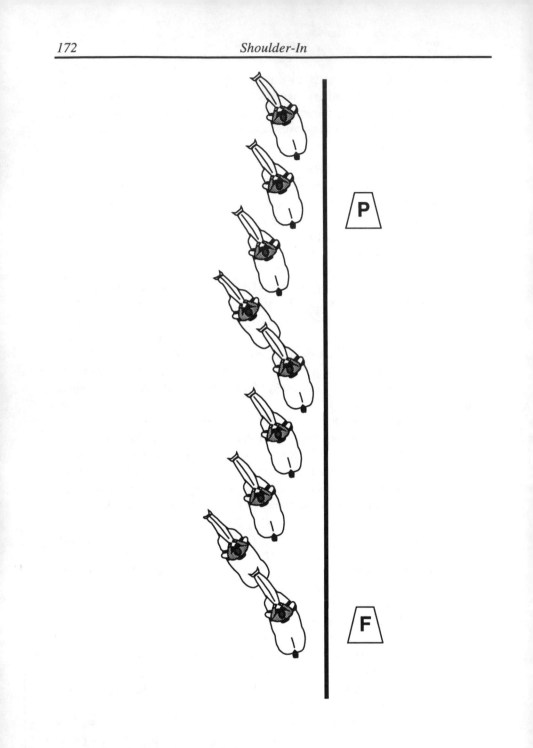

Figure 62. Shoulder-in entwickeln.

gentle flexion to the left, place the weight a bit more on the left seat bone, and drive with the left leg. The outside rein gives a slight half halt, while the outside leg helps with the bending.

The shoulder-in then proceeds back to the track along a very shallow line. Some might think of this as leg-yielding with bend, but it is better to ride as though an artificial wall exists at a slight angle to the real track. When then outside (right) hind leg arrives at the track, the horse is straightened to the shoulder again, and the movement starts over again.

The shoulder-in *entwickeln* can be done at all three gaits. At the canter, the rider must be very careful to coordinate the aids subtly, otherwise the horse is likely to put in a flying change when we ask him to come back into shoulder-in or to straighten. It is helpful at all three gaits to keep the angle relatively shallow, and to not over-do the bend. Also, be careful not to send the horse too strongly forward on the diagonal, just let the horse go forward as is done in the shoulder-in to lengthening on the diagonal. The important feature is to straighten, then bend, then straighten, and so on.

This movement must not be done until the horse goes willingly and easily into the shoulder-in, and can be maintained in a regular shoulder-in without always correcting and fixing the bend and angle. Obviously if the horse is always changing the angle, and the rider loses the shoulder or the bend when just trying to ride a simple shoulder-in, the *entwickeln* movement will complicate the communication, not clarify it. But when the shoulder-in is well in hand, the *entwickeln* is a great test of suppleness and communication, it adds brilliance and esthetic and ensures that the movement is being "ridden," not just survived.

As is true with all lateral movement, be sure not to practice this movement for more than two sides of the arena without riding the horse straight and forward to regain the swinging hind leg and back.

12.7 Travers

Like shoulder-in, travers (or haunches-in) is a suppling, bending, collecting movement, which should work all joints and muscles without tightness. In shoulder-in, the horse is bent with the arc of a 10 meter circle, with the haunches marching along the track. In travers, the bend is more like the arc of the 6 meter volte, and the front legs follow the track, while the hind legs are brought to the inside. In modern travers, the horse's hoofprints create four tracks with the outside hind leg coming to the inside of the inside fore: in travers left, the right hind leg moves along a line to the left of the left foreleg.[1] From the front, one would see all four legs of the horse as in Figure 54 and Figure 63.

---

[1] I learnt that travers and half pass were ridden on three tracks, not four. Three tracks permits a more forward movement and can be more collected, because the horse steps *under* his body. When the currently popular four-track movement is performed, the horse

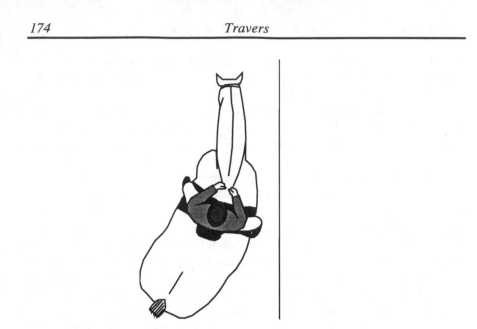

Figure 63. Travers. The front legs follow the track, while the hind legs are brought to the inside.

Travers is more difficult than shoulder-in for the horse to understand because we drive with and bend around the inside leg, while we expect the horse to move his haunches toward this leg. The horse is used to moving away from the rider's leg pressure, now he must accept the driving leg and bring his center of gravity over the inside hind leg, with increased bending. Here, the aids must be very well balanced and in harmony.

12.7.1 Travers on the Circle

As with shoulder-in, we start introducing the travers on the circle. At the start, we ride a circle in which front legs, shoulders and neck follow the line of the circle as well as the hind legs. In the travers, the outside front leg, shoulders and neck remain exactly along the line of the circle, while the hindquarters are brought slightly in.

In travers, the basic balance of aids—from inside leg to outside hand—still applies. The outside rein keeps the shoulders lined up along the path of the figure, while the inside leg drives the inside hind leg up under the horse. The outside leg is behind the girth giving the bending and sideways driving signals. These aids function in harmony because the horse is bent and well connected to the outside rein. The driving of the inside hind leg is received in the outside hand and directed around the circle.

To start, however, we need to increase the bend in the horse's body. For this, we drive from the outside leg to the inside hand. As one can

must step *over*, and crosses the legs. By over-doing the lateral movement, the collection is sacrificed, as is the forward impulsion.

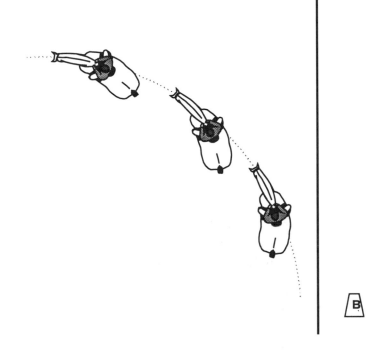

Figure 64. Introducing travers through travers on the circle.

imagine, starting this way can easily lead to riders continuing on in travers with a stronger inside rein, similar to the rider who tries to pull the horse into shoulder-in. It is therefore important to release the inside rein soon after starting the travers.

When we try to bend the horse around the inside leg with the outside sideways driving leg, it is common for the horse to think we want a canter transition. The aids are a little bit similar, although slower here, and the rider needs to learn to balance the outside leg with the inside hand to avoid this confusion.

When starting to introduce the travers on the circle, it is best to start the travers just when leaving the track along the long side of the arena. The exercise should not be ridden with too much bend, otherwise the horse will fall onto the outside shoulder. As soon as you have shown the horse the bend, let him continue the movement on his own.

Decreasing and enlarging the circle are movements which make the horse flexible and which require balance of the aids. Decreasing the circle is done in travers, enlarging the circle is done through shoulder-in.

To decrease the circle the rider should, in travers position, ride gradually toward a volte around the center point of the circle. It requires three or four times around the circle to get to the volte. Be careful not to

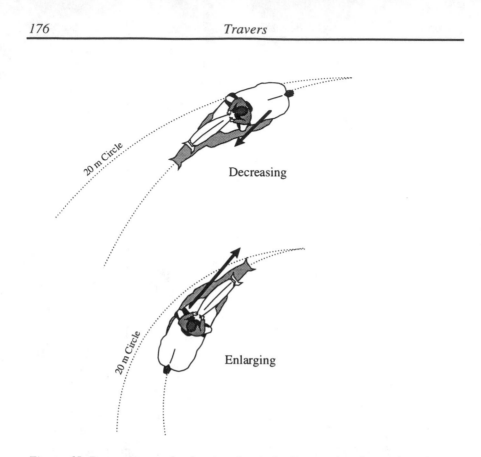

Figure 65. Decreasing and enlarging the circle. Decreasing the circle is done in travers, enlarging the circle is done through shoulder-in.

advance the haunches too much ahead of the forehand. The movement toward the volte is like the half pass; the forehand should lead very slightly.

The rider should sit well on the inside seat bone. The inside (left) leg is driving at the girth. The outside (right) leg is behind the girth and guarding. The horse is bent to the inside (left). The inside rein is actively used in an indirect way (turning the little finger to the opposite shoulder to give flexion and show direction) and then released slightly. The outside (right) rein contact is fairly steady and half halts are given on this side as the right hind leg of the horse moves forward. This keeps the right hind from falling out to the right and also stimulates the right hind to step over to the left by "crossing." The right rein half halts also determine the tempo.

When the volte is reached, the rider should put the horse on a single track and ride two to three times around the volte. Then the rider should develop shoulder-in position and enlarge the circle in three or four revolutions out to the 20 meter circle.

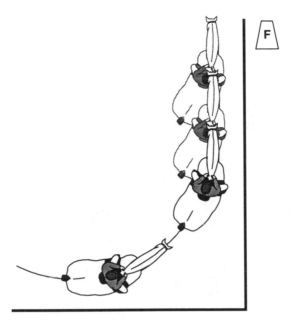

Figure 66. Starting travers along the long side.

12.7.2 Travers on the Long Side of the Arena

The travers along the long side of the arena is ridden essentially the same as that on the 20 meter circle. Here, the shoulders and neck remain aligned along the track, while the hind legs shift slightly to the inside. Be careful not to ride with too much outside right leg. The outside right leg is only the bending leg. To start, make use of the corner since it provides the necessary bend in the horse's body. Start the travers while the hind legs are still a little in the corner. (Using the corner to help start the travers points up how important it is to ride the corner correctly.) It is also helpful to ride the travers on the second track, away from the wall, so the horse is not leaning on the wall, and stays freer and more forward.

The volte can be used to correct or re-establish the bend, rhythm and relaxation. Make a volte in the corner, and when the hind legs are still on the volte, you start travers. If the rider becomes too anxious to start the travers from the volte, the hind legs can come in too much. When this happens, the power and swing are lost, so the movement becomes rough and unbalanced. When I was starting out, the old masters made clear that travers was a three track movement, in which the hind legs came in only slightly.

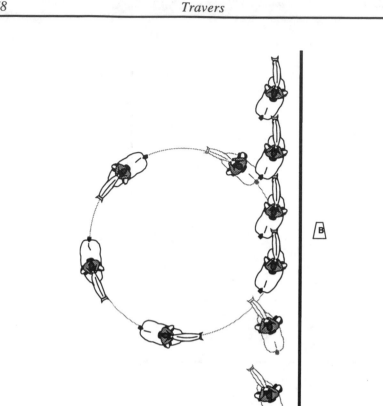

Figure 67. Shoulder-in-volte-travers.

Now there seems to be a desire to ride with larger angles and too much flexion of the neck. The gymnastic benefit of the exercise is achieved with a small angle, and it is easy to maintain a good forward, energetic movement with a smaller angle. As a proof of the training, larger angles can be used, but be careful not to lose the swing and power of the gait. Remember that movements such as travers are not ends in themselves, but means for training and developing the horse further. Only with swing, engagement and power can we make the horse light, balanced, collected and easy to ride.

A common fault is the horse leaning against the wall (or track) with his outside shoulder, because the rider drives too much with the inside leg. The inside hand doesn't give enough. The outside leg should drive the outside hind forward. The outside right hand gives half halts, and the inside hand should become softer. If the horse leaves the track, the rider should move both hands a little forward. The contact should not be lost, however. Both seat muscles and legs of the rider drive the horse forward. If the exercise is still too hard for the horse, the rider should make frequent voltes to improve the bend, rhythm and relaxation.

One should not ride travers for too long. Remember to straighten the horse at the last letter of the long side in order to ride correctly into the corner. Use your inside hip and seat bone with gentle flexion to the inside and give on the inside rein.

12.7.3 Shoulder-In-Volte-Travers

When the shoulder-in and travers are reasonably well understood by horse and rider, one can ride from shoulder-in to a volte and then progress in travers. This movement clearly establishes the bending through the shoulder-in and volte, and makes it easier for the horse and rider to understand that the travers has the same bending as the volte. Later on, one can ride from shoulder-in directly to travers. In this exercise, the direction of the bend through the horse's body remains the same while the degree of the bend increases slightly (from that of a 10 meter circle to that of a volte). In the shoulder-in, we ride the haunches straight down the track, then, increasing the bend slightly with the legs and hip, we bring the shoulders onto the track with the outside rein and leg and proceed in travers. For this exercise to go smoothly from one to the other, one must have a calm, quiet outside rein connection and a deep seat and legs.

12.7.4 Travers Entwickeln

As with shoulder-in, one can ride a travers *entwickeln*. In this movement, we start in travers at the start of the long side. This travers is ridden along a slight diagonal line leading into the arena, which brings the horse to the third track. When the haunches reach the third track, the horse is straightened to the haunches, and proceeds on a straight line diagonally back to the wall. When the head reaches the track, the travers is re-started, and the horse moves back to the third track in travers. As in shoulder-in, this exercise can be ridden on the centerline.

Many of my riders find travers *entwickeln* easier than shoulder-in *entwickeln*. If the lateral work is well in hand, the difficulty comes in stopping the straight travel. In shoulder-in, this movement is made away from the wall, so the rider must keep the horse from anticipating the full diagonal and get him back into the shoulder-in. In travers *entwickeln*, the forward riding is made toward the wall, which helps make the transition back to the lateral movement.

Of course, if the lateral work is not solid, it is always harder to make the travers away from the wall rather than making the shoulder-in back to the wall. The less experienced horse will seek the security of the making the shoulder-in *entwickeln* easier.

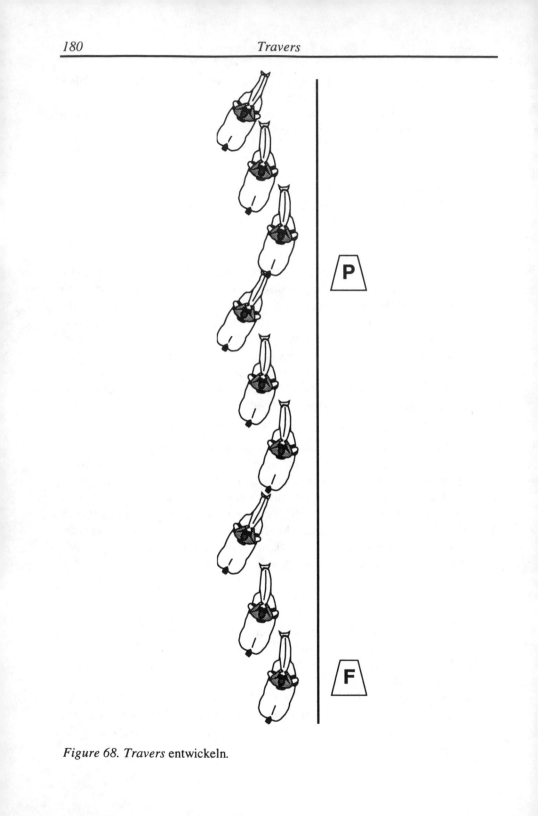

Figure 68. Travers entwickeln.

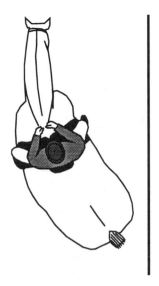

Figure 69. Renvers.

In travers *entwickeln,* do not confuse the travers along a slightly angled line into the arena with half pass. In half pass, the shoulders would lead slightly, while the haunches would remain parallel to the track. Here, the haunches are at a slight angle to the track, so when we straighten the horse to the haunches, we are automatically positioned along a line back to the track.

12.8 Renvers

Renvers (or haunches-out) is really nothing more than travers with the opposite bend. In renvers on the left rein, the horse's right hind leg is on the track, the horse is bent around the rider's right leg and the shoulders are moving on a straight line on the second track, parallel to the wall. The shoulders progress on a straight line down the arena, while the hind legs are taken to the outside. Think of an artificial wall along the third track of the arena. We ride the horse along this wall in travers right, executing a perfect renvers left!

There are technical differences between travers and renvers; in travers, the forelegs move along the track, while in renvers the haunches move along the track. A judge at C could tell whether a rider was doing travers or renvers on the centerline by looking at the path of the haunches. If they are on the centerline, the rider is executing renvers; if the forelegs are on the centerline, it is travers. These details are, as mentioned, technical.

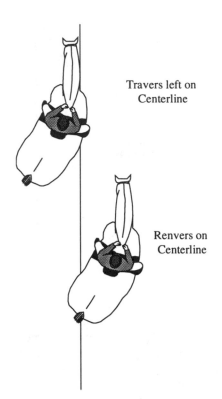

Travers left on
Centerline

Renvers on
Centerline

Figure 70. Travers and renvers on the centerline. Note the placement of the shoulders on the track in travers, the haunches on the track in renvers.

Functionally, renvers is more difficult than travers, and needs more skill. First, to start renvers, the rider must change the bend of the horse coming out of the corner. In travers, we made use of the bend of the corner to help the horse into travers, while in renvers we have no such assistance. In fact, one has to do more than change the bend. The shoulders must be brought in off the track, so that when the horse is bent through his body, there is space for the haunches to remain in the arena. In fact it is much easier for the horse when we ride renvers slightly in from the wall, with the haunches on the second track, and the shoulders brought more into the arena.

As we said above, to ride renvers when going on the left rein, the rider should think that the wall is on his left and there he rides travers right. The fact that the wall is actually on his right should be of no concern to the rider, but we will find that it is of concern to the horse. A horse that is quite willing to bring his haunches to the inside in travers may be more resistant to renvers, just because of the presence of the arena wall. This is another reason for riding renvers on the second track.

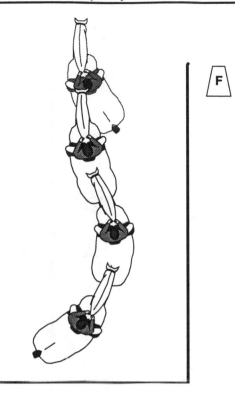

Figure 71. Starting renvers out of the corner. The horse must be ridden slightly off the track, then turned back onto the long side.

12.8.1　Travers, Renvers and Shoulder-In to Help Straighten the Horse

When a horse tends to move with his haunches to the left, the reason is that the shoulder falls out to the right. One always should correct the shoulder to the hindquarter, and although we have already discussed how the shoulder-in can be used to bring the shoulders over in front of the hind legs, I prefer using renvers to correct this problem. If the falling-out through the right shoulder is a persistent problem, it is because the horse's musculature is not symmetrically developed: the muscles on the right side are longer and those on the left side are shorter and tighter. By riding shoulder-in, we can bring the shoulders over, but the bending left remains, and we will not change the horse's fundamental development. By riding in renvers when going on the left rein and travers when going on the right, we will be loosening the muscles on the left side and firming up those on the right. This is not a correction which the horse "learns," nor is it one that is done quickly, but rather a basic alteration of the strength and suppleness into which the horse must grow.

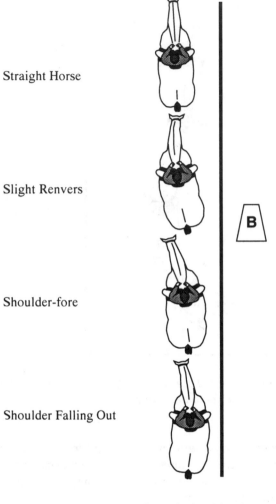

Straight Horse

Slight Renvers

Shoulder-fore

Shoulder Falling Out

Figure 72. Straightening the horse through shoulder-fore and renvers.

12.8.2 Renvers Entwickeln

In renvers *entwickeln*, it is easier to start on the right rein, because bending to the left is easier for most horses. Ride the horse out of the corner onto the diagonal. Before arriving at the third track, bend the horse to the left, and proceed in renvers right (like travers left) along a shallow line back to the track. When the left hind leg lands on the track, straighten the horse to the haunches, and proceed again straight on a diagonal line. The movement is similar to shoulder-in *entwickeln*, but with the opposite bend, and nearly identical to travers *entwickeln* ridden on the opposite side of the arena. Renvers *entwickeln* can be ridden in walk, trot, and counter canter.

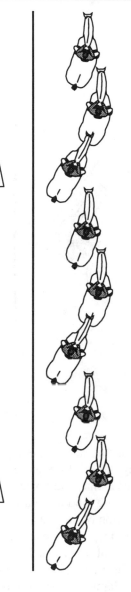

Figure 73. Renvers entwickeln

In renvers *entwickeln,* a common fault is for riders to allow their horses' shoulders to fall too quickly back to the wall, rather than proceeding with bend through the body and the haunches kept parallel to a diagonal line. It is especially important that the horse goes willingly in renvers along the long side before starting the renvers *entwickeln.*

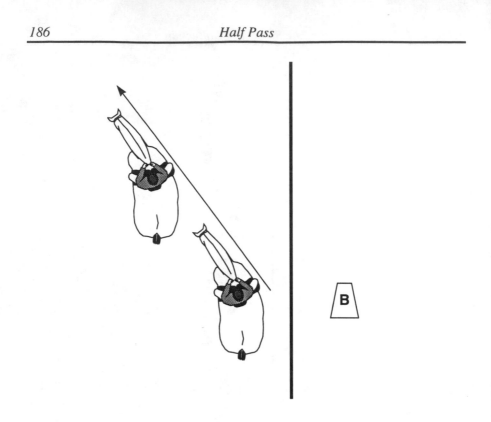

Figure 74. Half pass.

12.9 Half Pass

The half pass is a lateral, collecting movement which is characterized by a crossing of both fore and hind legs as the horse proceeds in a diagonal line across the arena. The horse is bent through his body in the direction of travel, so the inside hind leg must come well under the center of gravity of the horse. The action of half pass is very similar to that of travers, with the exception that at steeper angles, both the forelegs and hind legs cross. When introducing the half pass, it is best to make very shallow angles, in which case the half pass is essentially the same as a travers ridden along a diagonal line. The horse familiar with travers should have no trouble performing a gradual half pass, especially when ridden from a half volte and then back to the track. In such a movement, the hind legs cross while the neck and shoulders proceed along the diagonal line. At steeper angles, as required in Intermediaire and Grand Prix, the forelegs as well as the hind legs cross.

The gymnastic value of the half pass comes from the weight which must be "caught" and then carried by the inside hind leg. As the horse moves to the left, for instance, the left hind leg must reach out slightly and receive the weight of the torso coming over to the left. The right hind leg

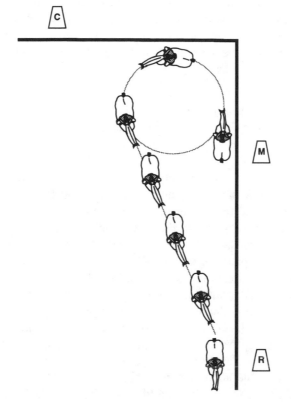

Figure 75. Half volte and half pass.

crosses under, but when it carries the weight, the torso is moving over and away from the foot. The steeper the angle, the stronger the inside hind leg must be. When the angle is shallow, the shoulders can proceed almost straight along the line of travel, but at steep angles, the lateral weight carrying must be taken up by the forelegs too.

It is very important that the half pass be ridden as a forward-sideways movement, with emphasis on forward. Be sure that the forehand goes slightly in front of the hindquarters.

12.9.1 Half Volte and Half Pass

We introduce half pass through the half volte and then half pass back to the track. This keeps the angle shallow, and brings the horse naturally back to the track, where he is most comfortable. Make the half volte with good bending. The aids are then the same as in travers. Sit into the motion, with the inside hip forward. Drive with the inside leg forward and sideways into the half pass toward the track. The outside leg of the rider is behind the girth helping to bend the horse and helping to drive him sideways. The outside rein gives half halts and is kept well against the horse's neck near the base. The horse should be gently flexed to the inside and made to go energetically forward. The forehand must lead slightly. Finish in a little renvers before you get back to the track. Otherwise the horse usually straightens himself out too soon.

12.9.2 Half Pass from the Long Side

When the half pass from the volte is familiar, we can make turns of 10, then 15 or 20 meters before making the half pass. Starting half passes from the corners (as from M to X or F to E , etc.) is the most difficult, because the horse is more familiar with staying along the track or going straight on the diagonal. If riding a half pass from H to F on the left rein, picture a wall connecting H and F on your right hand side. Now ride travers along this imaginary wall. On the next long side, ride forward on a single track to regain impulsion. But do not hurry. On the right rein if riding a half pass from M to K, picture a wall on this line to your left hand side. Now ride travers right on this imaginary wall from M to K.

Regardless of whether the half pass is started out of a volte or from the centerline or from the long side, the rider would do well to think first of riding a little shoulder-in—more thinking than riding—and then ride the half pass. This first step of shoulder-in should also be the first step of the half pass. When riding from the corner, use the quarter volte of the corner to bend and engage the horse. As in starting the shoulder-in, stay on this volte for an extra step, bringing the shoulders in off the track. With the shoulders slightly in front, the half pass is initiated.

It is important that we keep close attention to the *forward*-sideways tendency. If making a greater angle causes a loss of forward movement, return to the easier angle. Making a half pass from the track to the centerline offers a good challenge, while allowing one to keep a shallow, easier angle. This is good to confirm the movement and obedience while not over-stressing the horse.

If the hindquarters won't go sufficiently sideways in the half pass, do not drive harder! Most riders are already driving enough. My suggestion to riders is to bring the horse's shoulders opposite to the direction of the half pass. For instance, in a half pass right in which the haunches are trailing somewhat, the rider should bring the shoulders a little to the left. The problem is not insufficient forward driving but rather that the horse's shoulders have started falling in the direction of the movement, getting farther and farther ahead of the haunches, and the horse has lost the bend to the right. Thus the "haunches are trailing." This correction applies for half pass in trot and canter. Some horses have one side which is more difficult, and the haunches routinely lag behind. One should not ride shoulder-in first in this direction, but ride half pass immediately out of the corner.

Do not bend the horse too much in the half pass. This makes the movement very difficult for the horse. By riding a volte in the corner, you establish the proper bend. Keep this amount of bending through the half pass, by showing the horse what you want and letting him do it. Do not use overly strong and active aids, "overaiding."

Half pass is a collected movement, and you will need good engagement before starting it. Only with swinging hind legs is it possible to do collected work. After the half pass, the rider should not forget to ride forward again.

12.9.3 Half Pass – Straight and Repeat

A good exercise to confirm the coordination of the aids and the willingness of the horse is to ride half pass to the quarter line, then proceed straight for 10 meters or so, then half pass to the centerline, then straight, and so on. This can be done at trot and canter. It makes the horse well suppled, and gives him confidence. It is a close relative of the shoulder-in, travers and renvers *entwickeln*, and should be ridden with the same attitude of calmness, balance, swing, and communication between horse and rider.

For the rider, this exercise confirms that the aids are well balanced, and that he can easily straighten and bend the horse. Often riders pull the horse into the half pass with the inside rein. Such riders find this movement very difficult because they lack the steadying control of the outside rein which is needed to straighten the horse. In the correctly ridden half pass, the rider should use the inside rein to *show* the horse where to go, but then immediately give the inside rein to *allow* the horse to go. When the concept of half pass-straight-half pass is familiar, we can insert lengthening in the straight sections, followed by collecting and half pass. Again straight and lengthen, and so on.

The ability to perform this movement while keeping the horse in self-carriage, absolutely obedient, with fine elevation and good forward, swinging movement is a prerequisite to proceeding to change of hand or zigzag.

As with all exercises, we start with the side which is easier for the horse. Once the idea is understood by the horse, we can begin the other direction and continue to develop evenness in both directions. At the trot, it is then a relatively simple matter to do something like half pass left, then straight, then half pass right, then straight, etc. Use the straight sections to lightly re-position the horse for the new half pass. Later, the straight sections are reduced to produce the counter change of hand or zigzag.

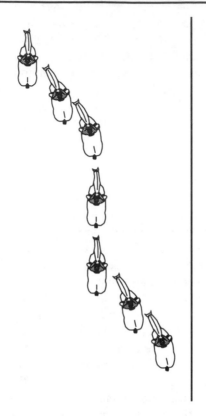

Figure 76. A good exercise is to ride half pass, then straighten, then return to half pass.

12.9.4 Counter Change of Hand at Trot

One of the most difficult movements is a counter change of hand ridden from F to X to M. Using the bending from the corner, ride a half pass left from F to X, again thinking of an imaginary wall along your right side. Arrive at the centerline a half-length before X, then straighten and re-bend to the right and start a new half pass to the right, again thinking of a wall on your left side from X to M. At M, be sure the horse does not straighten himself. It is better to ride a step or two of renvers at M. At the centerline you can think of a very slight renvers left just before re-bending and heading off in the new half pass.

This movement can also be ridden from F to E to M, as in the Grand Prix. This is very difficult because of the strong angle. If the rider gets too tight in the reins in order to make this steep angle, the horse can not be light and ready to respond when arriving at E. Again, it is a big help to think of a wall along the outside of the path.

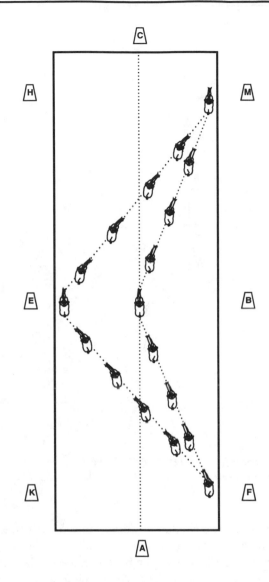

Figure 77. Counter change of hand.

12.9.5 *Zigzag at Trot*

To prepare the zigzag, ride half pass left from the centerline to the quarter line, then straight, then half pass right back to the centerline, as mentioned above. Then make the straight sections shorter and shorter until they are only a step. Only when this is 100% sure can we proceed to the zigzag.

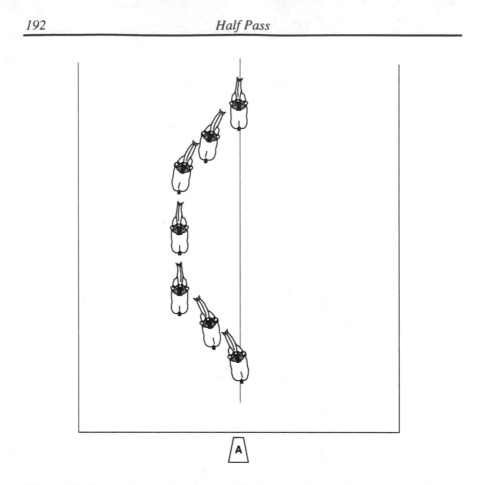

Figure 78. Preparing for the zigzag. Ride from the centerline to quarter line in half pass, then proceed straight. Follow by half pass from quarter line to centerline.

The first zigzags should be ridden only 5 meters each side of the centerline. From A ride half pass left for 5 meters, change direction, then ride half pass right for 10 meters, then back to half pass left 5 meters to C.

What is very important is that the swinging hind leg not get lost. Nothing is worse than this movement being ridden in a shuffling trot. If these easy angles are going very well, we can put more in (5 left-10 right-10 left-5 right, etc.). It is also important that the horse is not taking over and trying to make the exercise by himself. He must wait for our aids, and then we let him do it. It seems that this movement brings out riders' tendencies to use force and excessive aids. The apparent rush to change the bend and start off in the new half pass, combined with a desire to divide the arena up into equal sections easily leads to trying too hard. Riding this movement with force brings us nothing, on the contrary, the horse gets more and more frightened. This is a movement for which the horse must have understanding and careful preparation. Even when all the pieces are well-confirmed, an added difficulty comes in maintaining forward swinging movement throughout. This can only be done when the horse carries himself, is easily bent, and floats through the half pass. Every change of direction brings a potential loss of impulsion, swing and confidence.

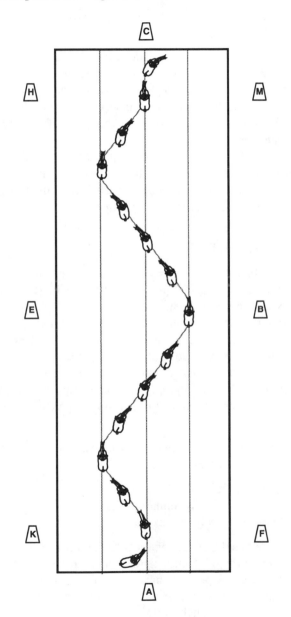

Figure 79. Zigzag at the trot.

Chapter 13
The Full Bridle

The full or double bridle was developed for the needs of the cavalry, where one occasionally needed a stronger controlling bit, but where the softer snaffle bit could be used most of the time. There is no doubt that it is more severe and controlling than the snaffle alone, but in the sport and art of dressage, its function must be elevated to the point of conveying extremely fine and delicate aids.

All Grand Prix movements should be able to be ridden in the snaffle bit. One sometimes hears of horses who are "curb-bit horses," who need to go in the double bridle. These are horses for which some great short-cut has been taken, and who have a fundamental mistake built in to their training—perhaps from the earliest handling.

13.1 Action of the Full Bridle

The full bridle permits the rider to ride with just the action of the snaffle (bridoon) or to bring into play the curb bit. The curb bit is a leverage bit which acts in two ways. First, when the angle of the shank increases in relation to the horse's jaw, the curb chain tightens, and the pressure of the bit on the tongue increases. The pressure of the curb bit can be **ten times** that of the simple snaffle. By having long shanks, this pressure is greatly increased over the pull on the reins. Shorter shanks lessen the pressure, but are still much stronger than the snaffle. The second action of the curb bit comes through the port, which can press up against the palate as the angle of the shank is changed.

Curb bits are available with a wide variety of diameters and port sizes. The most common are

1. A low port with relatively large diameter
2. A medium port, slightly thinner in diameter
3. A high port, relatively thin in diameter.

These are listed from the gentlest to the most strong. The situation is complicated by an array of shank lengths which are available, but again, one usually finds that the low port bits have shorter shanks, while the higher port has longer shanks. I always prefer only the gentlest, low port curb bit, with short shanks, since it is much softer for the horse. If the horse gets his tongue over the bit, it is sometimes helpful to have a slightly higher port, but it is better to not let it come to this.

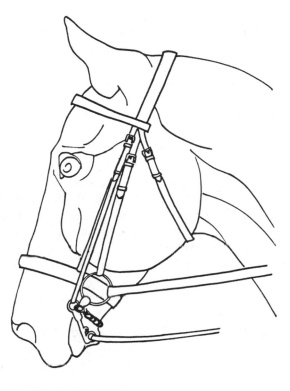

Figure 80. The full or double bridle.

13.2 Adjustment

First, the bridle should fit properly. The width of the horse's mouth and head have to be taken into account. The cheekpieces of the headstall should be buckled evenly on both sides and the browband must not press against the horse's head because of being too small, nor should it cause the headstall to cut into the back of the horse's ears. The throatlatch should be buckled so that a vertically held hand fits between it and the jaw. The cavesson should be one or two finger's width below the corner of the cheek bone. Sores can develop from the top of the curb bit and its cheekpiece rubbing against the cavesson. It is advisable to put Vaseline around the area of the cavesson and corner of the mouth before rubbing happens.

The curb bit should be wide. The mouthpiece should extend one half centimeter outside each side of the horse's mouth. The snaffle or bridoon should rest in the corners of the horse's mouth without pulling upward against the skin. It should lie in the horse's mouth approximately above the curb chain groove of the horse's chin and not pinch against the curb chain hook. The bit can be raised somewhat on horses who tend to overflex or who take the tongue over the bit.

The curb chain should lie properly under the horse's chin without pulling against the hooks, nor be so loose that the chain hangs too low. If the curb chain is fitted incorrectly, it might hurt the horse and cause tongue problems. The curb chain should be attached on the right side of the bridle and twisted to the right so that it lies flat and smooth against the skin. It should be adjusted so that the curb chain takes effect when there is a 45° angle between the shanks and the horse's jaw when the curb rein is tightened. If adjusted too tight, the horse never gets to escape the pressure of the chain, and if too loose, the port can rotate too high in the horse's mouth and create too severe an action on the horse's palate—this is less of a problem with low ported mouthpieces, but must be watched very carefully with high ports. When introducing the full bridle (to horse *or* rider), I use a low port and allow the chain to be adjusted somewhat looser than normal.

The curb chain hooks require attention in that the open part of the hook should be pointed forward and slightly away from the horse's mouth. These hooks are often installed incorrectly at the factory and need to be switched to point forward (I almost never see hooks installed properly). The points can be bent by using two pliers. If this is not corrected, there is a danger of injuring the horse.

Also, the loops at the top of the curb bit should be slightly deflected to the outside to prevent rubbing against the edges of the horse's mouth. Rubbing and chaffing is exacerbated by not having the bits very clean and smooth.

When choosing the bridoon, select a diameter that is not so thick that there is too much metal in the horse's mouth, and yet avoid such a thin bridoon that it acts like a wire. Remember that most of the time, the full bridle is used as a simple snaffle, and the size of the bridoon should not be greatly different from the horse's normal snaffle.

13.3 Holding the Reins

The normal way to hold the two reins of the full bridle is to have the snaffle or bridoon rein around the little finger and the curb rein between the little and ring fingers. This is the easiest for the rider and softest for the horse. The thumb presses down on the snaffle rein only. The curb rein lies freely inside the hand, pushed away a bit from the snaffle rein.

One often sees the curb rein become too tight. In fact, the rider seldom *tries* to make the curb tight, but rather allows the snaffle to slip through the fingers. One never sees the opposite, where the snaffle becomes tight and the curb slips through the fingers. This is easy to understand when we consider that the horse will tend to give light tugs or press against the reins. If the snaffle is shorter (as it should be), the tug of the mouth comes against the snaffle rein, not against the curb. But each tug can lead to a little slipping of the rein in the hand until both snaffle and curb are the same length—now the curb has become too tight! The rider must keep the snaffle

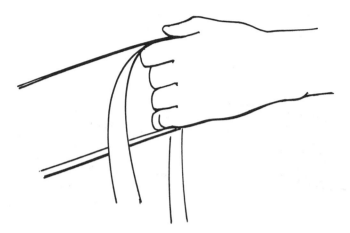

Figure 81. In the Fillis style, the snaffle rein is held over the forefinger. This makes the slightest rotation of the wrist affect the curb.

held well between the thumb and forefinger, and must continually be aware of any slippage to keep the curb rein from tightening.

Otto Lörke and Willi Schulthcis rode in the Fillis style, where the snaffle rein was held over the forefinger, and the curb bit was held under the little finger. Such a style can only be left to masters such as those two. It provides a great separation between the action of the snaffle and curb, but makes the slightest rotation of the wrist affect the curb. The years of learning in a snaffle, where the lower part of the hand connects with the horse's mouth are too likely to come back to the rider, who ends up riding on the curb rein only.

In the cavalry, the technique of riding with all four reins in one hand was developed. This left the right hand free for saber or lance. It also led to the "three-and-one" technique, where the left snaffle and both curb reins are held in the left hand and the right snaffle is held in the right hand. By simply transferring the right snaffle rein to the left hand, one can quickly ride with the right hand free. In this position, the left snaffle lies under the little finger. The left curb rein lies between the little finger and ring finger, the right curb lies between the ring and second fingers. The right snaffle rein is held between the forefinger and second finger. When held in this way, it is a simple matter to cross the right hand over the back of the left and pick up the two right reins into their correct positions on the right hand. Holding the reins in one hand is an interesting test of the horse and rider's communication and softness.

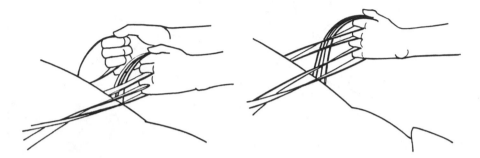

Figure 82. Holding all four reins in one hand, and the "three-and-one" technique.

13.4 Introducing the Full Bridle

I am often asked, "When is the right time to begin riding my horse in the full bridle?" First, it depends on the development of the seat and aids of the rider. The rider must sit correctly and be harmonious and effective with the aids. His balance must be completely independent of his hands. The horse must be easy to turn, easy to slow down and halt, and must go in correct collection in all three gaits. In other words, the horse must already work harmoniously and without force on the bit in the snaffle. He must be completely through in the aids, which means he must be fully suppled, and the driving aids and collecting aids should be easy in the snaffle. He must be straight and even on both sides in the hand.

I do not want to discourage riders from learning the correct use of the full bridle, but few are advanced enough to do so. A rider should not make the mistake of thinking that the horse can be made to go on the bit better through the use of the full bridle. This is a very bad mistake—and too common.

Extreme care must be taken the first time the horse is ridden in the full bridle. Choose a curb bit which is thick and which has a low port and short shanks. It is good to keep the curb chain fairly loose to give the horse a than the horse may be used to. Long straight lines and large figures should be ridden rather than small, tight turns. Sudden turns should be avoided so that the bits are not strongly used.

After a few weeks the horse should become accustomed to the full bridle and is stretching willingly into both bits. Then the curb chain can be tightened to the correct fit. Ten meter circles and voltes can be attempted now. When riding turns and circles, the outside curb rein needs to be softened since the curb bit is not jointed. On circles, we accept more contact in the outside snaffle rein, but we don't want to engage the curb bit, so the ring finger must open slightly to soften the curb.

When the horse accepts the large figures and stretches willingly, we can introduce the collecting exercises, shoulder-in, travers, renvers, half pass, etc. The rider should take care not to ride too much with the hand. He should not hurry to ride the difficult exercises with the full bridle, because if mistakes are made, it will take much time to correct them. He should concentrate on riding forward into a soft rein contact. "Ride your horse forward and make him straight" is again the best advice. *Überstreichen* or a stroke of the neck should be made frequently so the horse shows us if he is in balance.

When the horse becomes used to the curb bit, we should go again back to the snaffle and ride only once or twice a week—mostly to keep the rider in practice, and a little to keep the horse confident and familiar with the full bridle.

Chapter 14

Flying Changes and Canter Pirouettes

14.1 Flying Changes

Because the canter is an asymmetric gait, it is more comfortable and easier for the horse to balance on the right lead when going to the right and on the left lead when going to the left. In order to change the direction of a figure, young horses are brought back to the trot or walk and the new lead is obtained by asking for a new canter depart on the desired lead. More advanced horses can be taught to change the lead without interruption of the canter. This change is termed the flying change.

The flying change is accomplished by altering the sequence of footfalls during the moment of suspension. When changing from the right lead to the left, the left hind leg initiates the last stride of right canter. During the moment of suspension the horse re-organizes his legs so the right hind leg returns to the ground early and initiates the first stride of left canter. Similarly the right foreleg returns to the ground early. The left legs must continue swinging through the air longer than normal.

14.2 Preparing for Flying Changes

I am often asked "when can I start teaching my horse flying changes?" To begin with, the horse must canter with good impulsion and clear rhythm. The canter should be very active and have a jumping quality that allows the moment of suspension to be as long as possible. The horse must be confirmed in canter departs to both right and left from the slightest aids. The counter canter must be sure in both directions—in other words, the horse has to be absolutely straight and even in the canter. The rider must be able to ride 10 meter counter canter circles, serpentines, and left and right turns in counter canter and true canter with the horse remaining relaxed and free of tension. Finally, the horse and rider must be able to lengthen and shorten the strides easily and willingly without any resistance.

Without good suspension, the horse lacks the time in the air to re-organize the footfalls. A horse that needs to be bent in one direction or the other in order to obtain the correct lead is not ready to start flying changes. There is no time within the moment of suspension to re-bend the horse from one side to the other. Finally, since there is so little time to give the aids and get the response, the horse must be sensitive to the slightest aids of hip, legs, and hand.

While it is possible to teach both rider and horse the flying changes together, this requires a highly talented rider, horse and instructor. The best way for the rider to learn flying changes is on a schoolmaster that is already confident and happy doing changes. Just as horses make more progress when the rider knows the movement and has a feeling for the correct aids in the right moment, the riding student learns faster if the horse knows the movement and can give the rider the proper feeling even in the presence of clumsy or ill-timed aids.

Regardless of the training level of the horse, the inexperienced rider should first master the ability to start easily and effortlessly, first left, then right, then left canter with only a few canter strides between simple changes. In other words, the rider should be able to canter four strides of left canter, do a simple change, canter four strides of right canter, then simple change, and so on. Then they should be able to do this with three strides, and finally, two strides between simple changes. The aids for the simple changes should become second nature for horse and rider, with the walk steps correct and the horse remaining quiet.

These exercises confirm that the horse is ready to respond to the finest of aids, and that the rider is balanced and precise in the canter aids and half halts. The main objective here has to be to make the simple changes light and without effort. Short-cuts through rough aids will not help the horse to learn to count or in any other way help the overall goal, and will instill fear and lead to a lack of balance. Extra time spent on these movements to make them balanced and relaxed will be rewarded several times over when we address flying changes.

It sometimes happens that a young horse will volunteer a flying change by himself, when the rider is not asking for one. It is important at this point not to punish or correct the horse, since these are often the best changes. Afterwards, the rider should be watchful to indicate that the horse is to remain on the proper lead, but now is not the time to make the horse feel bad about having performed what we will ask in the future.

14.3 Aids for the Flying Change

We will now discuss the proper aids for the flying change. Unfortunately, the flying change requires at least six separate steps which must be done almost as one!

1. New light bending, flexion and giving;
2. Inside hip forward;
3. Outside shoulder a bit back;
4. Light half halt on the new outside;
5. New inside leg comes forward;
6. Outside leg goes back.

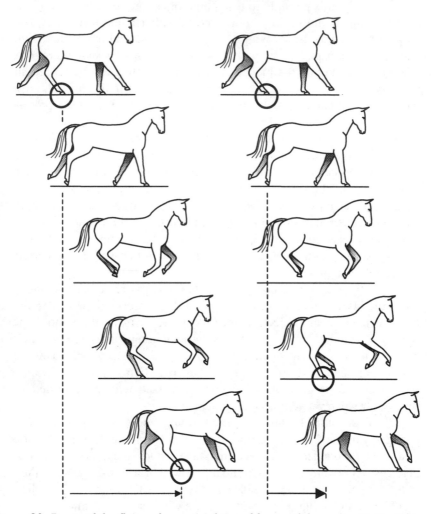

Figure 83. Beats of the flying change (right) and beats of the canter (left). Note how the right hind leg, which is just leaving the ground in row 2 is back on the ground in row 4 in the change, but does not return until row 5 in the true canter. Note also how much longer the left legs remain in the air in the flying change.

We can only discuss them one at a time, but in the final execution, they come almost to a single coordinated movement of seat, leg, hand, and shoulders.

In the right lead canter the rider should first emphasize the aids for that lead: right seat bone deep and pushing, left leg slightly back and well closed, right leg on the girth, closed and driving. In this movement, the body of the rider must remain quiet, and the aids must not be given in a rough and surprising manner. To make a change from right to left lead, the rider changes slightly the flexion to the left, sits well to the new inside (left) and simultaneously asks for the change: the rider pushes his left hip deep and well forward, stretches the left leg long and moves it slightly forward and with a deep heel, the right leg glides back, without leaving the horse's body, the right shoulder moves back slightly, giving a slight half halt on the new outside (right) rein. Never jerk the shoulder back nor swing the upper body left and right. To emphasize the aids, the rider may use the whip by using it in conjunction with the right leg when asking the horse to change from right to left. (In no case can we use the whip with sensitive horses, who would over-react. The whip can help with horses who are a bit more insensitive).

To understand the sequence of aids for the flying change, recall that the new outside legs return to the ground slightly early and the new inside legs must swing longer. In going from right to left, the rider has been progressing with a soft inside (right) rein, and good contact on the outside (left) rein. In order to shorten the new outside (right), the rider must change the flexion to the left and give a right half halt. Almost simultaneously, the rider must make room for the left shoulder and hind leg to swing through by giving with the left (new inside) rein—but don't throw the rein away.

The difficulty for the rider is in the rapid sequence which must occur. The aids should start between the second and third beat of the last left lead canter stride. This is just after the diagonal pair of legs has landed, just prior to the left front leg landing. In order to make the right half halt, the rider has to establish a firmer contact in the right rein. This is the step of changing the flexion. It involves a slight suppling with the left rein and leg. The horse must respond quickly and effortlessly to the half halt on the new outside (with *Durchlässig*). As soon as the right half halt is made, the left hand must give to allow the inside to swing through.

Often, riders starting to learn the flying change concentrate too much on changing the flexion that they pull or hold the new inside rein, or even try to give a half halt on the new inside. This does not look good, confuses the horse, and is counter-productive, since it pulls the new inside legs back to the ground just when they need to swing free, and the horse is afraid (or even unable) to jump through on this side.

This is also related to the problem of over-flexing or bending the horse between changes. The more the horse is bent to one side or the other, the more difficult it is to change the rein contact without pulling on the new inside rein. During the tempi changes, we will again see the need for maintaining straightness, where we can not spend several strides trying to bring a crooked canter into straightness before making a change.

The horse is only ready for the flying changes when he is straight and evenly balanced in the canter. By this I mean that the rider can maintain an even contact in both reins when cantering on both leads. This shows again how important it is to follow the precept "ride your horse calm, forward and straight."

The flying change requires far more than rein aids, however. The hip (weight aids) and leg are required almost simultaneously. The rider's old outside (left) hip has been back slightly. Immediately following the right half halt, the left hip and shoulder come forward. This automatically brings the inside hand forward to soften the new inside rein and allows the new inside shoulder (and foreleg) to swing. On the (new) outside, the rider's shoulder, hip and leg move slightly back.

In the canter, the inside leg at the girth activates the inside hind leg and encourages it to swing forward. Therefore, in the flying change from right to left, the right leg has been at the girth, engaging the right hind leg. To make the change, the left leg comes forward to the driving position to activate the new inside (left) hind leg while the rider's right leg comes off the driving position, sliding back to the holding and sideways-driving position and is now the new outside leg.

Of course the technical details of the mechanics of the aids are indispensable but incomplete. The final consideration is the timing—as we have always been taught: "the right aids at the right moment!" The process of making the flying change from right to left begins when the new inside (left) hind leg comes off the ground. This leg must remain in the air far longer than the right. To encourage the increased flexion and swing of the left hind, the rider drives with the left leg just as the horse's left hind is leaving the ground. This is the same moment when the diagonal pair is on the ground in the last stride of the old lead, and the right front leg is just landing.

The aids for the flying change should be almost invisible. The more one sees the aids, the less the horse and rider are in harmony. The horse and rider need to be focused and concentrating on a very good canter, with the aids crisp and precise. The horse is then waiting for every signal, and the rider can then ask for the change smoothly, without having to resort to contortions and flailing around. These are always counterproductive and confusing to the horse.

One often sees the rider giving the wrong aids for the flying change by looking to the left when asking for the change from right to left. This results in putting the right shoulder and hip forward instead of the left, and because of collapsing the left hip, the rider's weight is pushed to the right. The horse will try to continue the right lead canter even when he feels the rider bouncing around on his back.

It is hard for trainers and instructors when they have riders that have not been able to practice flying changes on a trained horse. It is a very great help to students to ride changes on a well-trained horse so they can feel what the changes are really like.

14.4 Introducing Flying Changes to the Green Horse

While some movements can be introduced to a young horse before they are truly ready, flying changes should not be attempted until the prerequisites are truly established. Horses that are not ready will start to jump late, or run away or jump to the side or almost come to a stop and then jump into the new canter. The horse will tend to jump against the rider's hands and learn discomfort and fear of the changes.

We begin asking for the change to the side that is the easiest for the horse. Usually this is from right to left. This is also usually the easier side for the right-handed rider, who is stronger in the right leg. Remember that most young horses learn to canter to the left more easily.

As always there is more than one way to approach this lesson. I have always prepared the horses for flying changes by asking for the following exercise: walk, right lead canter, walk, left lead canter, walk, right lead canter, and so forth. Here, it is very important to take patience with the horse and be sure that the aids for these transitions are quiet and precise. Only when the horse responds softly to these almost invisible aids is he ready for flying changes.

After riding across the short side of the arena on the right rein, I ride a very shallow serpentine along the long side of the arena to the quarter line. Arriving at the height of the loop (approximately 5 meters from the track) on the half school (E-B) line, the preparation begins. Starting to lead the horse back to the track becomes the first moment of the flying change. I have then the opportunity to ride back to the wall before the first corner of the short side. The horse's natural desire to return to the track helps in teaching the change at this point.

It is very important that the rider not overdo the aids. This is often the reason that the horse will become strong and rush away after the change. Therefore, the rider must be very careful not to override the horse. One sees this very often: the rider throws his upper body around, legs flapping backward. Everything is badly exaggerated! As usual, less is better.

It is important to continue the canter after the flying change, so the horse understands he is not to quit after a change but is to continue cantering, waiting for the rider's aids to ask for a transition. Continue riding the short side in counter canter. After the second corner the rider should ask for a transition to the walk, praising the horse and letting him rest on a long rein for a while. If the horse stays calm, the rider may repeat the flying change exercise every other day. It can be done the next day if the horse is very good and calm on the aids. Also, one can repeat the exercise with the same pattern but on the other rein. If the horse learned from right lead to left on the right rein, the rider asks for the change from right to left but now on the left rein.

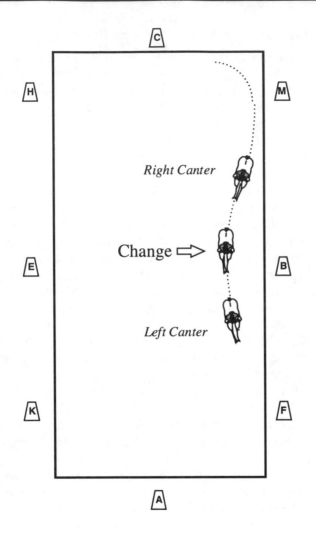

Figure 84. Introducing the flying change. It is usually easier to start from right to left rein.

Ultimately, the quality of the canter after the flying change should be as good as before the change with the horse jumping well off the ground with elasticity, staying forward and maintaining engagement. However, it is natural to lose some of the quality of the canter in the beginning when the horse learns the flying change. Few of them will be perfect at first; the horse may become stiff, tense and crooked. But, the rider should stop the flying change exercise immediately if the horse becomes afraid and rushes away. This is a sign that he is not yet ready for flying changes.

To refine the exercise just mentioned, the rider can do the following: ride a slight half pass from the beginning of the long side toward the centerline, straighten the horse, change the bend, ask for the change and half pass back to the long side. The horse instinctively wants to return due to his sense of security near the rail. This is also a very good correction for horses that come a little late with one or the other hind leg.

As soon as the horse can do this exercise of half pass, flying change, and half pass back to the rail quietly and reliably, the rider can try to ride across the diagonal with a flying change. I would advise the rider not to ask for the flying change at X. It is better to wait until shortly before the end of the diagonal. There, change the bend and give the aids for a flying change. It is best to ask for the change before reaching the rail, so the horse cannot run and lean away from the wall after the change. Instinctively, the horse will not rush away before the change since he is approaching the wall.

Again, we can do this exercise in both directions, beginning with his easier side and then the more difficult one. When the horse can do all these exercises in the flying changes calmly and correctly, we can begin with the series of tempi changes. Developing and confirming these single changes should take several months.

Many riders practice flying changes from one circle to another. I find this very difficult for the horse to do. The horse is positioned strongly to one side and when changing from one circle to the other, has a tendency to fall into the new lead and drift to the inside. Or the rider throws the horse from one side to the other. Of course, the poor horse can't perform a nice flying change in this manner. The same problem occurs when the rider asks for flying changes while riding a figure eight with a change in the center of the eight.

If a horse has difficulty understanding and performing flying changes, the following exercise over a low jump may help: set a low jump in the middle of the arena. Ride him a few times over the jump in a straight line, and then begin to approach the jump on a more diagonal line. Finally, coming from the right, approach the jump from a very flat curve. The rider's left leg should be well on the horse during the approach. During the jump, bring the right leg back (now the new outside leg), and change to the left, making a figure eight. It is easier for the horse to change over the jump, because he has a longer period of suspension during the jump.

If the horse is not used to small jumps, it is important to introduce the exercise with a pole laying on the ground. Remember that the aim is to keep the horse calm and on the aids, and not frightened and confused by the flying change. If the horse is frightened and confused by the jump, you can never expect to benefit from this exercise! This also means that the jump should be small enough so that the rider and horse have no difficulty staying together and in balance with the motion.

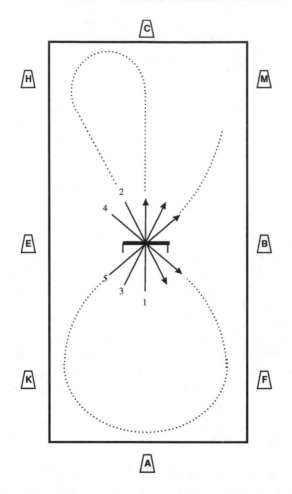

Figure 85. Using a low jump in the center of the arena for introducing flying changes. The steeper angle helps the horse with the flying change more than the shallow angles.

The rider can repeat this exercise frequently, but at the beginning he should be careful not to approach the jump too much from the side, or the horse may run out. It is important to use a strong driving outside leg, so the horse will feel the difference in the positioning of the leg. This exercise is specially good for jump riders so that they learn to make turns with the outside leg, allowing the horse to stay in better balance and keep the hind leg under—not letting the outside hind leg swing out.

Here is another, easy exercise for the flying change. On the short side of the arena, the rider and horse in the right lead canter slightly past the centerline. Then turn and ride a shallow serpentine up the centerline, staying close to the centerline (three meters on either side), and keeping a shallow bend, e.g., the bend of a half volte would be too much. The rider should change the bend and ask for the flying change each time he crosses the centerline. Don't forget that the canter must always be light and with impulsive and energetically forward (at the right tempo for that horse).

Let's go over the aids for flying changes for serpentine on the centerline.

The horse is in the right lead canter as he starts the flat serpentine up the centerline. Take care not to make the loops too deep. The horse should be well positioned to the right. The rider's right leg is well on the horse's side to engage the horse's right hind leg. The rider's left leg (outside) now becomes more active, placed well behind the girth. The rider's right hip is moving well into the movement like riding a half pass to the right. Shortly before arriving on the centerline, the rider positions his horse slightly to the new inside (left) after straightening the horse for a brief moment. All this must happen quickly but not so as to hurry the horse. As soon as the horse has the new position to the left, the rider pushes his left seat bone (hip) deep and forward and in the same moment the outside leg (right) glides back along the horse's body. The new inside leg (left) moves ever so slightly forward. The rider has almost nothing to do consciously with the left hand except release pressure, because the hand will automatically move slightly forward when we move our hip forward. This applies only if the hands were placed correctly parallel to each other from the beginning. The right hand gives a light half halt to stop the floating of the right leg.

The most important aid is moving the inside seat bone (hip) well forward. In other words, if the rider thinks about riding a half pass with his hips, then he will give the correct aid and make it easy for the horse.

When the horse has done the flying change well, then the rider should continue cantering on the left lead. The aids given for the change will stay the same but become even more assertive. The outside leg still stays stronger so that the horse gets to recognize the new inside leg more clearly.

When approaching the centerline, again position the horse slightly to the right. Just before the inside (left) front leg lands, push the new inside (right) hip deep and well forward. One big mistake riders often make when giving the aids is that they stand up in the stirrups instead of keeping a deep but not heavy seat. Don't lift your hip! Keep the hip (seat bone) deep and forward, and push the heel down on the same side. The left shoulder must be taken back slightly, the inside hand gives slightly, and the left leg glides back along the horse's body. Again, think of riding a half pass. This is an exercise for the flying changes that is easy for horses to understand, because it is easier for the rider to execute. The rider should not position the horse too strongly from one side to the other.

This exercise shows us that we should make it as easy as possible for the horse when teaching the flying changes. It is very important for the rider never to throw his upper body from one side to the other or move the lower legs too far back. All the aids must be distinct but never overdone. This would interfere with the horse. The rider must always stay quiet yet energetic.

It may sound quite easy, but depending on the horse's talent and that of the rider, it may take weeks, months or even a year for the horse to perform the flying changes. Don't lose your patience and expect the horse to do them perfectly right away. It is important not to demand more than the horse can give. What we teach him in a bad manner, we most often cannot correct later.

As soon as the horse can perform the flying changes correctly in the exercise mentioned above, we can begin to stay closer to the centerline. The loops become shorter and flatter until he can do the changes in a straight line. When the horse can make three, four or possibly five changes and stay straight on the centerline, the rider can begin to ride the tempi changes, starting with the four-tempi changes.

14.5 Tempi Changes

Tempi changes should only be begun when the horse can do single flying changes easily, without resistance or rushing. Tempi changes require much more precision, as reflected in an increased need for straightness and engagement. While riders first starting tempi changes seem to have the most difficulty with counting the changes, actually the most difficult problem is keeping the horse straight and engaged. When the rider concentrates so hard on getting the count right, he often swings the horse from side to side, and uses overly strong aids. This makes it much harder for the horse, and harder, therefore, for the rider to learn proper changes. For this reason, the focus should be on maintaining straightness. The counter canter should be very sure and easy for the horse.

The first work is to make changes in a series without counting. When the horse is balanced, light and ready, make a change. When he is again ready, make another. And so on. It is good to make these on the third track or quarter lines, away from the wall. This gives the rider a straight line to work on without inhibiting the horse from changing to the outside lead. If changes are done too frequently on the diagonal, you will often see the horse becoming tense and cramping his canter in anticipation.

I am often asked "My horse's changes are always more difficult from left to right. What can I do?" We must understand that if the natural crookedness of the horse has not been dealt with in the basic training, there will always be a problem with the horse's crookedness, especially when we ask for new things from the horse, even if we position him straight. Horses are just like humans in being left- or right-handed. The rider must simply straighten his horse by getting the hind leg to be more energetic, and the rider must become softer on the horse's stiff side. When the horse is stiff on the left, he should always be ridden in a slight shoulder-in position when going to the left, to correct the shoulder to the hind leg. When we ride this horse to the right, it should be in a tiny travers position—without any force! This horse will always try to balance himself on his stiff side by leaning on the rider's left hand. Therefore, always lighten the contact on the horse's stiff side. Otherwise the vicious circle is unavoidable: when the horse is stiff to the left, the rider's hand pulls back and, because the horse raises his right hip, the rider sits on the left side. This makes changes to the right very difficult because the rider cannot bring his right hip forward. This is why the rider should always soften the contact on the horse's stiff side and engage the horse's stiff hind leg. The horse that is stiff on the left is naturally bent too much to the left, and the muscles on the left side of his body are shorter. For this horse everything that goes from right to left is easier, like travers left, half pass left, changes from right to left. Exercises to the right will be more difficult since bending to the right requires the left muscles to stretch and the right muscles must shorten. The right side is higher because the right hind leg is straighter, so everything pushes more to the left. We see again how important it is to have the horse absolutely straight, and we see the importance of basics to avoid problems in the future.

After each flying change the rider must make sure that the horse is well on the aids and under the rider's seat, and not worry too much about the horse being "on the bit," or try to force him into a frame with the hands. Also, we must not get anxious and stubborn if the horse does not understand the tempis right away. Remember to ride only to the horse's limit on this point, then change to an easier exercise and later come back to the harder lesson.

14.5.1 How to Count in Tempi Changes

When the series of changes on straight lines is understood by the horse and rider, the work of counting the strides can begin. When counting strides in the tempi changes, the rider should count for every stride that he wants the horse to stay in that lead of the canter. Since the canter aids are given with each stride, it is best to count the aids—often the rider only counts, and forgets to give the canter aids for each stride. The horse then loses impulsion and straightness and can not make the changes when asked.

When the rider needs to count the series of tempi changes, it is best to count in the following manner. For five four-tempis: **1** - 2 - 3 - 4, **2** - 2 - 3 - 4, **3** - 2 - 3 - 4, **4** - 2 - 3 - 4, **5** - 2 - 3 - 4. The first number is the series number, the others are the strides of the canter in the series. This should help the rider to keep track of the number of changes he has done during the series. On the 4 beat, the rider must think of landing and changing almost at once. An experienced ground person can be of a great help to the rider starting the changes.

The same technique can be used for five three-tempis: **1** - 2 - 3, **2** - 2 - 3, **3** - 2 - 3, **4** - 2 - 3, **5** - 2 - 3. And for seven two-tempis: **1** - 2, **2** - 2, **3** -

2, **4** - 2, **5** - 2, **6** - 2, **7** - 2. The one-tempo are the easiest to count: the rider just has to count the canter aids.

To help yourself with counting, practice canter-walk transitions as follows: four canter strides right, half halt, walk; four canter strides left, half halt, walk. The fourth stride is the one during which the half halt is given and later the position change takes place. It is important in doing this exercise not to hurry. If the horse becomes nervous, stay in the walk longer and forget temporarily about the tempi changes.

Doing an even number of changes on the quarter line (2, 4 or 6) will leave the horse on the true canter for the following short side. When the changes are ridden on the diagonal, an odd number will be needed.

Once more, I want to emphasize that it is far more important to ride the horse correctly than to be a slave to the counting. You can often see riders practicing tempi changes over and over—but without a single one truly correct! Without balance, impulsion and straightness, the horse will become more and more frightened and upset about the tempis, with the rider becoming more frustrated and sour—in a vicious circle.

14.6 Four-Tempi Changes

We begin again with the right lead, cantering well forward and energetically with lots of suspension—as if the horse is cantering on hot coals. Begin the four-tempis on the quarter line or third track, as has been done with the random series of changes discussed above. After riding well engaged through the corners of the short side, the rider turns onto the quarter line by giving soft half halts with the outside (left) hand. The rider's outside (left) leg is well on the horse's side and is active so the horse cannot fall onto his outside shoulder. The horse must be absolutely straight. Only then can the rider give the correct aids.

Now the rider should begin to count the aids for the right lead for four strides. Just before the horse lands the right front leg from the fourth stride, the new aids for the left lead begin. The fourth stride is also the basis for the depart for the flying change. What makes this so difficult is the need for promptness in giving the aids for the change immediately upon landing, as the horse begins the suspension phase. Give the aids for change by positioning the horse slightly to the left, pushing the left seat bone deep and well forward, then slide the new outside (right) leg lightly back along the horse's body and half halt on the new outside (right) just before the old inside (right) front leg is landing. Then count the canter aids four times in the left canter and again position the horse to the right during the fourth stride, take the new inside seat bone well forward and deep, the right heel deep and leg forward just before the old inside (left) front leg is landing, the new outside leg slightly back, and then the flying change occurs when the fourth stride is completed. The next stride is the new first stride.

Again, the rider counts the canter aids four times in the right lead, changes the horse's position during the fourth stride just before the old inside (right) front leg is landing, and gives the aids for the change. The change comes during the suspension between the fourth and next strides.

Changes can be begun on the diagonal when the work on the quarter line is comfortable. Even so, go back often to riding tempis on quarter lines and riding diagonals without changes. It is not necessary at first to make 5 four-tempi changes on the diagonal. It is better to do only three changes and get them placed perfectly, so the second change is at X. Then go to making 5 changes. Should the horse become excited and rush on faster, then you should forget the changes and continue on until the horse is calm and quiet. As with everything in riding, the use of force leads to fear and mistrust and sets us back, not forward.

14.7 Three-Tempi Changes

We are now coming to the three tempis. As always the horse must be straight. I must mention here that the four-tempis and three tempis are the hardest. The two-tempis and one-tempos are really the easiest. They have a normal rhythm, and one does not have to count so much. We make it hard on our horses, because we get too focused on our counting! We count and count and miss giving our correct aids.

Go onto the diagonal on the right lead after riding the two corners of the short side with good engagement in the canter. Give a half halt with the left rein (outside), and the aids are the same as in the four-tempis.

About two horses' lengths onto the diagonal with the horse straight, the rider asks for the first change, counts three canter aids, straightens and positions the horse into the new direction just before landing from the third stride and asks for the change. Again, count three canter aids, straighten and position the horse into the new direction and ask for the change just before the old inside (right) front leg is landing and keep repeating. It is important that the horse canter with good engagement, well on the rider's aids and that the rider not hurry the horse.

Most of the time the horse will do the first three-tempis very well. If horse and rider are close to the short side, the rider should be satisfied with two of the three-tempis and not try to cram another pair into the series. It is important to praise the horse before we ask him to do this exercise again. We must ride the horse forward during these tempi changes and not let him change the rhythm and tempo of the canter. The rider will again experience the horse trying to fall out on his weak side. Therefore, he must take care to keep his leg secure on the horse's side which shows stiffness and remain soft in the hand.

For example, if the horse wants to fall or swing out to the right, the rider should not—under any circumstances—take his right leg off the horse. He must catch the sideways movement with his right leg, of course not so strongly that the horse mistakenly continues to canter in the previous lead, but enough to keep him from swinging sideways during the flying change. Naturally, the same technique is required from right lead to left (using the opposite aids) if the horse has a tendency to fall or swing out to the left in his changes.

Sometimes this swinging out with the haunches is caused by positioning the horse too strongly to the new side. Then the haunches swing sideways to maintain balance. The correction must be only to change the position in front slightly for the flying change. Another reason for swinging haunches can be that the rider uses too much outside leg pressure, and therefore, the horse breaks away in the opposite direction.

14.8 Two-Tempi Changes

We start on the right lead. The rider gives a clear half halt on the outside rein (left) before turning onto the diagonal. The outside leg of the rider stays in good contact with the horse's body and takes care that the horse does not drift off the desired straight line of the diagonal. Then when the horse is nicely straight and is not trying to wander left or right, and the canter is steady and energetic, the aids for the first change can begin.

The rider gives the horse the new position, to the left when the old inside (right) front leg is landing, without pulling. It should happen with a very light hand. The new inside seat bone (left) is pushed down and forward in the saddle. Automatically, the rider's left leg moves slightly forward also, without losing contact with the horse's side. The right leg slides a little back, also staying on the horse's body. And the first change is done. Most importantly, the canter should be maintained.

The rider counts the aids and changes the horse's position to the right after stride number one when the old inside (left) front leg is landing. Then the new inside seat bone, (right), is pushed down and forward in the saddle while the right leg moves slightly forward along the horse's body. The right leg is now the forward-driving leg. The outside leg moves back, the final signal for the change.

These aids are used repeatedly every two strides. The rider should remember to concentrate on the good springy canter.

14.9 One-Tempo Flying Changes

The one-tempo changes were a source of great controversy in the 1950's. Bastions of classical riding, such as the Spanish Riding School in Vienna, had earlier refused to make one-tempo changes because they violated the purity of the canter stride. Many felt that they represented circus movements which had no place in the development of the horse. While the theoretical discussion on the true value of the one-tempo change has never been fully resolved, the eye-catching beauty of a well-performed series of one-tempo changes won the day, and it is now a featured part of the "classical" repertoire, found in the Olympic tests as well as the Spanish Riding School.

One should start with the one-tempo changes only when the changes to two are well confirmed. I always introduce the one-tempo changes to my horses on the short side of the arena.

In the right lead canter on the right rein, I would engage the horse in the canter very well, so that he felt active and steady and ready to do a flying change at any moment. On the short side after the first corner, when the horse is straight, I would ask for a flying change. As soon as the change is completed, and the horse lands in the new stride, ask for one change back to the original lead. For success, you must pay careful attention to keeping the horse straight, and must time the aids precisely. The aid for each flying change comes on the last beat of the canter, when the old inside front leg is just landing.

This usually works well for the first two changes. The reason for doing the changes to one on the short side is that the horse is usually calm on the short side while at the same time accustomed to being engaged more there. The short side is the place where the horse is often brought back together after an exercise has fallen apart a little on the long side or diagonal. So the horse has additional confidence in his rider and surroundings on the short side.

The two changes to one should be done several times on the short side. Then they can be tried on the diagonal coming from the right rein with a change to the left and back to the right. It is important that the horse stay straight and calm. Otherwise, the rider should forget the changes for a while. Then let the horse continue in the right lead for a few strides and do another two changes to one. Then the horse can be asked to do these pairs of changes closer and closer together, with fewer and fewer strides of right lead canter between the pairs. Finally, the rider will have the sequence of several changes to one.

The pairs of changes to one are not very difficult. The difficulty comes with adding the third change to one. When this change comes easily, the following changes to one will also come easily, because the rider does not have to worry about interruptions in the rhythm. Nor does the rider have to worry about losing the quality of the canter between the changes as in the changes to four, three and two.

It is, however, of utmost importance in the one-tempo changes to ride the horse well forward. The neck of the horse must remain straight and not too short with only a slight new flexion. It should not be pulled to the left and right during the changes, and the rider should not throw himself to the left and right, lifting the seat off the saddle, thus separating the seat from the horse's back. It is better to work with the seat bones more than with the legs. It is not necessary to swing the legs back and forth too far, since the change must come out of the hip, especially because the aids must be changed so rapidly. I have trained horses to do one-tempo flying changes in side-saddle, and it works quite well if the horse is schooled to the rider's weight through the seat.

In teaching the one tempo changes, it is sometimes useful to start the changes from the counter canter to encourage the horse to stay on the track near the wall. The same principle applies here as when we were teaching the horse to leg-yield from the quarter line or second track back to the track. To ask for the flying change from the counter canter to the true canter and then back to the counter canter will go along with the horse's natural tendency to move back toward the track.

The rider has his greatest difficulty in starting the one-tempo. A common mistake is to give the aids too quickly at the beginning of the series. What happens is that the rider gives the aids for the "second" change before the first change has happened! Therefore no change occurs. The horse has made no mistake and forgives or ignores the rider's gyrations and stays in the original lead of the canter! The rider must give the horse the chance to do the first change before the aids for the next change are given. This mistake is frequently seen, even at big shows.

14.10 Placement of Tempi Changes

The placement of the sequence changes on the diagonal is important. For instance, if riding three changes every four strides on the diagonal, the second flying change should be at X. The third change should be placed on the second half of the diagonal. The sequence changes should lie symmetrically on the diagonal around X.

If riding five changes to three, the third flying change should be exactly at X. There would be two changes before X, the third at X, and two after X. When doing nine changes to two, the fifth flying change should be at X with four changes before X and four changes after X on the diagonal. When riding fifteen one-tempis, the eighth stride is at X.

In preparing the placement of the sequence of changes on the diagonal, the rider should take the length of his horse's canter stride into consideration. With a shorter-strided horse, the rider should not start too soon on the diagonal with the changes. If the horse has a large stride, the rider should start earlier on the diagonal. It is not a pretty picture to see the horse executing the final change on the diagonal in the corner. This probably often happens when the rider delays starting the changes until just before X.

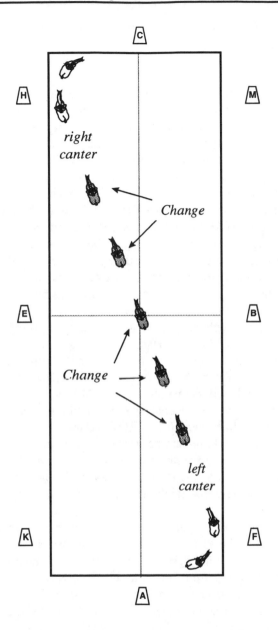

Figure 86. Placement of tempi changes. The middle change should occur at X. Shown are 5 changes every third stride.

When riding tempi changes on the centerline, similar attention must be paid to locating the middle of the strides at X.

14.11 Counter Change of Hand

The counter change of hand is a set of two half passes separated by a flying change: as in half pass right, flying change, half pass left. This can be a very beautiful exercise, but is very difficult to execute: to the six different aids for the flying change we must add the additional aids for the half pass, straightening and second half pass! In Chapter 12, we discussed the counter change of hand at the trot. As at the trot, a prerequisite is a good floating half pass in both directions without resistance. The exercise of half pass-straight-half pass (all in the same direction) should be well in hand. The horse must be very obedient and balanced and relaxed. Next comes the half pass-straight-flying change-straight-half pass back. So many riders are sure they can do each of these elements that they jump immediately to trying the counter change, without spending the time to try this simple, but revealing exercise. Straightening after a half pass is a difficult and delicate process, and our exercise of half pass-straight-continue in half pass can be done with a somewhat sloppy straightness. If we simply add the flying change, as in half pass-straight-flying change, the rider will really discover whether the straightness is true. (The judge at C gets a close look at this movement in the Prix St. Georges test). Either the horse will refuse to make the flying change or will swing the hindquarters in a poor flying change.

To start the counter change of hand, I like to make the half pass from K to the quarter line, then proceed straight, make the flying change and half pass back to the track, remaining in counter canter. After the change, it is good to remain straight to regain impulsion so one has the power for the sideways movements. Only when the horse has confidence in the movement, can we make the moment of straightness shorter and shorter, without losing *schwung*.

As the period of straightness becomes shorter, we can make the half passes further across the arena, as in K to slightly before X , change at X, then back to H. In the Grand Prix, the most difficult change of hand comes with a very steep half pass from H to B and back to K. In this movement, the straightness must be achieved in the stride which initiates the flying change—and the half pass must start right away out of the change. A few strides straight on the track would make the angles so steep that it becomes difficult to maintain *forward*-sideways movement. Nevertheless, it is always difficult to execute this change so quickly as one would desire. It is better to plan on arriving slightly before B. Thinking of walls along the diagonals still makes the half passes easier, even at the Grand Prix.

To make the counter change of hand, be sure that each stride of the half pass is springy, with each stride ridden as if it were a new starting of the canter and half pass. Since the flying change is simply a new canter depart

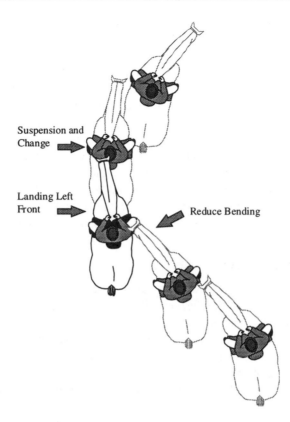

Suspension and
Change

Landing Left
Front

Reduce Bending

Figure 87. Counter change of hand. During the moment of suspension in the last stride of the half pass, the horse is straightened in preparation for the flying change upon landing.

on the opposite lead, this will prepare the flying change. If the horse takes over the half pass, he will not be ready for the flying change.

When arriving at the track, the horse is straightened during the moment of suspension of the last half pass stride. Then when the horse lands the inside front, he will be ready to make the flying change and start back in the other half pass.

Usually the difficulty starts when the rider tries too hard to make the change and second half pass too quickly. He gets a bit excited and the horse loses balance and confidence. In the first half pass, the horse does not remain springy, forward and lightly on the aids. The trouble is that when riders start exercises such as these, they try to make them perfect from the start, just as laid out in the test or how judges say they would like to see them. This is a prescription for disaster. The rider should stay with the plan of gradually shortening the number of straight jumps, always keeping a careful eye to balance, relaxation and harmony.

The correct counter change of hand comes when the horse and rider are completely harmonious in the aids of flying change and half pass so that the flying change is made out of the last half pass stride, and the new half pass is made directly out of the flying change. This coordination will become especially important when performing the zigzag at the canter. To the six facets of the flying change we add the sideways movement *in the change*. When going from left half pass to right, the aids for the change are given when the left fore leg lands (just before the moment of suspension). The change is made with an additional sideways-driving aid of the left leg. The horse must stay relaxed and calm. This degree of skill comes from very careful attention to the balance of the aids and the correct aids in the right moment.

14.12 Zigzag at the Canter

When the single counter change of lead is well understood and harmonious, we can begin the zigzag at the canter. The zigzag at the canter is a series of canter half passes separated by flying changes. In tests, zigzags at the trot are ridden a certain number of meters on either side of the centerline (usually 5m.), while zigzags at the canter are ridden for a certain number of strides each way (4-8-8-4 or 3-6-6-6-3).

The zigzag introduces three major new problems for the horse and rider:

1. The counter changes of hand are not done on the track, but away from the wall.
2. The half pass after the flying change must be kept floating and springy, since it sets up the next flying change.
3. The movement requires extended periods of lateral work combined with 3 or 4 flying changes.

In the normal counter change of hand, arriving at the track gives the horse and rider a single point where they can both plan the flying change. In the zigzag, the horse must wait for the rider's aids, and then respond promptly. (In the counter change on the track, we of course want the horse to wait for the rider's aids as well, but the horse will come to expect something to happen upon arriving at the track.)

At the start, the rider should not think about the number of strides or count. He should concentrate on the quality of the flying changes and the changes of direction, focusing on the coordination of his aids. This will make the exercise easier for the horse.

The rider must strive to maintain a good clean 3-beat canter. The demands of the half pass and the flying change each can lead to disruption of the rhythm, putting them both together in the zigzag simply makes things harder. The aids must be precise and the horse must react very easily and willingly. It is easy for the horse to become frightened, and the rider to rush and throw his body to one side or the other. If the horse goes too much against the hand, then he will come up behind, and will not react easily to the rider's aids. As with any complex movement, it should only be attempted when each of the components (the half pass and flying change) are easy and correct.

In all the flying change work, there is a real danger that the rider starts to demand too much from the horse. The emphasis on counting the strides and on making the zigzag in the right number of strides leads the rider to try to force the horse to behave or to learn to count. It takes a long time for the horse to understand what is going on. Through repetition, the horse learns "Oh, I know what this is all about," but there is a real difference between calmly repeating carefully executed changes and a forced rough repetition. Force never leads to elegance and beauty. Repeating careful, calm, balanced changes lets the horse think "I know what this is all about, and there is no problem!" Repeating rough, forced mechanical changes leads to the horse thinking: "I know what this is all about, and I am in real trouble!" at this level of training, the horse and rider have come so far that it is a pity to see the destruction of a horse's confidence that comes from so-called short-cuts.

When the horse and rider are comfortable with the zigzag without counting, we need to begin the counting. By counting, we increase the difficulty in many ways: first, we must be prepared to make the change at a specific time (we can't wait a stride or two to bring the horse into better balance), second, the counting shows whether the lateral movement is the same in each direction, and finally, the change must be made right in to the opposite half pass, with no opportunity for strengthening.

A common problem is that most horses move more easily to the left, so that the zigzag gets further and further to the left with each change. The rider must be careful to know his horse and not over-drive with the right leg.

For the 4-8-8-4 zigzag of Intermediaire II, upon turning onto the centerline coming from the left, after one length of the horse, we start the half pass to the left. With the horse well flexed to the left by shortening and releasing the left rein, the outside rein makes a half halt and then releases. In the same moment, the rider's outside leg drives the outside hind leg sideways while the outside hind leg is lifting up. The rider's inside hip is pushing the horse into the half pass. The rider's inside (left) leg is driving the inside left leg forward. The rider now counts the canter jumps.

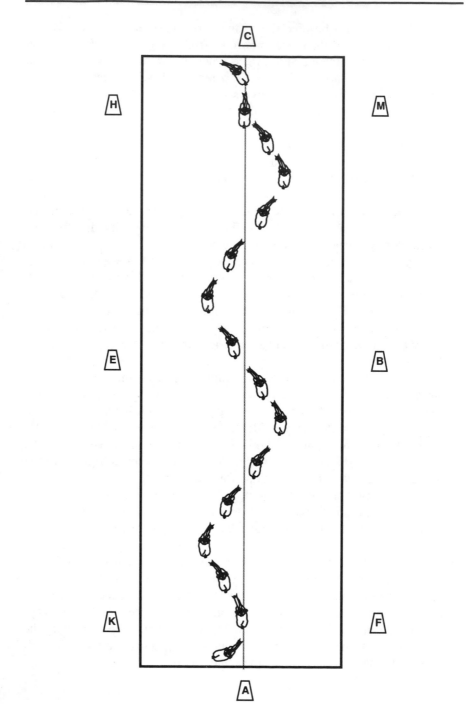

Figure 88. Canter zigzag of 3 - 6 - 6 - 6 - 3 strides.

Half pass left. Make four strides of half pass left. When the left fore leg lands in this fourth stride, give the aids for the flying change. This is just before the moment of suspension.

Half pass right. In the change, we establish the new half pass and begin the counting of 8 strides to the right. In the landing of the 8th jump, when the right fore leg is on the ground, give the aids for the flying change to the left.

Half pass left. In this change again we give the aids for the sideways movement of the half pass left. Again count the 8 jumps, and give the aids for the flying change to the right when the left fore leg lands on the 8th stride.

Half pass right. Now we count 3 strides to arrive back at the centerline.

Straight. In the fourth and last jump of the half pass to the right, the horse must be straightened, so he can progress straight on the centerline. The exercise of half pass-straight-half pass (all in the same direction) that we made when beginning the half pass now has its reward in a smooth transition from the right half pass to straight on the centerline.

In the flying change in the zigzag, I give the aids slightly earlier than I would when riding tempi changes. Remember that the change is itself a stride, so I count the landings of each stride: "1-2-3-4-change-2-3-4-5-6-7-8-change-2-3-4" and so on. That is, the landing of the change is counted as the first stride in the new direction.

It is also very important to ride forward between these exercises to get the hind leg swinging again. Only with a swinging hind leg can we keep the horse up and light through the half passes and changes. Once again, "ride your horse forward and make him straight."

14.13 Canter Pirouettes

This is one of the most difficult exercises, but when correctly ridden, one of the most beautiful ones in dressage. Many riders say that canter pirouettes are difficult for their horses. Again, the quality of the canter is the first priority. The canter pirouette is a jumping, cantering movement. The collection must be good. The horse must be well elevated but relaxed. The canter pirouette will only work when the horse is easily in command of the collected canter, volte, shoulder-in, and half pass. One often sees horses trying to do pirouettes who do not know how to do correct voltes and half passes at the collected canter. It is no wonder they can't do pirouettes! Again, this is an example of a mistake created long before it shows. It will not help at all to try to improve the pirouette. One must correct the original mistake.

A good preparatory exercise is to make transitions from canter to walk to canter, etc., on a circle. By each transition, both to the canter as well as to the walk, decrease the circle slightly, bring the shoulders in slightly. Otherwise, it will create a leg-yielding effect, and the pirouette will be too large. The rider should be thinking of keeping the horse in shoulder-in position. By this I mean that the horse's forehand is ridden slightly to the inside. The half halts are given with the outside rein and leg. Should the horse begin to come in too fast and too much, then the half halts are carefully given with the inside rein which should be well against the neck and inside leg to control this. Thus the circle gets smaller and smaller. Then on the very small volte, when the horse feels calm and obedient, take the canter, making the very first stride the beginning of the pirouette. The first stride of the canter in a good departure is the most engaged with the horse stepping farthest under, and the rider can give the aids for the pirouette. The horse should be positioned well to the inside. The rider gives the half halt on the outside and pushes with his outside knee and leg to bring the horse into the turn. The rider's inside leg and seat bone drive to maintain the jump of the canter.

I try to explain the canter pirouette to my horses by approaching it in half pass. The horse should be started in this exercise on his easier side, on his better canter. First, make a canter volte in the corner at the beginning of the long side, then ride canter half pass until a distance of approximately eight meters from the opposite long side. At this point, ride straight ahead briefly, to avoid throwing the horse around. Ride a half volte and immediately half pass again to a distance of eight meters from the track, and again half pass, etc. The half voltes should be made smaller and smaller until the horse realizes that he is practically executing half pirouettes, and that he can do it. It is important for the rider to sit into the movement and that the horse does not fall out with his hindquarters or in with the shoulders. The half pass must be correct, with the shoulders leading into the movement. The rider should keep the horse well positioned to the inside, still think about half pass, but actually discontinue the half pass. Carry the feeling for half pass into the small volte. Repeat this until the rider has the impression that the horse has confidence in the small volte done in this way. This technique is continued until the half volte is a real half pirouette by making the half volte even smaller. The rider should realize that the few strides of half pass and likewise the few strides of the half pirouette can be ridden going in any direction out of the volte.

Another good preparatory exercise for the canter pirouette is to ride canter eight to ten strides left lead, walk, and immediately turn on the haunches left without hurrying. Take your time! Then make a right lead canter depart promptly but not hurriedly. Canter again several strides (perhaps eight to ten), walk, half turn right, and again left lead, etc. The horse must wait for our aids. This way the horse learns that after the walk transition there will be a turn on the haunches and a canter depart. I must emphasize the importance of calmness and not hurrying through this

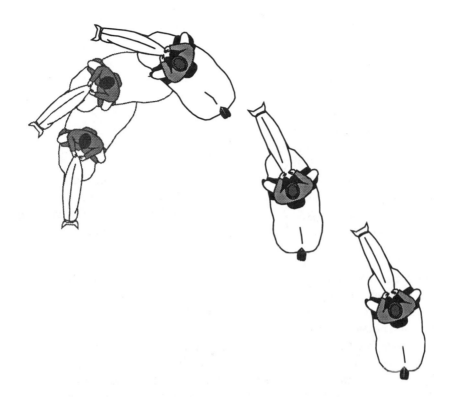

Figure 89. Introducing the canter pirouette through half pass.

exercise. Otherwise, you will be creating an ugly picture so often sadly seen at shows.

When riding pirouettes, the canter and the half pass (at the canter) should be quiet and very much on the rider's seat. In entering the pirouette, the rider should pay attention to keeping the inside leg well at the girth, outside leg behind the girth—but not too far back in the soft area behind the ribs, the outside knee actively helping the turn, the inside rein well against the horse's neck, as well as the outside rein, so that the horse is truly between the leg, _Kreuz_, and rein aids. As soon as the horse makes a few good strides in the pirouette, the rider should ride him out of the pirouette and praise him so he knows he has done well. This should be repeated and practiced on both reins. It is important to start this exercise on the horse's easier side. Every horse has a good side and a bad side.

One of the frequent mistakes in riding canter pirouettes is to give the aids too strongly. When this happens, the horse throws himself around. Probably the most important thought for the rider is to keep the rhythm of the canter steady. The three-beat quality must be maintained.

If the horse enters the pirouette going too fast, the rider will be forced to give a half halt with the inside rein so that the horse will not run against that rein. The outside leg is "standing guard," so to speak, and the inside leg is driving. Then the horse stops or almost stops, and the rider must give up on the first attempt and try to establish the canter again and to put the horse on the aids. When the horse ceases to canter properly, it is a clear sign that the tempo was not correct for the exercise.

Another mistake is to ride too large a curve or arc in the canter pirouette. Half halts should be given on the outside to keep the pirouette small while retaining a clear canter rhythm.

Once a horse has learned pirouettes, it is often found that he will have difficulty with a volte, falling in on the second segment of the figure— he thinks this is a pirouette. To correct this, the rider should plan to ride the horse a little more forward at this point. This will prevent the horse's confusion.

In preparation and execution of the canter pirouette, it is very important that the rider keep his hands together and low and quiet. When riders saw left and right, swinging the horse's head from left to right, it becomes obvious that the frame of the horse has been done with the rider's hands, and not well or correctly at that!

Another common pitfall for execution of the canter pirouette is for the rider to collect the canter more and more as he approaches the spot where he wants the horse to perform the pirouette. This shows that the collected canter is not correct. The collected canter should be established well *ahead* of the approach to the pirouette, not *in* the approach. The description in test guidelines is, after all, "collected canter and pirouette."

If the horse becomes disunited, changes lead behind, during the pirouette, it means that the rider does not have the horse sufficiently on his inside seat bone and inside leg. The outside leg of the rider should be slightly behind the girth, ready and on guard. But the inside leg should be driving, while the half halt is given on the outside. The rider sits well on the inside seat bone and should keep his outside leg well against the horse, so that the horse cannot swing out with his haunches, thus escaping the rider's aids. If the horse continues to change leads behind, the rider should ride the pirouette larger (on to a volte) until the horse develops his confidence. Only then should the rider decrease the diameter of the pirouette, gradually attempting the smallest volte around the supporting inside hind leg—the canter pirouette!

It would be a serious mistake for the rider to force the horse to do a canter pirouette. The horse would become frightened by the aids for the pirouette, and this would lead to resistance and confrontation, which no rider wants. When problems arise in the canter pirouette, this means that there were problems in the preparation. In other words, the problems existed long before the pirouette was even begun! For instance, the quality of the canter

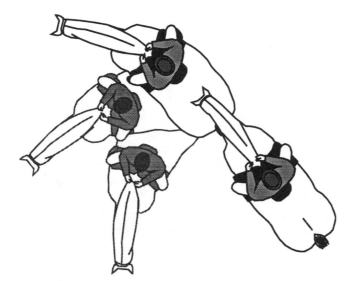

Figure 90. Canter pirouette on the diagonal.

was not correct; the position in the horse (degree of bending) was not correct; the outside leg and knee of the rider were not sufficiently against the horse. The rider's weight was too heavy to the outside so the rider couldn't sit properly to the inside and could not use the inside seat bone correctly. The inside leg of the rider wasn't driving enough; the half halts to the outside weren't quite right, etc., etc.

Half-Pirouette on the Diagonal. In the Prix St. Georges test, a half-pirouette is executed on the diagonal, between H and X, followed by a flying change at H, then a half pirouette on the diagonal between M and X, with a flying change again at M. This sequence requires that the horse be well collected and on the aids. The success of the pirouette starts with a correct corner and turn at H. There must be correct bending through the corner, so that neither the shoulder falls out nor the hindleg swings out. At H, the rider indicates the turn with light turning aids. The inside rein must shorten, but then give almost immediately—show, then allow. It is so important to make the horse straight right from the beginning of the diagonal. There are so few strides between the corner and the pirouette, that if you have to take several strides to make the horse straight, there will be no opportunity to prepare the pirouette.

On the diagonal, continue the *collected* canter, with a uniform tempo. Two of the most common mistakes are that the horse accelerates on the diagonal—ready for medium or extended canter, which will come next— or the rider takes the horse into shorter and shorter steps, losing the impulsion that will be needed for the pirouette.

Keep the horse straight on the diagonal. When the horse falls over the outside shoulder in the corner, riders often do not pay attention, and proceed to the diagonal, with the horse ending up in travers.[1] The mistake in the corner now means that the rider is in real trouble: i) there will be trouble turning off at H, ii) the collected canter is impossible when the horse falls over the shoulder, iii) if the rider tries to correct and straighten, he may easily get a flying change.

Just before the point where the rider wishes to make the pirouette, the aids for the pirouette begin. Give good flexion to the left and a half halt so that this canter jump is almost on the spot. The inside hip comes deep and forward. The rider's inside leg activates the inside hind leg of the horse. Then the aids lead the shoulders around the inside hind leg: a half halt on the outside joins with outside knee and leg pressure and an inside rein that guides the shoulders to the inside. It is important that both reins enclose the neck, so the rider can make any correction quickly and efficiently.

Just before reaching the 180° of the turn, we need to i) stop the shoulders from coming around in the pirouette, ii) correct the straightness and iii) ride out straight on the diagonal. In the last pirouette jump, an inside (left) half halt stops the shoulders from continuing on the turn. The outside rein must remiain taut so that the effect of the inside half halt is to stop the shoulders, not to bend the horse further left. The outside leg and knee must become passive. Next, the inside rein gives, while the outside rein straightens the horse. At the end of this last jump of the pirouette, use both seat bones and ride out of the pirouette, with a continued good collected canter. Here begins the preparation for the next movement, the flying change at H, because only when the canter is correct can the flying change be correct. Often in the piroutte, the collection and energy is lost, since the rider is thinking only of the turning and not of the cantering. Without the quality of the canter, the horse can not be straight, and without strightness, the flying change can not be correct.

The flying change sets the stage for the canter across the short side, and the preparation for the second pirouette. In this test sequence, it is easy

---

[1] I have suggested that you use half pass into the pirouette to introduce the movement to the horse. When the training has achieved very correct pirouettes, it is not necessary, nor desirable to ride half pass or travers into the pirouette. At the point of showing Prix St. Georges, the horse should be confirmed and willing to do the pirouette from a straight canter.

to see how one mistake or careless movement can snowball into bigger and bigger trouble. The sequence of movements is really quite compressed, and there is little time to recover from any mistake.

The second pirouette, between M and X is a mirror of the first. The important differences are that the horse now is more sure of what is coming, and that one side or the other may be more difficult for the horse.

Full Pirouettes on the Diagonal. There is no major difference between a full pirouette on the diagonal and the half pirouette, except in the full pirouette, straightness on the diagonal is much more apparent. When ridden from F to H, with a pirouette between F and X, a flying change at X, and a pirouette right between X and H, the quality of the flying change becomes of paramount importance, since there is almost no time between the change and the second pirouette. The quality, rhythm, tempo and straightness of the canter must remain true through the change.

Full Pirouettes on the Centerline. The 1995 Grand Prix test, calls for a canter pirouette left at L, a flying change at X, and a pirouette right at I. The Grand Prix movement is like that done on the diagonal in Intermediaire II, but the precision of the turn and the straightness on the centerline are much more apparent.

In the Grand Prix Special, a pirouette right at D is followed by nine one tempo changes followed by a full pirouette left at G. This involves three movements which require excellent collection, engagement and energy, and each of these three can tend to lose collection, engagement, and energy. The pirouette at G is usually well-prepared by the turn onto the centerline at C. Again, the difficulty is associated with the loss of canter purity and energy in the pirouette. This will compromise the one-tempo changes. By their nature, the one tempo changes make it difficult to maintain energy and power. After the changes, the collected canter must immediately be very clear and powerful and correct, for shortly afterwards comes the pirouette left.

In the musical Kür, we now see pirouettes done several times around. When well-ridden, they can be very nice, but most of the time, I have the feeling that the horse needs help to keep cantering. It would be better to stop with a good single pirouette than to prolong it into badness.

Chapter 15
Piaffe and Passage

These are two of the most difficult exercises in dressage. In order to ride these two movements correctly, it is necessary to recognize their essential characteristics, to know the correct aids in the right moment, and to be aware of mistakes that should be avoided at all costs.

It is extremely difficult to teach the rider piaffe and passage without a well-schooled horse from which he may learn the feeling of the movements. Both the piaffe and passage, as well as the transitions in and out, require a lot of tact and finesse on the part of the rider.

Not all horses can perform piaffe and passage very well. Those with a naturally high knee action are particularly suited for piaffe and passage; the Lippizaners and Andalusians are common examples. Those without a particularly high knee action will require much more work on collection and development of the hind leg and lightness on the forehand to achieve a brilliant piaffe or passage.

15.1 Piaffe

The piaffe is essentially a trot movement executed almost on the spot with diagonal pairs of legs moving with accentuated elevation. With a high degree of collection and strong flexion of the haunches, the horse's legs are lifted vertically in held cadence. This cadence is produced by the horse holding each diagonal pair up for a relatively long moment. The legs are lifted and lowered on vertical lines. The forearms of the horse's front legs almost reach a horizontal line when each is lifted in the piaffe. The hind feet stay very close to the ground, enabling the haunches to carry much of the horse's weight. The hind hoof should raise only to the level of the opposite fetlock. When it rises too high, then the forehand takes up too much of the weight in order to keep the horse in balance, and the forelegs are unable to elevate enough, or start to cross, swinging left and right.

An important requirement for the correct piaffe is absolute straightness. Rhythm, relaxation and impulsion must be present, and it must be apparent that at any second the horse could go forward. If the horse can not immediately go forward out of the piaffe, it is a sure sign that the piaffe is not correct—it is mechanical. This brings us back to the old saying, "Ride your horse forward and make him straight!"

Figure 91. Piaffe. The hind feet stay very close to the ground, enabling the haunches to carry the horse's weight.

15.1.1 Rider's Position and Use of the Aids.

The correct seat of the rider is key in the piaffe work. The rider's weight should be evenly distributed on both seat bones, but not too heavy, the legs should be long and quiet, activating the horse in the right-left rhythm of the piaffe. The hands should be still, but supple in order for the horse to accept the rein contact correctly. The horse must step confidently to the flexible hand. The hand needs to be ready to give or receive. The piaffe is correct when the rider feels the cadence of the hind leg flowing smoothly over the back, into the hand and then back to the hind leg. The rider should feel he has the horse in front of him.

Most of the time riders over-aid their horses in piaffe. It is important to study and communicate with the horse to find out just how much aid is needed. It is a terrible fault when the rider hops up and down or side to side in the saddle during the attempts at piaffe. Usually, the horse is doing little or no piaffe, but the rider thinks the piaffe was good, because he was almost jumping up and down in the saddle! The quieter the rider sits, the more careful he can be with his aids, the more the horse will pay attention to the rider, and the better the horse can respond.

15.1.2 On Use of the Whip

I recommend that the rider not rely on the effect of the whip too much for work in the piaffe. At a show the whip cannot be carried at all in the FEI tests. The rider should not force the horse with the whip when at home. Although sometimes it very helpful to have a knowledgeable ground person use the whip, the horse should not learn that he only has to do the piaffe when he feels the whip. Throughout his training, we have limited use of the whip to reinforcement for the leg. We should not give up this principle now.

It has happened even at World Championships and Olympics that horses have been "helped" from the ground with a whip right up to entering the arena. Unfortunately, the result is that either the horse is hysterical or completely numb to the piaffe aids and, understanding that he is finally free from the whip, does not do the exercise!

We are reminded that force brings us nothing, at least nothing beautiful.

15.1.3 Spurs

When the horse does not react enough to the rider's leg, he can use the spur briefly to engage the hind leg. While we wish to avoid the hind leg coming too high, it is sometimes necessary to activate and engage the hind leg to keep the horse from stopping the two-beat movement altogether. The same rule applies for spurs as for the whip. The spurs should be used precisely and in just the right moment, and not as a substitute for correct training and careful aids. Over-use of the spur will lead to dullness, or resistance and fighting, perhaps with explosive results. Spur marks or sores are inexcusable, and a mark of dissonance, not harmony.

15.1.4 Developing Piaffe Through Short Step Trot

To begin with it is wise to make the piaffe appealing to the horse. This holds true for all exercises the rider wants to teach the horse. The horse should find joy in the exercises just as he does in nature in performing the movements.

We start with developing a short step trot. In the teaching process of the piaffe, riding forward is essential. In the beginning the rider should not think of the piaffe—he should just think of shortened, collected trot steps. From a lively collected walk, we take three or four short, but lively, trot steps, then back to the collected walk, with good engagement of the hind leg throughout. Ride the horse forward into the walk, not pulling him back down to the transition. The first walk must be engaged and active, the trot must be light in the hand and active in the hind leg, and the final walk must be engaged and powerful, ready for another transition. The walk must be correct: not tight, but powerful, not rushed but ready to go forward into the trot at any moment. It is very important not to ask for too much at this stage, so the horse does not become frightened or jumps away. If the horse

Figure 92. Short step trot.

becomes excited and the walk is not clear and calm, then we have to wait and re-gather the horse. It is our objective to go from walk to trot to walk and right back to trot, but the rider must be very honest with himself and sensitive to the horse. If the rider's error or horse's excitement result in a walk which is not active, up, and light, as well as relaxed, then it is best to forego the next series of short steps. The horse should be engaged and ready for any step to be a trot, canter or short step. The rein contact must remain very light and soft, and the hind legs must remain active and lively. There must always be a tendency forward.

Let us assume the horse is on the left rein. The rider goes on the long side of the arena and engages each hind leg as the hoof leaves the ground. Therefore, when the left hind hoof is leaving the ground, the rider drives the left hind. But in the same moment the rider drives, he also gives a slight half halt left to transform the energy created by the driving aids from a longer stride into a shorter, more activated step. The same then follows with the outside or right hind leg. This is then repeated. The driving aids should not be so strong that the rider has to hold with a heavy rein contact. The rider should use the right dosage of aids! It is also very important that the horse does not step sideways. The rider's hands should enclose the horse with the reins on the right and left so that he cannot evade to either side. The rider's legs should drive the horse forward and not sideways. Therefore, when the rider is using one leg, he should take care to hold against it with the other leg so as not to create sideways movement of the horse. The rein on the passive side must also hold against the horse's sideways movement.

The rider should take the time to perfect this technique of collecting steps and thus prepare the horse over a period of several months until the horse offers a respectable piaffe. When the horse is well on the aids and accepting the short step work easily, willingly and staying straight, this exercise can be practiced a little bit every day. The horse should think of this as fun.

In summary, begin slowly, do not try to hurry the training. Praise the horse when he first offers a little piaffe or the collecting steps nicely. Ask for these steps in the middle of the long sides a few times, and then change the rein, and ask for the same in the other direction. Do this also on the quarter line, diagonal and centerline to check that the horse is straight and on the aids. Remember how important it is for the horse to go forward in this exercise and not to drift to the left or right. This is perhaps the most important aspect and requires constant vigilance from the rider. As with all collecting work, remember to stretch the horse forward after a few repetitions to re-establish a swinging hind leg.

15.1.5 Problems in Piaffe

Jumping too high with the hindquarters. When the piaffe is correct, the horse shifts almost all his weight for a moment onto each hind leg as it is on the ground. But when the whip is used to hurry the process of teaching the horse the piaffe, and it is often used quite harshly, the result is that the horse jumps up and down rapidly with each hind leg.

A horse can lift his hind hoof in the piaffe only to the height of the fetlock of the other leg if he is correct. Do not be impressed by a horse who is lifting his hind legs higher than this in the piaffe, because this causes him to lighten the weight on his hindquarters. This means that he has to put more weight on his forehand. Horses who jump high with the hind legs in the piaffe can hardly lift the front hooves out of the sand. Crossing of the front legs is often seen, sometimes the horse steps on his own hooves. No wonder he begins to fear doing the piaffe! This is also a sign that the horse is working so hard with his forehand to stay in balance that in effect he is seeking contact with the ground again as soon as possible after lifting each hoof. Because he has not correctly shifted his weight to the hindquarters, he must balance himself mostly with the forehand.

Quick steps. Quick steps in the piaffe is a sign that the horse is frightened. This should be avoided, naturally. In this case it is important to build up the horse's confidence by asking for only a few steps, giving much praise, and doing the exercise in different places in the arena. It is not easy to give a horse his confidence back in the piaffe if it was taught the wrong way. I have heard often that a horse can only do a good piaffe when he is mad. This is absolutely wrong: the horse will never do a good piaffe under these conditions.

Hindquarters too far forward. Another fault in the piaffe is for the hindquarters to stay too far under the horse. The ugliness of this picture is compounded when the horse's front legs are drawn back under the body. In this instance the horse usually has his hind legs widely separated while the front legs just shuffle, hardly lifting, and he looks like a goat on a rock. The horse is afraid he will step on his own feet. He has shifted most of his weight onto the forehand, unfortunately! This horse should be asked only to do piaffe by very gradually shortening the passage. As soon as the horse falls into his old bad style, ride forward into the passage immediately.

Of all mistakes, the greatest is to make a horse do the piaffe with his head against the wall in the corner of the riding hall. Some bad trainers provoke horses in this tragic position. The horse's response is at best to frantically move his legs in no steady rhythm and lose all desire to go forward which is so important in the correctly executed piaffe. We should consider the horse's natural instinct to flee from danger and pain by running forward. Confronted directly by the wall, the horse does not believe he can escape, and becomes worried and frightened. We must never forget in all training that the horse must feel that he can go forward—that for him, the door is open to the front. We are asking the horse to trust us based on years of good, reliable handling and the development of a long-lasting partnership, but these few years can not negate millennia of instinct and natural selection.

On the other hand, however, the rider will be amazed at how quickly the horse will learn to do the piaffe correctly if the classical approach is taken. The collecting steps exercise described earlier, when ridden daily will produce a correct piaffe that the horse takes joy in, partially because it feels right and partially because he was not forced beyond his ability too early. The horses gradually are able to shorten their trot steps more and more through this exercise. Suddenly, after much time and diligent work, the piaffe will be there! Just as after endlessly watching the grass grow, it is suddenly there!

It is extremely important to praise the horse whenever he does something well. In training the horse to do the piaffe, the rider should not make the horse do too many steps too soon, otherwise the horse will not enjoy the piaffe. He will become tense, perhaps leaping away—the horse's attempt to flee from the aids altogether.

Behind the bit. One more pitfall in the piaffe is for the horse to get behind the bit, a sign that the rider used too much hand and too much spur. The rider should be more cautious and not demand so much piaffe so early when the horse simply cannot grasp it. The horse should go confidently to the hand, and not be afraid of the hand. If he avoids the contact, he will go behind the bit to escape.

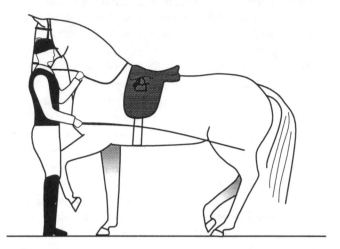

Figure 93. Training piaffe in-hand.

Croup high. If the horse's croup is too high in the piaffe, the basic correction is to move forward. The piaffe should be ridden forward in the tempo of the collected walk.

Front legs not lifted vertically. If the horse stretches his front legs out in front of himself in the piaffe, this shows that the horse was forced in the training and that there is considerable tension. The horse takes this stance in an attempt to balance himself. The correction for this is to engage the hindquarters more and to ride the horse more forward in the piaffe. This will help the correct cadence of the piaffe to return.

15.1.6 On Training In-Hand

Another way to train the horse in piaffe is in-hand. This takes the feeling and experience of a great master. One of them is Riding Master von Neindorff. He can make horses dance in hand! He is also a master of work on the *Pilaren* (pillars).[1] Some believe that the horse's first experience in in-hand work can be the piaffe. This is like trying to ride piaffe first without learning leg-yielding, shoulder-in, half pass, and so on. These activities can all be done in-hand given sufficient patience and time, and should be done before attempting the work in piaffe. Then, when the horse is carefully introduced to the piaffe in-hand, going willingly and with proper movement,

---

[1] Reitmeister Egon von Neindorff is one of the few of the masters who uphold the classical traditions. In his Karlsruhe Reitinstitut, he offers to the public two shows each year demonstrating the classical equestrian art. Many German and foreign riders have gone through his school. I have had the honor to ride in this demonstration.

introduction of the rider's weight can be added. Next, the horse must learn to move from the leg aids, and not the whip. We can see how difficult this in hand training is, and I recommend it only for very experienced trainers. When used, the whip should be an aid to understanding. One must be very careful, so the horse respects the whip, but is not frightened by it.

15.2 Passage

The passage is an elevated, floating trot movement, with relatively little length of stride. The horse continues in the two-beat rhythm, but slows the tempo, creating a slow-motion effect. The passage is a beautiful movement when done correctly.

I consider the passage more difficult than the piaffe, because the horse must have the maximum engagement of the haunches and go forward also. In the piaffe with the same level of engagement, the horse can stay almost on the spot with very little forward thrust.[1]

The horse's front legs from the knee down should be perpendicular to the ground when lifting. The forearm should come almost to the horizontal as it should in the piaffe. Unfortunately, one sees this seldom. Horses usually do a sort of Spanish walk, holding the front legs almost completely straight. To correct this, the rider collects the tempo, thinking more of piaffe. As in the piaffe, the hind leg should rise only a little above the opposite fetlock. By the lowering of the coup to carry the weight, the joints of the hind leg are already well articulated. If we bring the hind foot too high off the ground, we must be lifting the croup, and decreasing the carrying power. The neck and head of the horse should become more elevated, and the forehead and nose can come close to the vertical. It should never be behind the vertical. The neck must not be made too short, otherwise he will not have enough freedom in the shoulder to lift his front legs. The rider should have the feeling of riding up hill.

The collection should be maintained in the passage just as in the piaffe. These exercises demand the greatest lowering of the haunches, thereby producing the greatest thrusting power and carrying power possible in the horse. The energy is directed forward and upward.

15.2.1 Rider's Position and Use of the Aids

The aids for the passage are essentially the same as those for the piaffe. This is especially important in making smooth transitions from piaffe to passage and back. In the passage, the rider emphasizes the driving aid of the seat slightly and lets the horse move forward into a giving hand. As in the piaffe, he should sit deep but not heavy, sitting quietly with the motion, not swinging left and right.

---

[1] Remember that the piaffe must have the *feeling* and *tendency* of forward thrust, even though it is barely visible. Nonetheless, passage requires more forward power.

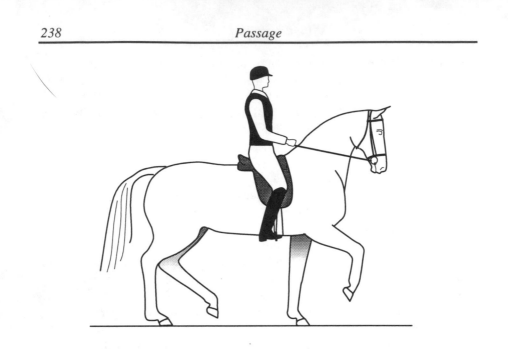

Figure 94. Passage.

As always, it is critical that the rider knows exactly which of the horse's hind legs is just about to move forward. The rider needs to know with which hind leg the horse will move into the passage in order to give the correct aids. Only when the rider knows this moment can he drive the horse into the passage correctly, making a good transition. Just as mentioned in the beginning of the book, the rider must know which hind leg is where for the correct timing of the aids.

During the passage, the rider should drive with each of his lower legs in the moment the hind leg of the horse on the same side is just about to push off the ground. In other words, left for left, right for right. At the same time, however, the outside leg and rein must guard against the possibility of the horse drifting sideways away from the pressure of the active lower leg of the rider. Again, as we see throughout the training of the horse, the straightness of the horse is indispensable.

It will be noticeable in the piaffe and passage that the horse is better in one direction than the other. Therefore, the rider should take care to be SOFTER on the side where the horse tries to lean more heavily and use STRONGER AIDS on the side where the horse does not seek contact. Here, too, the corrections should be made forward.

If the horse is lazy, the aids should enliven the horse a little. A high priority in the passage is to maintain the impulsion without the horse fleeing from the rider's seat and legs.

Once the horse is in the passage, the rider will soon meet an obstacle: the corner! Do not ride deep into the corner. Shortly before the corner the rider should give slightly stronger half halts on the outside, without the horse losing impulsion. The rider will have to use a stronger outside leg to prevent the horse from drifting out through the corner. These aids should be given when the horse's outside hind leg is in the air. The rider should remember to ride each corner and every turn this way. Throughout the passage the rider will have to give continuous driving aids with the lower legs, left then right, etc. The rider must have good contact with the horse's mouth, with giving tendency.

15.2.2 *Introducing the Passage*

The classical technique is to develop passage from the piaffe. When the piaffe is relaxed and powerful, and the horse maintains a good tendency to go forward, we can start introducing the passage. For this we simply let the horse utilize his forward tendency and let him move out into passage. The idea that the horse is allowed out into passage defines what I mean by a good tendency to go forward in the piaffe. This is the same as the transitions made from collected to medium or extended trot: the horse is allowed to go forward, not chased or pushed. Thus we see that the foundation for the passage starts far, far earlier, in correct transitions from collected to medium work, or even from the working trot to lengthened trot and all the way back to the transition from walk to trot. That is where the fundamentals of the right aids at the right moment begin.

As with the introduction of medium and extended trot, the first passage steps are maintained only so long as the horse keeps a clear rhythm and balance. As soon as the horse loses the slightest amount of balance, bring him back immediately to piaffe. Over time, the horse will gain familiarity and confidence in the passage and be able to hold his balance longer and longer, until he becomes fully accomplished. The passage demands the most strength and engagement, and it takes a long time to develop the muscles needed for this new work.

One can teach horses who have naturally high knee action a passage-like movement from the trot, without first developing the piaffe. But the danger then exists that whenever the rider tries to collect the trot, the horse offers the passage-like steps, which is very undesirable and incorrect in the collected trot.[2] One can also teach the passage from the extended trot by riding strong half halts to slow the trot extension and strong alternating leg aids (right, left, right, etc.). The rider lets the horse extend only for a few strides and brings the horse back with these strong aids, thus producing the passage. But here one often sees unevenness in the use of the hind legs. This usually results because the rider used leg and rein aids that were too strong on one side. The rider must be very careful to give the aids properly to get the horse's hind legs to lift the same height and in the same rhythm. This

---

[2] When this happens, the rider should correct by riding shoulder-in without driving too much.

approach to training the passage from the extended trot also contains the danger that when collection is asked of the horse at the trot, he may offer passage-like steps instead of a pure collected trot.

The pitfalls of teaching the passage from the collected or extended trot explain why one often sees a working tempo with high elevation of the frame instead of a truly collected trot at FEI level competitions. The rider knows that the passage-like steps will start if he collects the horse too much and therefore avoids this by riding a working trot. This is why this approach is not advisable.

It is also important that the horse does not get too heavy in the rider's hands during the passage. This happens usually when the rider drives too much or the horse is leaning on the hands, looking for support. The horse can only lean on the rider's hand when the rider allows this to happen. The rider should give the aids more cautiously, not so strongly. If the horse goes above or behind the bit, it is a serious concern. The right "dosage" of the aids should be given in order to put and keep the horse as exactly as possible on the bit.

15.3 Transitions

15.3.1 *From Piaffe to Passage*

If the horse does a good and correct piaffe, the transition to the passage is generally not too difficult. The rider should always have the feeling that he can ride *out* of the piaffe *at any time*. The rider starts the transition to passage as if he wanted to continue in the piaffe, giving the same aids, but now he uses the seat somewhat stronger and puts the hands slightly forward to allow the horse to go forward into the passage. The rider must simply ride forward more energetically.

The rider needs to have great sensitivity, or feel, at this point. He should not push the horse too much so that he is forced to jump away. The rider should try to get the horse to gain ground forward by continuing the piaffe aids while encouraging the horse to go more forward. The rider's knowledge of which of the horse's hind legs is about to leave the ground is the most important piece of information, especially in the transition from piaffe to passage. The leg aid for sending the horse forward into passage must be given when the horse's hind leg on that side is coming off the ground.

When the first few passage steps come, the rider should praise the horse very much to show him that he has done the right thing. After doing this a few times, the rider should be quite pleased with only a few passage steps. If one is patient, these transitions can become the beautiful work of art that they are capable of being.

Under no circumstances should these exercises go on for too long. The horse has to be physically and mentally ready. Build up to the work slowly. Short rest periods should be made frequently. These are particularly strenuous exercises for the horse. The rider should take care that the horse is participating happily in this work and is not becoming frightened. One often sees horses leaping away stiffly (*Lansaden*) and rearing because the training has gone on too long. Ridden too long, passage does not make the horse strong, but instead causes him to lose brilliance, and can easily injure the horse. So many good, talented horses were broken down by being over-ridden. Impatience is the worst enemy of the horseman.

15.3.2 From Passage to Piaffe

The rider should give the aids for continuing the passage, only gradually asking for a slower and slower passage. It is very important NOT to ask too soon for the piaffe steps on the spot. This is almost never a success. It is better to ride the passage slower and slower, less and less forward, but in the same rhythm. The rider in getting into the piaffe should NOT give the piaffe aids in a faster rhythm. The alternating leg aids going into the piaffe should be gradually a little slower. Otherwise, the resulting piaffe will be like a sewing machine.

If the rider has the feeling the horse is going to stop in the transition from passage to piaffe, the rider should ride forward back into the passage immediately and try again in a few moments for the transition to piaffe. The rider should be careful that he is not asking for too much too soon. These transitions take several months to a year to develop.

The most common mistakes in the transition from passage to piaffe are that the rider drives with leg aids that are in a rushed rhythm and that the rider sways left and right with the upper body. The rider must remember to be very careful with the leg aids and the weight distribution. Be very careful with the hands and under no circumstances allow the contact to become hard or rough. The horse must accept the rein contact in complete trust. It is the rider's responsibility that the horse continue to enjoy these movements and all the training.

Never try to ride both the piaffe to passage and the passage to piaffe transitions the first day. Much repetition will be needed to show the horse that he should be steady and regular and forward at all times. It is extremely important to ride the transitions correctly. The rider should be pleased and satisfied when the horse can execute three or four strides of each with good transitions! The horse should be praised. The horses will understand quickly and make fluid transitions if they are not forced.

15.3.3 Passage-Piaffe-Passage-Piaffe

Making more than one transition from piaffe to passage or vice versa, it becomes immediately clear whether the balance, engagement, and desire to move forward is maintained. The somewhat too abrupt transition into piaffe can put the horse out of balance and cause him to fall on the forehand. Then the transition out of piaffe is almost impossible!

When schooling these transitions, don't allow the horse to lose rhythm. If the horse starts to lose rhythm in the piaffe, go back to passage immediately. The horse must keep the rhythm clear throughout the transition. One often sees the horse brought from passage into an almost complete halt and then activated into piaffe. This break in the rhythm should be avoided at all costs. It is better to make shorter and shorter steps in the passage, while keeping the rhythm, until the horse has confidence in the passage-piaffe transition. Only then will he maintain the balance needed to proceed back to passage. Again, remember to go back to lengthened and medium work to regain the swinging hind leg.

The aids for repeated passage-piaffe-passage-piaffe work must be extremely balanced between driving and receiving aids, and correctly timed. The same can be said for transitions between medium and collected trot or canter, and the careful rider who has practiced those transitions with balance and rhythm over the years will be on familiar ground. The rider who "got away with" unbalanced transitions (covering mistakes in rhythm with excessive leg or hand aids) will be unsuccessful with the same techniques here.

The piaffe-passage-piaffe-passage transition is a distillation of horsemanship and a culmination of the seven elements of training: Rhythm, Relaxation, Contact, Impulsion, Straightness, Suppleness and Collection. When this is achieved, there is nothing nicer in the whole world! Happiness for the rider and horse.

15.3.4 *Walk or Trot to Passage*

Transitions from walk to passage or trot to passage may also be ridden once the passage is well confirmed. From a movement with very little swing, we need to make an immediate transition to one with the ultimate amount of engagement. The transition is like that from walk to trot, but the driving must be more emphatic and the half halt must be stronger, all without roughness or sloppiness. It is especially important that the walk is lively and energetic, because we have to go from a non-swinging movement into the most powerful. At first, this may be surprising to the horse, so do a few steps of passage and then stop to praise and re-assure the horse that this is what you intended. As in all transitions, the first steps are the important ones, and should be harmonious and comfortable, but powerful and sure.

15.4 Piaffe Pirouette

We are seeing more and more the piaffe pirouette and passage half pass movements done in Grand Prix Freestyle competitions. While a classically trained horse and rider can successfully accomplish these movements, I want to warn that these movements should NEVER be practiced until the piaffe and passage (and transitions between them) are 100% perfect and reliable. (One can count on one or two hands the number of horses and riders in the world who can meet this standard). While I am very concerned that premature attempts to perform the piaffe pirouette will ruin many that have potential to be great horses, I acknowledge that this exercise could be a true pleasure to see when it is correct.

If the piaffe is insecure, the piaffe pirouette will certainly make it worse, not better. This destroys the piaffe and compromises the pirouette. Consider how difficult the correct piaffe is in the first place. The engagement of the hindquarters must be superb, and the horse must lift and hold his forelegs while supporting most all his weight on one hind leg. As mentioned above, we often see horses crossing and swinging their forelegs because of a lack of balance. Now if we ask the horse to move his shoulders around the inside hind, we complicate the balance issue. The horse is likely to stop the piaffe or lose rhythm at best, and the rider hops and jerks around to keep the piaffe coming while hauling the horse around in a pirouette-like turn.

For the pirouette to be successful, the piaffe needs to be 100% powerful and there must be a constant tendency forward. The horse must be very soft and well on the aids. Only make one or two good steps of pirouette with good flexion and bending, giving a very slight outside half halt and applying the outside knee and leg. The inside leg is very important in order to keep the engagement of the inside hind leg because this has to provide all the power and weight which is carried from the forehand. The inside hind leg makes the steps on the smallest radius of a volte. When the walk and canter pirouette were introduced, we used a training pirouette that was not too small, and made the turn step-by-step. The same applies here. This is not the time to think the horse "knows" the pirouette or that the movement is a simple rotation within the piaffe.

After the two steps of pirouette, we need to maintain the rhythm of the piaffe, and then repeat again two or three steps (depending on how the horse reacts). Should the horse lose his confidence and balance, we must stop immediately with the turning and concentrate again on the correct piaffe.

Attempting to do this movement with force will lead to disaster.

15.5 Passage Half Pass

As with the piaffe pirouette, it is essential that one waits until the passage is 100% reliable, and the half pass is perfect at walk, trot and canter in both directions. The passage itself demands an extreme amount of strength and suppleness on the part of the horse. Straightness in the passage is essential in order for the horse to carry and suspend himself through this difficult work. In the half pass, we complicate the work by introducing both bending and crossing. The extra loading of the inside hind leg can lead to loss of rhythm or even stopping of the inside hind.

When the horse is strong, supple and the rider's aids are refined and harmonious, the passage half pass can be introduced. The aids are exactly the same as in trot half pass. Ride with good bending, but not too much, taking and giving the inside rein, keeping the rein well against the neck. Occasionally one will need an inside half halt to keep the shoulder from falling in too quickly, but in general the outside half halt together with the outside leg is needed to move the horse sideways. Always maintain more forward than sideways movement, with the front legs leading slightly into the direction of the half pass. The rider must sit very quietly to avoid disturbing the horse in his back and in his movement. The movement must remain swinging.

This exercise can look very beautiful when ridden correctly, but many times the movement is a mistake, with the rider asking something that the horse is unable to do or understand.

Chapter 16
Conclusion

Dressage in Harmony is the result of careful, thoughtful application of classical principles. These principles have been developed over thousands of years and have been handed down to us through a series of very experienced masters. This gradual evolution of the sport and art of riding is expressed today in the upper level work of a harmonious horse and rider. But each new student starts with no experience, and must find his way to the highest level within a single lifetime. For this, we need the intelligent, guiding hand of masters to show the way. Each new generation always thinks that there can be shortcuts or technological improvements to make faster and better progress. So many other sports seem to routinely set new records and achieve new breakthroughs, (mostly through better skis, or better shoes, running tracks, and so on.)

Through better breeding, management and nutrition, better and better sport horses are being produced today, but the tools we need to improve the quality of our sport over the levels we commonly see today are already in our hands. Most riders have barely scratched the surface. Fortunately, we have our whole lives to plumb the depths of wisdom available to use—and the rewards are real and great. Fortunately too, horses are never too old to keep learning. When in Munich, I got a very beautiful 18-year old Hannoverian stallion in training. He did many of the movements, in a wishy-washy fashion. But he never did one-tempo changes. When I first rode him, everything went quite well. But when I came to the canter, I was very surprised. It was a classic four-beat canter, and I felt like I was sitting on a hopping rabbit. He did not go forward at all, but only in the hopping canter. The poor guy, he thought he was doing well. At first I did not even try the flying changes, how could he ever do it? But the owner asked me to ride changes to two tempis, which he did quite well, she said. "He never learnt the one-tempis," she added. I was not very happy to try these changes, but felt I had to make the owner happy. Right away, I was sure that with such a hopping canter, there could never be beautiful changes. After I made the first flying changes, I was not surprised over the results. All changes were difficult because the poor guy would not canter forward. Every change went more sideways than forward, beginning with four-tempis. When I got to the two-tempis, I felt like I was dancing with a terrible dancer who was throwing me from one side to the other. It was horrible!

How could I convince the owner that her horse first needed to learn a good three-beat canter and that he must respond more to my forward driving aids? To my surprise, she told me I should do everything I could to help the horse learn the one-tempis. She would not have any time to ride the horse for the next two months, since she was getting married, and I would have the horse to myself. Of course I had to tell her that it would take much longer than two months to retrain a horse who goes in such a terrible canter, and he was no longer the youngest horse, making it harder for him. For him and for me then started a very hard schooling time. Fortunately, he was very willing and went readily to my aids. After some initial sore muscles for him (from the freer canter we needed to bring him back to his natural movement), he started to respond more and more to my forward driving aids, especially when I could ride him on the big canter ring on Haus der Kunst.

Of course, at the beginning I had to be very careful because he was so happy to gallop outside that he would easily over-stress himself. But after four months, he did a rather nice three-beat canter. I put a flying change in here and there, but only in almost medium canter. Through the medium canter he had no possibility of making the changes sideways. After another two months, we could ride two-tempis, and they were very nice and straight forward. At the end of the year, I could make the one-tempis as long as I would like. He felt very good, and was a most happy horse—even at 19 years old. The mistake was not in the flying change, but way back, in the canter, which was not forward enough. From this and other examples, you can see that with correct training, it is always possible to "teach an old dog new tricks." You should have seen how happy the owner was when she rode her stallion for the first time in one-tempis. I had a hard time to stop her, so happy was she! After she married, she sold the horse to a friend of hers who came every morning at 7:00 after driving two hours. He came several more years, enjoying every ride.

It has been my very great pleasure to share my knowledge and experience with you. I wish you a lifetime of harmonious rides.

As expressed in an Arabian proverb:

For so long as people love horses, the gods will love people.